MARK TWAIN

Also by Charles Neider

Susy: a childhood
Naked Eye, a novel
The Authentic Death of Hendry Jones, a novel
The White Citadel, a novel
The Frozen Sea, a study of Franz Kafka

MARK TWAIN

by CHARLES NEIDER

HORIZON PRESS   NEW YORK

ACKNOWLEDGMENTS

I wish to thank Frederick Anderson and Henry Nash Smith of the University of California, Berkeley, for kindnesses and courtesies extended to me over a period of years. I am greatly indebted to the late Jacques Samossoud for his generosity in allowing me to quote, in part or in their entirety, from Mrs. Clara Clemens Samossoud's letters to me.

I wish to thank Doubleday & Co. for kindly permitting me to reprint material which originally appeared in various volumes of Mark Twain's work, and I wish to thank Harper & Row for permitting me to reprint material which appeared in *The Autobiography of Mark Twain*. Parts of "Mark Twain and the Russians" appeared in *The Literary Gazette* of Moscow. The full text appeared in pamphlet form over the imprint of Hill & Wang and was later included in the Washington Square Press edition of the *Autobiography*.

CONTENTS

CONTENTS

PREFATORY NOTE

The majority of these chapters were published as introductions to volumes of Mark Twain's work. "On Mark Twain Censorship" and "The Notebooks" have not been published previously.

THE NOVELS

O NE OF THE first things we can say about Mark Twain as a novelist is that he did not regard novel-writing as his essential "calling"—in the way that Flaubert, James, Mann, Dostoyevsky, Faulkner, Hemingway and other writers did. Mark Twain came to novel-writing almost accidentally and did not give to it the major part of his literary energy. He did not *begin* as a novelist. He wrote his first novel, *The Gilded Age*, only after he had poured out a great deal of literary energy on his first two books of non-fiction, *The Innocents Abroad* and *Roughing It*. And when he did begin, he began as only a half-novelist, inasmuch as he co-authored *The Gilded Age* with Charles Dudley Warner. *The Gilded Age* was conceived, as we shall see, not only as a sort of accident but as a kind of joke as well.

Few great novelists have had such an inauspicious beginning, and the history of the novel does not reveal for us many prominent examples of co-authorship. But if Mark Twain was eccentric in his beginnings as a novelist it should not surprise us. He had a reputation in his day for being eccentric which he thoroughly enjoyed and encouraged. And if his beginnings were, shall we say, weak, that should not surprise us either, for if he lacked any great instinct as a novelist it was that instinct which we call the artistic conscience. Mark Twain did not hesitate to take liberties in his novels, and in his fiction in general, which he would have hesitated to take in his non-fiction. He had a respect for non-fiction which he often seemed to lack for fiction. He told Rudyard Kipling in 1890, "I never read novels myself except when the popular persecution forces me to—when people plague me to know what I think of the last book that everyone is reading. . . . Personally I never care for fiction or story books. What I like to read about are facts and statistics of any kind. If they are only facts about the raising of radishes

1

they interest me." Clemens regarded himself from first to last as a reporter who had clear and quite stern responsibilities to his public, whatever the jigs and high kicks he performed in an overflow of good spirits, health and a desire to amuse. He thought of himself as an entertainer, but as a serious one; and, as he said in his last years in his autobiography, his humor was only incidental to his purpose—if it came, good, if not, it could be dispensed with, for he was concerned primarily with discussing a moral.

In general this purpose is true for his novels also. The difference is that his conception of the act of writing novels and of the act of reading them lacked that rigorous sense, that discipline, that artistic conscience, which one finds in his non-fiction books, loosely constructed though the latter may at times be. It was as if non-fiction books were a man's fare and novels a woman's. We note a significant pattern in the extraordinary years of his literary activity: two books of non-fiction preceded *The Gilded Age;* many of the nostalgic and by far the best chapters of *Life on the Mississippi* preceded *Tom Sawyer; A Tramp Abroad* preceded *The Prince and the Pauper;* and the composition of the major part and the publication of the whole of *Life on the Mississippi* preceded the completion and publication of *Huckleberry Finn.* The sense we have that Mark Twain poured out vast literary energy for his books of non-fiction and a lesser energy for his novels is supported not only by the matter of ebullience, scope and linguistic energy of the books of non-fiction but also by their greater length. But we must not push this comparison far, inasmuch as it is obvious that the fiction may be more compressed and more potent than the non-fiction.

So much of Mark Twain's work, fiction and non-fiction together, is indebted to the American yarn and the American vernacular that a few reflections on the yarn and the vernacular may illumine for us his salient qualities as a vernacular stylist and remind us that far from being the originator of a humorous vernacular style he was its culminating point.

A number of differences have been noted between the style of President Johnson's administration and that of President

Kennedy. One of the significant differences lies in the approach of the two presidents to humor. President Johnson, it has been observed, is an eager and apt yarn spinner, who likes to tell stories with a political point. The President's manner is casual, almost homespun, in his speeches. He enjoys phrases like "I'm in tall cotton tonight" or "My old daddy used to say." President Kennedy, on the other hand, was an intellectual, detached man, who enjoyed wit more than comedy and a wry aphorism more than a yarn. He has been aptly called the first Irish Brahmin. On occasion his wit was aimed at himself, as when he introduced himself in France with, "I am the man who accompanied Jacqueline Kennedy to Paris."

Both Brahmin wit and yarn humor have had a long history in the United States and have suggested two aspects of the American mind and character, one related to urban life and formal learning, the other to rural life and homespun learning. The classic centers of these two somewhat antipodal styles were New England for wit and the Old Southwest for yarn humor, and the classic confrontation occurred in the campaign which saw the election of Andrew Jackson (himself no humorist) as the first president from the western lands. It is interesting to note how Mr. Kennedy, from Boston, represents the first style and how Mr. Johnson, from the New Southwest, the second, despite the fact that they are of the same party and of the same political persuasion.

It was not until the Jackson administration that the printed yarn came into its own. Before then the yarn had flourished mostly in its oral form and was related by yarn spinners known for their skepticism and for their droll and deadpan manner. Skepticism seemed to flourish naturally in the back country. The ideas and experiences of Europe were tested in the proving ground of the unsettled land, and the result was a lasting skepticism regarding Europe, ideas and many things besides, including Easterners and their ways. If the yarn spinners seemed to recognize no limits in their will to exaggerate, this was understandable, at least to some foreign observers, in view of the vastness and mystery of the new country. Anything seemed possible in a country so unknown and so full of surprises. Hyperbole was the stock in trade even of the early guidebooks, which presumed to offer factual knowledge. It was great to take in the suckers, whether you were a land speculator or a yarn spinner. The yarn spinners were the chief entertainers in a rural society which had a surplus of time and where much time was spent in gregariousness and in travel—in the country store, the meetinghouse, the courthouse, in the stagecoach, on the river boat, at the campfire: heavy time if empty, delightful time when yarns could be swapped and could be heard from the mouths of the local artists.

"Well," goes an anonymous Down East yarn, "Uncle Zeke and I took it into our heads on Saturday afternoon to go a gunning after ducks, in father's skiff. So in we got and sculled down the river. A proper sight of ducks flew backwards and forwards, I tell ye, and by'm-by a few on 'em lit down by the mash and went to feeding. I cotched up my powder-horn to prime, and it slipped right out of my hand and sunk to the bottom of the river. The water was so clear I could see the horn on the bottom. Now I couldn't swim a jot, so sez I to Uncle Zeke, 'You're a pretty clever fellow, just let me take your powder-horn to prime.' And don't you think, the stingy critter wouldn't. Well, says I, 'You're a pretty good diver, 'un if you'll dive and get it I'll give you primin'.' I thought he'd leave his powder-horn but he didn't, but stuck it in his pocket and down he went—and there he stayed. I looked down, and what do you think the critter was doing? There he was, setting right on the bottom of the river, pouring the powder out of my horn into hizen."

The rise of the penny press in the Jacksonian decade encouraged the change from the oral to the written form of the yarn. The penny press, unlike the old "blanket-sheet" newspaper, was interested in local color and welcomed the work of the regional humorists—the Down Easters like Seba Smith and Benjamin Shillaber, and the humorists of the Old Southwest like Augustus Baldwin Longstreet and George Washington Harris. It was the latter who wrote the famous stories which he collected under the title of *Sut Lovingood's Yarns*. Men like these early humorists carried on the tradition, but in print, of the oral yarn spinners, in manner and matter alike.

One of the first yarn spinners in American politics, surpassed in fame only by Lincoln, was Davy Crockett, who used the yarn as he did the whiskey treat, to obtain votes. Crockett was a great one for the tall tale, as he was for invective used for political ends. Like Lincoln he was skeptical, quaint, unhurried as he told his yarns. Once, when he found himself running for Congress against an opponent with a very winning smile, Crockett decided that the smile was costing him votes, so he made the following stump speech about it.

"Yes, gentlemen, he may get some votes by *grinning*, for he can out-*grin* me, and you know I ain't slow. And to prove to you that I am not I will tell you the following. You all know I love hunting. Well, I discovered a long time ago that a coon couldn't stand my grin. I could bring one tumbling down from the highest tree. I never wasted powder and lead when I wanted one of these creturs. Well, as I was walking out one night, a few hundred yards from my house, looking carelessly about me, I saw a coon on one of the highest limbs of an old tree. The night was very moony and clear and old Rattler was with me. But Rattler won't bark at a coon, he's a queer dog in that way. So I thought I'd bring the coon down in the usual way, by a grin.

"I set myself, and after grinning at the coon a reasonable time found that he didn't come down. I wondered what was the reason and I took another steady grin at him. Still he was up there. It made me a little mad. So I felt around and got an old limb about five feet long and, planting one end on the ground, I placed my chin on the other and took a *rest*. I then grinned my best for about five minutes but the coon hung on. So, finding I could not bring him down by grinning, I went over to the house, got my ax, returned to the tree and began to cut away. Down it come and I run forward, but damn if the coon was there. I found that what I had taken for one was a large knot on a branch of the tree and, upon looking at it closely, I saw that I had grinned all the bark off and left the knot perfectly smooth.

"Now, fellow-citizens, you must be convinced that in the grinning line I myself am not slow. Yet when I look upon my opponent's countenance I must admit that he is my superior. You must all admit it. Therefore be wide awake—look sharp—and do not let him grin you out of your votes."

There are several points of resemblance between Crockett and Lincoln. Both were backwoodsmen, both had charm and great physical strength, both were master folk storytellers, and both were politicians who used yarns and other forms of humor tellingly in electioneering and in debate. Lincoln was very fond of humor of a rather broad taste, and when he was president delighted in the work of such humorists, skeptics and political satirists of the day as Artemus Ward, Petroleum Vesuvius Nasby and Orpheus C. Kerr. The story is well known that he read a chapter from Ward to his cabinet before reading to them the final draft of the Emancipation Proclamation. William Herndon, Lincoln's law partner and after Lincoln's death his biographer, relates a typical Lincoln yarn, this one about an old-line Baptist preacher in a backwoods meetinghouse who had for his text on one occasion, "I am the Christ, whom I shall represent today." A little blue lizard ran up beneath the preacher's coarse linen pants and although the preacher slapped away at his legs while continuing the sermon the lizard went on about his business. The preacher, growing desperate, loosened the button which held his pants up, and suddenly he kicked his pants off.

"But meanwhile," Lincoln is supposed to have said, "Mr. Lizard had passed the equatorial line of the waist-band and was calmly exploring that part of the preacher's anatomy which lay underneath the back of his shirt. Things were now growing interesting but the sermon was still grinding on. The next movement on the preacher's part was for the collar button, and with one sweep of his arm off came the tow linen shirt. The congregation sat for an instant as if dazed. At length an old lady in the rear of the room rose up and, glancing at the excited object in the pulpit, shouted at the top of her voice, 'If you represent Christ then I'm done with the Bible.' "

Ward, Nasby and Kerr were members of a new breed of

humorist, who had added something new to the old skepticism—
theatrics. After the Civil War the country had more leisure, more
easy money, and people wanted entertainment. The minstrel
show, the lecture platform, the show boat and touring com-
panies all came into their own, although they had their origins
before the war. The theatrical humorist was not slow to take
the hint. More often than not he used a pseudonym, performed
on the lecture circuit and had a bagful of theatrical tricks such as
illiterate spelling and atrocious punning. Like an actor, he pre-
ferred to hold up a mask of ambiguity between his private self
and his audience. The theatrical humorist's range was more national than regional and he did not specialize in creating local
types.

Mark Twain, the crowning point of American humor, benefited thoroughly and consciously from the work of his predecessors and from the fashions of his time. Among his several
accomplishments, he brought the yarn to a state of near-perfec-
tion. His retelling in print of the jumping-frog yarn which he
had heard in California gave him his first national fame. In his
travel books he often stopped the narrative to insert a favorite
yarn, such as "Buck Fanshaw's Funeral" in *Roughing It* and
"Baker's Bluejay Yarn" in *A Tramp Abroad*. His yarns were almost always long. He seemed to luxuriate in his power to make
them long but not tedious. The American yarn had important
influences on Mark Twain. It is well known, for example, that
one of his triumphs in *Huckleberry Finn* was his introduction in
breadth and depth of mock-oral language into the American
novel, and his mastering the American spoken idiom in print.
In this accomplishment he was aided by an incomparable ear and
a subtle memory. This particular triumph was dependent on
his decision to tell the story from the point of view and in the
language of its protagonist. His decision had major consequences
for the hairy-chest branch of the American novel, no better
proof of which is needed than Hemingway's cocky statement of
indebtedness, "All American literature comes from one novel
by Mark Twain called *Huckleberry Finn*."

Clemens's stylistic achievement probably did not seem novel

to contemporary American humorists, since for a generation or more American humorists of the yarn-spinning stripe had been busily writing in the vernacular for the popular press. Even an amateur writer like the anonymous author of *Sketches and Eccentricities of Col. David Crockett* was able to suggest the way, although unconsciously, when he set down four vivid hunting stories told him by Crockett, and set them down as nearly as he could in Crockett's own words. *Sketches* was published slightly more than half a century before *Huckleberry Finn,* yet the hunting stories sound almost contemporaneous with the novel.* Clemens's singularity resided in the fact that he applied his training as a humorist to the medium of the novel. This seems now like an easy and fairly obvious transfer of energy. That it wasn't so even in the case of a writer as gifted as Clemens may be judged by the fact that not many of his novels have the released, vernacular style of *Huckleberry Finn.* Clemens's taste was uncertain enough to allow him to declare late in his writing career that his favorite among his books was *Joan of Arc,* whose antique style is only one of its unattractive features.

In 1895 Clemens published a brief essay, "How to Tell a Story," in which he contended that the humorous story is American, the comic story is English and the witty story is French. Although he did not mention the yarn as such, in the context it is clear that what he had to say about the humorous story could also be applied to the American yarn. His comments on the humorous story revealed some distinctive aspects of American humor and the American yarn. His comments may be summarized as follows. The art of telling a humorous story (he meant by word of mouth, not print), "was created in America, and has remained at home." The humorous story depends on the manner of the telling, the other two depend on the matter. The humorous story may be spun out to great length, it may wander as it pleases, and it need not arrive anywhere in particular. The other two must be brief and end with a point. The humorous story is the only difficult one to tell, for it is a work of "high

* See the Appendix for the hunting stories.

and delicate art," and can be properly told only by a master of timing, the pause, mimicry, suggestion and self-control. The other two can be told by a machine. The humorous story is told gravely and with a deadpan style. The other two are told with pathetically eager delight and sometimes with guffaws, which is enough to make one want "to renounce joking and lead a better life."

This patriotic view of humor (at least some of it offered with tongue in cheek) contains a surprising turnabout, for Clemens is accusing the British and the French stories of being obvious and left-handed, the things which early travelers to the United States, notably British ones, charged American humor with being.

It is worth noting that in Mark Twain's explanation the humorous story is told in the guise of an imagined and droll character, and not straight out in the manner of the comic and the witty story. This creation of "distance" between audience and story, in which the teller pretends to be an unaware and innocent middleman, is typical of yarn humor. For Mark Twain the special charm of the humorous story is that it is projected, dramatized. The teller is an actor whose function it is to give the illusion of standing aside while the story unfolds itself. Clemens's complaint about the tellers of comic and witty stories is that they get in the way of the stories. This insistence on the teller's modesty harks back to an ambiguity of the backwoods. Although men like Crockett were admired for their individualism it was still required of them, for the democratic game, to be modest and retiring at certain times, as when Lincoln, asking a crowd of people to vote for him, said he would appreciate a victory but that if the people did not elect him, it was no matter. There was an ambiguity for Englishmen too. Visiting Englishmen in the early years of the American nation were displeased by the boasting, excessively individualistic behavior of the backwoodsman. Yet the English had their own brand of rugged individualism, which was manifest in the many eccentrics who had affected a humour or an odd habit of mind.

Mark Twain kept telling yarns most of his life, down to the last pessimistic years, during which he dictated his autobiography. In the autobiography he told yarns about bowling, pool, dueling, and he retold the old yarn from *Roughing It*, "His Grandfather's Old Ram," to show how he had told it on the lecture stage. These yarns were dictated in the new century. Even before the closing of the previous one the yarn had begun to seem old-fashioned and no longer adequately representative of one American way of life—the non-urban way. It was no longer in the main stream of American humor, which took a turn for subtlety, sophistication, urbanity and a measure of open narcissism. The poor if not pure fool of the regional and theatrical humorists and of Mark Twain became the pure if not poor neurotic of twentieth-century humorists like Thurber. Finley Peter Dunne and Will Rogers were carry-overs from the school of social critics like Ward and Nasby. By the time of Will Rogers homespun humor was reduced to pithy sentences or brief disconnected paragraphs. The drawl and the understated manner were still in evidence but the spinning rope which was Will Rogers's trademark seemed largely to have replaced the spinning yarn.

The tempo of American life which accompanied the increasing urbanization, mechanization and finally the suburbanization of the country gave a quietus to the old yarn, at least for general humorous consumption. The brisk comedy of vaudeville, radio and television could better reflect the nation's urgent tempo. Perhaps, however, the yarn is more viable than one thinks. It is still, at any rate, alive in electioneering, in legislative debates, in liars' clubs and in its original activity in the mouths of locally famous yarn spinners here and there across the country.

For some time before he began *The Gilded Age* Clemens had considered writing a tale based on the visionary character of his mother's cousin, James Lampton, but, as his biographer later explained, he was "unwilling to undertake an extended work of fiction alone." One evening early in 1873, when Clemens and his wife were dinner hosts to the Charles Dudley Warners, their neighbors in Hartford, the husbands made some slighting remarks about the quality of the novels their wives were currently reading. To which the wives responded with a challenge: all right, then why didn't the husbands write a better novel and improve the public's taste? The challenge was accepted in a spirit of fun and the two men conferred about a plan. Clemens proposed the tale he had had in mind, which pleased Warner, and without much ado Clemens set to work and quickly completed the first eleven chapters of the novel, which he read aloud to Warner. Warner then wrote the next installment of chapters. The book, begun in February, was completed in April and was published shortly before Christmas 1873. Long afterward Clemens recalled that he and Warner had worked alternately "in the superstition that we were writing one coherent yarn, when I suppose, as a matter of fact, we were writing two *in*coherent ones." In this casual, almost haphazard way, Mark Twain began his career as a major American novelist.

The Gilded Age is a very spotty book, as we might expect it to be. There are gross differences in style, tone and characterization, due to the fact that two different hands were at work, showing Mark Twain's broad strokes, earthy humor and backwoods setting together with Warner's deft, sophisticated touches, urbane humor and in general urban setting. The novel is a mongrel work and it is a pity that Mark Twain didn't write it alone, for the best things are his, including the creation of the fabulous Colonel Sellers, the first of a panel of great characterizations. Although Warner's prose is witty and sensitive, the weakest characterizations are by him. He was working on Clemens's terrain and was at a disadvantage in any comparison with Clemens. As far as the social theme was concerned, however, the two men worked harmoniously. Both were inspired by a profound skepticism regarding the course the nation was taking, and they produced a portrait of the feverish, overblown, corrupt Reconstruction period. The title of the novel is a superb epigraph on that time. For all its obvious faults The Gilded Age is often a very entertaining book. It was very popular when it first appeared. A little more than a month after its publication it had sold 26,000 copies, and four weeks later it had sold a total of 40,000 copies, which made it a best seller by any standards, those of its own time or those of today.

From the beginning Mark Twain had the good sense, the instinct, to rely on familiar materials. Squire Hawkins is in some respects modeled on his father; Washington Hawkins is modeled on his brother Orion; Senator Dilworthy is modeled on Senator S. C. Pomeroy of Kansas; and Uncle Dan'l is apparently modeled on the real Uncle Dan'l of Clemens's boyhood, who later became the great figure Jim in *Huckleberry Finn.* The motif of the Tennessee Land is based on real events. The description of the steamboat race is based on Mark Twain's knowledge of the river, and the description of Washington society and of Congress is based on personal experience and observation.

Clemens's great ability to hear and write dialogue and dialect authentically are in obvious evidence in the novel. We rarely *see* characters in *The Gilded Age;* mostly we hear them. At times, however, Clemens's dialogue is embarrassingly melodramatic and naive, especially when he is dealing in "psychological" moments. Like Hemingway, Clemens was a master of the external life and weak when he was dealing with the internal one, or with sensitive psychology. His, like Hemingway's, was essentially a man's world, and women are for the most part shadowy figures in it. The emotions of his characters are usually primitive, even when the characters are not supposed to be primitive. The characters of *The Gilded Age* are largely cartoons, entertaining at times but too often letting us reflect that they are not seriously concerned with the business of life and literature. Not unexpectedly, Clemens begins a habit of dropping footnotes to assure us that he has a real reality in mind, that he is not merely writing a fairy tale, a fable. Non-fiction seems more important to him, and he assures us of the importance of his fiction by pointing to its "real" origins.

We ought not to assume that whereas Clemens worked from authentic materials Warner did not. Warner had once been a practicing lawyer and it is partly for this reason that the courtroom scenes are so well done. He had once been a railroad surveyor in Missouri and was familiar with the Missouri setting and with surveying. Even the motif of inherited land was not foreign to him. His father was a farmer in western Massachusetts and

when he died virtually all that he left his widow and sons was
the some two hundred acres he owned. Warner was a good,
sensitive stylist and some of his share of the novel is intelligent
and well imagined. He was able to portray women subtly and
intellectually, and his portrait of the woman struggling to eman-
cipate herself is admirably done.

There was a third co-worker in this vineyard: J. Hammond
Trumbull, who supplied the chapter mottoes. He was reputed
to be the most learned man in Hartford of his time. Clemens,
a choice practitioner and connoisseur of swearing, claimed with
awe that Trumbull could swear in twenty-seven languages.

Tom Sawyer is the great river idyll, the American song of
innocence, the fable of the Great Valley before industrialism
changed it, whereas *Huckleberry Finn* is a kind of anatomy of
conscience, a moral investigation, and a great realistic evocation
of the river basin and of the pastoral yet essentially violent life
that flourished in it before the Civil War.

Tom Sawyer is, no doubt, a lesser book than *Huckleberry
Finn*, but in some ways it is superior to *Huckleberry Finn*. It is a
more unified novel, more of a piece, better constructed and with
fewer flaws. It is a lesser novel for reasons of theme and language, but it is better controlled than *Huckleberry Finn*. The
large, adult themes are only hinted in it, Jim is absent from it,
and Pap is mentioned only briefly and he is off-stage. Some of
the episodes strike us as being too convenient for the author—
for example, Injun Joe's escape from the courtroom. Joe es-
capes with ease, and apparently without pursuit, which shows
what can be done in fiction. Joe seems to have almost supernatural powers—until he dies in the cave in an episode of retri-
bution, the just vengeance of heaven—and the convenience of
the author. Occasionally there are lapses of style but on the
whole the language is clean and strong, although it is not the
wonderful, fragrant vernacular of *Huckleberry Finn*. In *Tom
Sawyer* the more conventional style suits the more conventional
Tom. *Tom Sawyer* is a bright, cheery book despite the amount
of adult violence in it, and Tom is a pleasant boy. Huck isn't

well developed in Tom's book. His character, language, point of view and conscience are shown in detail and in depth only in the book of his name. _Tom Sawyer_ was written during a relatively affluent, healthy and happy time in Mark Twain's life.

So much has been said and written about *Tom Sawyer* and *Huckleberry Finn* that they hardly need an introduction. We all know that they are based on autobiographical materials and that *Tom Sawyer* gave its author little trouble but that *Huckleberry Finn* gave him so much trouble, balking and languishing, that at times its very existence was threatened. And we know that Clemens never correctly judged *Huckleberry Finn* as his greatest novel and as one of the great novels produced in America. What is not so well known, perhaps, is that Tom and Huck represent, to a degree which is fascinating, two conflicting aspects of Clemens's mind and personality—the theatrical-romantic side (Tom) and the skeptical-iconoclastic side (Huck). The conflict is controlled and subdued in *Tom Sawyer*, for the reason that one of its elements, Huck, exists only in embryonic form there. The conflict flares out of hand in *Huckleberry Finn* and leaves the novel greater than *Tom Sawyer* but with a vast flaw. It is Huck who makes *Huckleberry Finn* the greater novel but in a sense he does it in spite of the author. The author's intellectual preference is for Huck, although he never ceases to have powerful emotional ties with Tom.

If we study Tom throughout the four Tom-Huck novels we reach the conclusion that he grows progressively more unpleasant and that at the same time Clemens becomes more fond of him. Certainly it is Tom and the author's fondness for him which are responsible for the maiming of the final quarter of *Huckleberry Finn*—that explosion of burlesque and vaudeville antics at the expense of everything that is important and serious in the novel. It would seem that the older Mark Twain became and the more he used up the materials of the boyhood river idyll the more he clung to Tom as representing the passing of youth and innocence in his own life.

Hemingway said that the real end of *Huckleberry Finn* is where Jim is stolen, and that that is where the cheating begins.

In my opinion he was only approximately correct. It is in character for the "King" to steal, or rather to sell, Jim. And the fact
that Jim can be stolen and sold like that heightens our sense of
the plight of the Negro in the South. The true cheating begins
with the *deus ex machina* of Huck suddenly finding himself
taken for Tom. All through the novel Clemens brought in long-
ing references to Tom, and always they were an intrusion. Now
at last he has his desire granted: Tom can be brought back on
stage, the story can be taken over and managed by him, and the
serious, profound, original, moving novel can become a comedy
of errors, a minstrel show, and merely a boy's book. Tom is
invariably the character who encourages Clemens to indulge in
practical jokes and twaddle. The real world of ugly, difficult
problems—the father-son conflict, Jim's attempt to free himself,
Huck's rebellion against the Village morality—can be ignored
and all the beautiful "justice" of fairy tales can be arranged: the
two bums get their desert, Jim is miraculously freed, Pap is revealed to be dead, and everyone lives happily ever after, except
the reader, who is stunned by the size of the sellout. The reason
we care, the reason we are astonished, is that the novel has been
so wonderful most of the way, and the people and their problems so real, our people and our problems. Some of that last
quarter or, to be exact, twenty-three per cent, of the novel is as
bad as anything Mark Twain ever wrote in fiction.

If we were not familiar with the uncertainty of his artistic
taste and the shallowness of his artistic conscience we would be
surprised by this great flaw. But we are not wholly surprised
and not surprised by further evidence of his subordination of
fiction: his tossing an important chapter, the raft episode, of
Huckleberry Finn into *Life on the Mississippi* to fill out the latter, and his failure to rescue the chapter when he prepared
Huckleberry Finn for publication. It was typical of Clemens
also that he was willing to risk cheapening the characters of
Tom, Huck and Jim by putting them through the lightweight
situations and performances in the sequels, *Tom Sawyer Abroad*
and *Tom Sawyer, Detective*. Didn't he understand that he could
not hope to capture the feel and the magic of *Tom Sawyer* and

Huckleberry Finn again—at sixty and in the midst of a thoroughly polished way of life? And didn't he realize that our impressions of Tom, Huck and Jim can be affected by seeing these figures—who are so alive for us—acting weakly, vaguely and sometimes cheaply, as they act in the sequels? Apparently not. Mark Twain was one of those wayward geniuses whom it is not always easy to defend or to understand.

There are amusing and engrossing things in the sequels but the sequels are only sequels, faint echoes of the greatness of the major novels. Unfortunately, although they are "written" by Huck they are all centered on Tom. Tom is now no longer a talker, he's a doer, and Huck is only a shadow, an amanuensis to report on Tom's glory. Tom is now more respectable than ever, even pompous, and ever so theatrical; and Huck, without his nature lore, his skepticism, his conscience, his flight and his quest, seems little more than a country ignoramus. Even Jim shrinks in stature. Perhaps this is the price of success—the three characters have "made it," and the tension of their development and their growth, their strivings, has disappeared.

It is curious, the gulf which existed between Clemens's moral conscience and his aesthetic one. Apparently he did not see how offensive it was to make Jim the butt of practical jokes, and how callous Tom was to withhold the news of Jim's freedom. Tom knows that Huck is willing to be a "nigger-stealer," and is outside the Village code, and he pretends that he is too, lying to Huck so he can indulge in his histrionics. Jim is portrayed marvelously and it is an artistic crime to use him purposelessly as a pawn for Tom's high jinks. It's as though Mark Twain didn't believe in Jim's existence—he had "made him up," it was only fiction, not solid stuff, not real stuff like *Life on the Mississippi*. The only value one can see in these Tom chapters is that they serve to reveal how callous Tom's conventional conscience is where Jim is concerned. Tom was not callous about Muff Potter and eventually his conscience caused him to tell the truth about Injun Joe. But Potter was white and in danger of being hung. Jim is black and technically free. Tom's sin is that although he knows that Jim is no longer a slave he permits him to continue

living as a slave and he encourages him to escape from the cabin
at danger to his life—for his, Tom's, own theatrics, glory and
limelight-hogging. Tom never repents. He is smug and self-
satisfied. Huck would never have behaved like that. Huck is full
of empathy and humanity, even toward the two ragamuf-
fins who have misused him.

We might suppose that Clemens has arranged all this to show
the difference between Tom's "morality" and Huck's. The
trouble with this idea, however, is that Clemens so obviously
enjoys and approves of Tom and of his tomfoolery; and besides,
an even greater difficulty is the low literary quality of it all: the
padding, the jawing, the bad jokes, and even, and inevitably, the
degeneration of language. Tom's antics are an artistic crime, as
we have noted, but Mark Twain doesn't have enough of an artistic conscience, apparently, to know that a crime has been
committed. Even having Tom shot in the leg is not a gesture of
punishment but only an opportunity to make Tom more romantic, more glamorous and more theatrical than ever, an opportunity that Tom adequately exploits in the beginning of *Tom
Sawyer Abroad*.

Tom is a romantic boy who loves to stage "effects." There are
many echoes of him in Clemens's own life—the white suit, the
long, unruly hair, the sealskin coat, the grand house suggesting
the shape inside and out of a Mississippi steamboat and containing the famous fireplace under the famous window; the deliberate stage manner: drawl, deadpan, quaint delivery, monotonous
voice, frequent use of anti-climax; the adoration of Joan of Arc,
the defense of Harriet Shelley, the nostalgia for the American
and European past, the love of costume and archaic language.
Tom is a western boy but in his mind, through books and daydreams, he is fixated on the fairy tales of older cultures, and it is
no accident that in *Tom Sawyer Abroad* he travels eastward to
the places of "romance," and takes Huck and Jim with him, "up-
rooting" them. Huck, on the other hand, is indigenous, both in
body and mind, and anything but romantic. In Chapter 2 of
Tom Sawyer, Detective he puts the case plainly. "It was always
nuts for Tom Sawyer—a mystery was. If you'd lay out a mys-

tery and a pie before me and him, you wouldn't have to say take your choice; it was a thing that would regulate itself. Because in my nature I always run to pie, whilst in his nature he has always run to mystery."

Huck is a skeptic from beginning to end. He is heir to the skepticism of the backwoods and to the skepticism of American humorists and to Mark Twain's own skepticism and social criticism. He is a realist because his existence depends on the quality of his realism. Tom likes to go by what's in books, or what he thinks there is. Huck goes by what's in nature. Tom, for all his truancy and lies and pranks, belongs to the Village, and his conscience is a sound, Presbyterian, Village conscience. Huck, for all the Widow's and Miss Watson's attempts to reform him, remains a social outcast, but with a conscience more profound and more tormenting than Tom's. Huck is outside of the Village society and has an outlander's, an almost anthropological, view of it, which is why some of the social forms of the Village, such as home prayer, seem funny and illuminating when seen through his eyes. Tom still has a chance for social grace. He desires social grace. Huck does not desire it. Tom has a foot in each of two worlds: Huck's and that of the Village. He plays at being a rebel. Huck, being a rebel, doesn't feel the need to play at being one. Tom has more imagination than Huck and it is more likely, in real life, that *he* would have written a book than that Huck would have. Yet he doesn't write one, whereas Huck writes three. But if he had written one it would have lacked the tension of Huck's. Huck also lives between two worlds, but his position is full of tension. He lives between the Village and the world of the total outcasts: criminals, slaves, drunkards; between the Village and the world of his father. Huck has real problems and doesn't need to invent any for himself, the way Tom does. He is more mature than Tom. The more Tom strays from home the more theatrical and unpalatable he becomes, a pattern which is true in reverse for Huck. In his own book Tom is an interesting and admirable boy. In Huck's he's a visitor, an intruder, and callous, almost cynical, not merely toward his uncle and aunt and toward Jim, but toward his good friend Huck too.

Conscience does not bother Huck about the minor infringements of the Village code as it does Tom and the other boys of the gang, because his life as a semi-outcast keeps him infringing many times and he has become used to infringing. But in the important matters, such as Jim's efforts to escape from slavery, his conscience does bother him. Huck treats Jim as an adult. Tom treats Jim as a child. Huck knows that he is not square like Tom. He says, "I was playing double." He sees the Village society with almost a Northerner's view. Tom is the truer Southerner.

The second half of *Life on the Mississippi* is inferior to the first half, and similarly, the second half of *Huckleberry Finn* in no way matches its first half. In 1882 Mark Twain returned to the river country to collect material for *Life on the Mississippi*. It is well known that this return to the place of his boyhood and young manhood inspired the completion of *Huckleberry Finn* after the novel had languished for years. Perhaps that visit, with its load of facts as against memory and nostalgia, had as unhappy an effect on the novel as it had on the travel book.

We recall that in the novel Huck finds himself taken for Tom, and Tom disguises himself as his brother Sid. Both are incognito at the Phelps farm in the final quarter of the novel. In *Life on the Mississippi* we learn that Clemens also traveled incognito on that visit. He did it for greater freedom to collect material. "I remembered that it was the custom of steamboatmen in the old times to load up the confiding stranger with the most picturesque and admirable lies, and put the sophisticated friend off with dull and ineffectual facts . . ." This is what Tom did. He loaded up Huck and the Phelpses and Jim with picturesque lies. Clemens was "sold" by the lies of a pilot. "The pilot warmed to his opportunity, and proceeded to load me up in the good old-fashioned way." And the young man from Wisconsin, who knew little about boats, tried to "sell" Clemens about the steamboat they were traveling on. "He gave me a world of misinformation; and the further he went, the wider his imagination

expanded, and the more he enjoyed his cruel work of deceit."
But the young man was "sold" himself. "Idiot! if he had not
been in such a sweat to play his witless, practical jokes upon me,
in the beginning, I would have persuaded his thoughts into some
other direction, and saved him from committing that wanton
and silly impoliteness." These words could be applied by Huck
and Jim to Tom.

But despite the great flaw in the novel and despite what
Hemingway has called "cheating," *Huckleberry Finn* remains a
marvelous, magical evocation of a people, a place and a time
central to our history and our folklore.

It may be said with some justification that the last quarter of
Huckleberry Finn marked a turning point in Mark Twain's
career as a novelist. The curve was upward until then. It leveled
out in *A Connecticut Yankee* while the two conflicting elements
in Clemens's mind and character achieved a precarious balance.
After *A Connecticut Yankee* its direction was downward as the
theatrical-romantic side of Clemens became ascendant and produced such minor works as *The American Claimant* and *Pudd'n-
head Wilson*, the utterly theatrical, clownish and tasteless *Those
Extraordinary Twins*, and the super-romantic and gyneolatrous
Joan of Arc, the latter Mark Twain's grand effort to write a
"serious" novel. It is interesting to observe that together with
the absence of the vernacular style in *Joan of Arc* there is the
absence of that broad and refreshing, that saving humor which
is usually associated with the vernacular, especially in the American yarn. *The Prince and the Pauper*, which was published between *Tom Sawyer* and *Huckleberry Finn*, is a fairy tale for
boys and girls, with almost no irony in it. It was written in the
sort of reverential mood which controlled the writing of *Joan
of Arc*, and with the same deficiency of vernacular style and
humor.

A Connecticut Yankee is the first of Clemens's novels which
does not follow an important work of non-fiction. It is chiefly
for this reason, I believe, that it possesses a great amount of energy: in invention, in the speed of delivery of its humor, in the

multiplicity of themes, in the venom and sweep of its social criticism, in the acreage of corpses, in the ebullience of language, in
the free and easy characterizations. It seems to me that this is one
of the most successful of Clemens's creations, with fewer flaws
than is usual in his books, and that it is one of his most important
works for several reasons: the degree of success of its fancy,
its coherence as a work of the imagination, the essential seriousness of its themes, and its purity and ease of language, despite
the fact that the language is not the wonderful vernacular of
Huckleberry Finn. With *Tom Sawyer* and *Huckleberry Finn* it
completes the trio of Mark Twain's major novels. None of the
others comes near these three in scope, in style, in characterization, in imagination and in truthful rendering of subject
and scene.

It does have its flaws. One may ask why Chapters 15 and 19
were not omitted by the author, for as comic relief they are
rather sad failures, being neither comic nor a relief. One may ask
why Hank Morgan so conveniently dies at the very end of the
book, when he gave no sign earlier in the day that he was ill or
even indisposed. Demented he was, as a result of the blow on
the head we hear about in the novel's beginning; and we do not
doubt that his was a dual personality, the two parts "dwelling" in
different centuries; but why does he choose to die at a moment
so convenient to the author? And if Merlin is the magician-fraud
he is supposed to be how is he able—also for the author's last-
minute convenience—to put Hank Morgan into a sleep of
thirteen centuries?

A Connecticut Yankee is a kind of thematic sequel to *Huckleberry Finn*, at least in terms of the slavery motif. In *A Connecticut Yankee* Mark Twain expresses a degree of venomous
indignation about the institution of slavery which he did not attempt in *Huckleberry Finn*. Perhaps the extent and intensity of
his passion has something to do with the fact that he badly let the
subject down in the last quarter of *Huckleberry Finn*, as though
for some reason it was still too hot to handle in public, although
by the time of the appearance of *Huckleberry Finn* the Civil
War was distant by some two decades. Not that Mark Twain

openly condemns American slavery in *A Connecticut Yankee*.
He does it by implication, allusion, parallels, and only far along
in the novel, in Chapter 30, does he bring his southern theme
and allusions into the open and discuss the "poor whites" and
their degraded condition, and their relationship with the slaves
and with the slave-lords; and only in Chapter 34 does he speak
of the freemen who were often sold into lifelong slavery. We
note that the hero of this novel, who is so vociferous on the
evils of slavery, who sounds like a passionate Abolitionist, is, as
we might have expected, a Yankee.

Just before and after the appearance of *Huckleberry Finn*
Clemens was engaged in an extended lecture tour with George
Washington Cable, the New Orleans writer. Cable was small,
delicate, a pious Presbyterian and a fanatical Sabbatarian. He
was also a thoroughly reconstructed Southerner who because
of his liberal views was despised widely in the South. It is possible that the discussions which the two authors had on the subject of the South were a stimulus to Clemens when he came to
write *A Connecticut Yankee*. Also that the degree of heat which
Clemens worked up on the subject of the Church and religion
was inspired by memories of Cable. Near the tag end of the
lecture tour, which began November 5, 1884 and which ended
February 28, 1885, Clemens wrote to Howells in his best vein
of invective:

"Tonight in Baltimore, tomorrow afternoon and night in
Washington, and my four-months platform campaign is ended
at last. It has been a curious experience. It has taught me that
Cable's gifts of mind are greater and higher than I had suspected.
But—

"That 'but' is pointing toward his religion. You will never
never know, never divine, guess, imagine, how loathsome a
thing the Christian religion can be made until you come to
know and study Cable daily and hourly. Mind you, I like him;
he is pleasant company; I rage and swear at him sometimes, but
we do not quarrel; we get along mighty happily together; but
in him and his person I have learned to hate all religions. He has
taught me to abhor and detest the Sabbath-day and hunt up new
and troublesome ways to dishonor it."

Consistency was never one of Clemens's limiting hobgoblins. If he hated "all religions" and had a distaste for religious types, he nevertheless counted among his closest friends Reverend Joseph Twichell of Hartford, an admittedly unusual variety of minister, who shared Clemens's amusement with the latter's bawdy *1601.* In fairness to Cable we ought to remember that the lecture tour was a long and arduous one, the two men were physically and temperamentally very different, and they were thrown upon each other's company to an unnatural degree, so it is a wonder, really, that an explosion did not occur, especially when one considers Clemens's easily ignited temper. Cable idolized Mark Twain, whereas Mark Twain found release in frequent letters to his wife, in which he criticized Cable for certain items of behavior which seemed to him to evidence beyond doubt a smallness of soul.

Clemens's resentment and fear of the power of the Catholic Church, which appear so prominently in *A Connecticut Yankee,* were not inspired by the Protestant Cable. Clemens was a steady hand at writing diatribes against the Roman Church. In his first travel book, *The Innocents Abroad,* he excoriated the priests of Rome, and as late as 1906 he dictated the chapters of his autobiography, "Reflections on Religion," in which he derided various aspects of the Catholic Church, incidentally confusing the dogma of the Immaculate Conception with that of the Virgin Birth. *A Connecticut Yankee* is a subversive book, and what Clemens is saying is that almost all laws and customs are relative, even our own, and that none are excusable if they are cruel. Nothing so enrages and finally disheartens him about "the damned human race" as its willingness to endure torment without resistance, and nothing so disgusts him as the priestly misuse of the conception of God, the use of God and religion to buttress a particular social structure based on subordination.

Yet despite Clemens's increasing pessimism there is still a strain of optimism in *A Connecticut Yankee.* "A man *is* a man, at bottom," he asserts. "Whole ages of abuse and oppression cannot crush the manhood clear out of him. Whoever thinks it a mistake is himself mistaken. Yes, there is plenty good enough material for a republic in the most degraded people that ever existed—even the Russians; plenty of manhood in them—even in the Germans —if one could but force it out of its timid and suspicious privacy, to overthrow and trample in the mud any throne that ever was set up and any nobility that ever supported it." This is the prophet Clemens reading a very clouded crystal ball, for it was precisely these two peoples who overthrew their monarchies and nobilities—and lifted themselves up to be the prime movers of a conflagration of terror and mass murder unexampled in history. Whether they achieved this distinction just because they had been "degraded" we leave to the historians of degradation to discover.

As in *Huckleberry Finn*, Clemens holds to an outsider's view. Hank Morgan is an outsider in the most extreme sense, a seemingly impossible sense because of the difference in centuries —or at least impossible except in dreams—but not actually impossible psychologically, given a sufficient measure of moral sensitivity, moral indignation, intellectual insight, and disagreement with the prevailing culture. It is this outsider's view, perhaps, which inspires the degree of release which we feel in the author in *A Connecticut Yankee*.

Whatever may have been the influence of Cable on the treatment of slavery and religion in *A Connecticut Yankee*, there is no doubt that he had a significant although perhaps accidental influence on the choice of the Arthurian time. The novel was inspired by Thomas Malory's *Morte D'Arthur*. Clemens's biographer says that Cable introduced Clemens to the book and presented him with a copy. But if the contemporary stories about Cable's miserliness were true it is more likely that Clemens paid for the copy himself. *A Connecticut Yankee* was first published in December 1889. Clemens's own publishing conpany was in need, for financial reasons, of a new work by him, and Clemens himself felt it was more than time, for reasons of his literary reputation, that he appeared before the public with a full-size book.

The choice of the Arthurian time was a happy one for Mark Twain. Here was an age of chivalry which could be burlesqued as essentially unchivalrous; of romance which could be derided as childish, blind and sentimental. And at the same time Clemens, ever a Tom Sawyer at heart, could have his cake and eat it too: he could wear the plumes of knighthood in his daydreams and be as romantic as he wished. Also, the social institutions of that distant time could be scarified as inhuman, unjust and hopelessly superstitious; and Clemens in his daydreams could be as inhuman and unjust as the rest, committing mass murder by means of dynamite, electrocution and Gatling guns. But superstitious he was not, not even in his daydreams, unless his growing penchant for determinism could be labeled superstition.

The novel was an extended opportunity for jokes, tall tales, a delightful roaming in time past, and a pleasure in tasting, mimicking and burlesquing an archaic language, which was almost as much fun as taking off on the absurdities of the awful German language. Clemens had a field day and wrote with verve and gusto. One of the most delicious things in the novel, to my taste, is the item called "Local Smoke and Cinders," with its nightmare typos, in Chapter 26. The style is American territorial and the sound is that of the old penny press. Clemens, who had worked for the territorial press, and very successfully, knew the style and no doubt had scrapbooks which could help refresh his memory if they were needed. Whenever his humor returns to his southwestern origins and his far-western experiences it is unsurpassed in bounce and surprise.

There was much satisfaction to be derived from childish nonsense, the childish nonsense which always fascinated him. The setting, with its contrast with the nineteenth century, was a gold mine for him. Colonel Sellers had come into his own. There were crazy language, fireworks, explosions, lassoing knights in a tournament, the cream of knighthood on bicycles, and all the rest of it, just as though Clemens had stumbled upon an undiscovered primitive people, with all the opportunity to play God which such a situation implies. There was a powerful strain of Katzenjammer humor in Mark Twain, with its attendant cruelties. On the other hand there was the great humanitarianism, which called forth bursts of Jovian anger and satire, and gave birth to impassioned brief essays on the injustices inherent in certain social institutions; on man's willingness, perhaps desire, to be ruled or enslaved; and in general on man's inhumanity to man.

The descriptions are very vivid and this does much to make the novel succeed. The reader is projected into it as though it were a motion picture. The author's suspension of disbelief is contagious. The descriptions of the town and castle near the beginning of the novel, and the descriptions of the interior of the castle, with their palpable phrases, show how strongly Clemens's imagination was stirred and involved. Yet there is always, despite the realism, the sense of a fairy tale being told, and with the trappings of a tour de force. Not that the novel came all in a rush. It grew tired around its middle and he had to put it aside for some two years before his tank, as he called it, filled up again. The experience of having his tank run dry while working on a full-length book was not a unique one for Clemens. In 1906 he recalled in his autobiography:

"There has never been a time in the past thirty-five years when my literary shipyard hadn't two or more half-finished ships on the ways, neglected and baking in the sun; generally there have been three or four; at present there are five. This has an unbusiness-like look but it was not purposeless, it was intentional. As long as a book would write itself I was a faithful and interested amanuensis and my industry did not flag, but the minute that the book tried to shift to *my* head the labor of contriving its situations, inventing its adventures and conducting its conversations, I put it away and dropped it out of my mind."

Pleasant though the novel must have been to write, judging by the elasticity and bounce of its style, and delightful though it is to read, it has many somber, painful passages in it dealing with man's cruelty, his superstitions and his willingness to be oppressed. Although on the surface Clemens was attacking the inhumanity of that more primitive time of the sixth century and of the lowly man's rotten condition in it, he was also, and obviously, making savage comments on the modern British system of nobility, preference, a powerful church, and oppression of the unwashed classes. In addition he was subtly but unmistakably alluding to the economic abuses of his own country—to the effects of capitalism, with its underpaid and overworked wage earners, its sweatshops—and to the social abuses of the South, both before and after the Civil War.

It was not an accident on the author's part that the hero of the novel was an important employee of an arms factory. His knowledge and experience in warfare give him a tremendous advantage when he is in the sixth century and permit him to destroy the institution of knight-errantry and to damage the old-time chivalry, which did not extend to the lower and oppressed classes. (One recalls the effect of gunpowder in bringing the Middle Ages to a close.) This is one of the leading plot reasons for Hank Morgan's connection with a northern arms factory. A symbolic reason is that Clemens can hint at the novel's subordinate theme by suggesting that it was northern industrialism and force of arms which conquered the South and put to sleep its outmoded code of honor, its aristocratic system based on a slave class and its restricted chivalry.

Clemens like Cable was a reconstructed Southerner. Howells characterized him after his death as "the most desouthernized Southerner" he ever knew, adding, "No man more perfectly sensed and more entirely abhorred slavery, and no one has ever poured such scorn upon the second-hand, Walter-Scotticized, pseudo-chivalry of the Southern ideal."

Howells read galleys of the novel and relieved and gratified Clemens by praising the book handsomely, at first in private and then, shortly after its publication, in a review in *Harper's Magazine*. Howells wrote in the review: "Mr. Clemens, we call him, rather than Mark Twain, because we feel that in this book our arch-humorist imparts more of his personal quality than in anything else he has done. . . . The delicious satire, the marvellous wit, the wild, free, fantastic humor are the colors of the tapestry, while the texture is a humanity that lives in every fibre. . . . We can give no proper notion of the measureless play of an imagination which has a gigantic jollity in its feats, together with the tenderest sympathy."

In view of the novel's burlesque of Arthurian times and legends and its harsh and unmitigated criticism of the institution of nobility it is not surprising that it found only a lukewarm welcome in England. The English publishers, Chatto & Windus, had feared this when they asked Clemens to edit the novel for their edition. He replied that he had already made certain changes which had been suggested by his wife and he indicated that he was not in the mind to make any further changes. He implied that Livy had toned down passages in the novel and that this softening was sufficient for the English edition also. He wrote, ". . . the book was not written for America; it was written for England. So many Englishmen have done their sincerest best to teach us something for our betterment that it seems to me high time that some of us should substantially recognize the good intent by trying to pry up the English nation to a little higher level of manhood in turn." The book was published without changes.

It is strange that Clemens, who was careful not to offend certain areas of public opinion in his lifetime—he suppressed a chapter of *Life on the Mississippi* out of fear it might offend Southerners, and he (and his daughter Clara) effectively suppressed his "Reflections on Religion" until its publication in 1963 for fear it would inflame the religious community—should have been willing to risk offending the English, whom he liked so well and who liked him in turn. His reference to the "many Englishmen who have done their sincerest best to teach us something for our betterment" and his inclination to square things recall the literary battles fought between English and American writers after the War of 1812.

It is strange too that Clemens did not admit in his letter that the novel was also written for America. Probably it was inconvenient for the purposes of his reply to mention that he intended the book for a much larger audience also. His larger purpose is reflected in his autobiography. Discussing the novel near the close of his life, he wrote, "*A Connecticut Yankee in King Arthur's Court* was an attempt to imagine, and after a fashion to set forth, the hard conditions of life for the laboring and defenseless poor in bygone times in England, and incidentally contrast these conditions with those under which the civil and ecclesiastical pets of privilege and high fortune lived in those times. I think I was purposing to contrast that English life, not just the English life of Arthur's day but the English life of the whole of the Middle Ages, with the life of modern Christendom and modern civilization—to the advantage of the latter, of course."

We note the irony of that appendage: "to the advantage of the latter, of course." Having seen what bestiality man is capable of in modern times, the spectacle of which Clemens fortunately was spared when he died in 1910, we are not likely to dissent. If Mark Twain thought it was a "damned human race" in his own lifetime, what would he have thought if he had lived in a time which has witnessed the eradication of almost whole peoples, and in that most "civilized" of all continents, Europe.

Princeton, New Jersey
March 1964

THE ADVENTURES OF
COLONEL SELLERS*

O F THE TWO paragraphs which Mark Twain
contributed to the preface of *The Gilded Age*, one, the last of the preface, was the following:

"One word more. This is—what it pretends to be—a joint production, in the conception of the story, the exposition of the characters, and in its literal composition. There is scarcely a chapter that does not bear the marks of the two writers of the book."

The paragraph was designed to reassure the subscription reader (the volume was meant to be sold by subscription only) that the product was not a hodge-podge, a mish-mash, a conflict of styles, settings and characterizations; that it was a sensible, reasonable, harmonious joint production. The paragraph was less than candid, for some of the chief characters, Colonel Sellers, Laura Hawkins and Washington Hawkins, were Mark Twain's sole creations, as was the backwoods Missouri setting, and more than fifty of the sixty-three chapters were written not by two hands but by one. If we are to believe Mark Twain's friend and official biographer, Albert Bigelow Paine, even the basic story was Mark Twain's alone. Mark Twain almost gave the game away when he said, "This is—what it pretends to be—." The idea of a thoroughly joint production was a dubious one, for it is difficult to see how two minds and two styles as different as those of Clemens and Charles Dudley Warner could be depended on to bring forth anything but dissonance.

If Mark Twain—perhaps guilelessly—misled the prospective reader, he did not mislead certain of his friends. Shortly after

* The title of a book comprising Mark Twain's share of *The Gilded Age*, the novel which he wrote with Charles Dudley Warner.

The Gilded Age was published he wrote to his friend Mrs. Fair-banks (February 25, 1874), "I think you don't like the Gilded Age,—but that's because you've been reading *Warner's* chapters. I wrote chapters 1, 2, 3, 4, 5, 6, 7, 8, 9, 10, 11, 24, 25, 27, 28, 30, 32, 33, 34, 36, 37, 42, 43, 45, first three or four pages of 49,—also chapters 51, 52, 53, 57, 59, 60, 61, 62 & portions of 35 & 56. You read *those*." Three days later he wrote to Dr. John Brown, "My dear friend—we are all delighted with your commendations of the Gilded Age—& the more so because some of our newspapers have set forth the opinion that *Warner* really wrote the book & I only added my name to the title-page in order to give it a large sale. It is a shameful charge to make. I wrote the first eleven chapters—every word & every line—Warner never retouched a sentence in them, I believe. I also wrote chapters 24, 25, 27, 28, 30, 32, 33, 34, 36, 37, 42, 45, 51, 52, 53, 57, 59, 60, 61, 62, & *portions* of 35, 49, & 56. So I wrote 32 of the 63 chapters *entirely*, & part of 3 others beside.

"The fearful financial panic hit the book heavily, for we published in the midst of it. But nevertheless in the 8 weeks that have now elapsed since the day we published, we have sold 40,000 copies—which gives £3,000 royalty to be divided between the authors. This is really the largest two-months' sale which any American book has ever achieved (unless one excepts the cheap edition of Uncle Tom's Cabin). The average price of our book is 16 shillings a copy—Uncle Tom was 2 shillings a copy. But for the panic our sale would have been doubled, I verily believe. I do not believe the sale will ultimately go over 100,000 copies."

In July 1874 Mark Twain noted in a copy of *The Gilded Age* for his friend William Seaver the chapters and parts of chapters which he had written. It is clear from the letters and the marked copy that the novel is not the joint production which Clemens claimed it to be in the preface. This judgment is supported by an examination of a substantial portion of the extant manuscript. I have not been able to discover in the manuscript anything which challenges Clemens's ascription of authorship in the two letters and in the Seaver copy. It is for this reason—Clemens's

authoritative statement of his contribution to the novel—that
it is possible to publish his contribution separately. It is worth
noting in passing that whereas in the letters to Mrs. Fairbanks
and to Dr. Brown, Clemens claimed all of Chapter 53, in the
Seaver copy he indicated a few brief passages by Warner in that
chapter. There are other small differences between the Seaver
copy and the letters. It is clear that the Seaver copy has a higher
authority than the letters.

The Gilded Age has lived because of Mark Twain's share of
it, although most readers did not and do not know which parts
were his. It has lived because his genius is in it, at a youthful and
vigorous stage. It has lived despite Warner's contribution. It was
an error for Mark Twain to seek Warner's help. There can be
little doubt that had he undertaken the work alone he would
have produced a good novel and one which would have spared
him from living under the cloud of joint authorship. As it happens, his share of *The Gilded Age* is the central share and the
text is cohesive and extensive enough to be printed separately if
certain sections by Warner are synopsized to carry the story
along.

To the possible objection that Mark Twain's work ought not
to be "tampered with," we can recall that Bernard DeVoto
modernized the punctuation of a masterpiece, *Huckleberry
Finn*, and inserted a chapter into it which Clemens never put into
it. Yet nobody consigned DeVoto to hell for doing it. He was,
by the way, literary editor of the Mark Twain Estate and the
outstanding Mark Twain scholar at the time he did it. I have
not changed one word of Mark Twain's text. My sole purpose
has been to rescue his text, not to change it; to let the reader see
as clearly as possible just what it was that Clemens put into *The
Gilded Age*. Clemens himself set a kind of precedent by extract-
ing his share of *The Gilded Age* when he made the play called
Colonel Sellers, which was a great success, with John Raymond playing the colonel. The method I have used in synop-
sizing Warner, printing him in a denser type than Clemens, and
bracketing him, follows Clemens's method when he lifted
Those Extraordinary Twins out of *Pudd'nhead Wilson* and

printed it separately, with portions synopsized and printed in smaller type than the main text.

Clemens's and Warner's criticism of contemporary novels to their wives in 1873 was echoed later the same year by the *Saturday Review* in some comments which were reprinted by the New York *Daily Graphic* under the title "Modern Novels."

"Nobody can look upon the stream of fiction which is constantly poured forth upon the public without some doubts as to the intellectual habits which it fosters. Every day brings forth some new aspirant to the pulpit. If we could believe, which indeed would be a rather rash assumption, that they all succeed in obtaining some kind of hearing, we should be awestruck by the revelation of the waste of human energy. It is bad enough that so many people should write such trash, that so many printers should waste so much paper in circulating it, and that so many critics should be doomed to give it at least a cursory glance. It would be still more lamentable if we could believe that a large class of readers derives its chief intellectual sustenance from these monotonous reproductions of old materials. How can standard literature—or, not to use a term which has unfortunately become associated with much that is wearisome, how can the thoughts of men who have really had something to say about the world—receive a due share of attention when swamped and overwhelmed in this torrent of vapid literature? Nobody, of course, would be puritanical enough to deny to hardworked men and women the right of unbending their minds over innocent, if insipid, literature at odd moments. We cannot all fill up the interstices of our lives with metaphysical or scientific or historical researches. But certainly it is a natural impression that the habit of endless story-telling and endless story-reading is hardly likely to encourage strenuous thought. If not demoralizing in the sense of actually encouraging vice, it is perhaps demoralizing in the sense of softening the intellectual fibre. A man raised upon rice-pudding and water-gruel would not have strong bones and firm muscles; and a mind nourished by modern novels would hardly be fitted for vigorous intellectual labor. In spite of the outcry about sensationalism, the bulk of our novel literature is dull and colorless enough in all conscience. The objection to it is not that it is vicious, but that it is enervating; and when Mr. Trollope was delivering an address to youths who had won prizes in some kind of intellectual competition, he would perhaps have spoken more to the purpose if, instead of proving that Dickens does not teach us to be misers and debauchees, he had shown under what conditions Dickens and other modern writers may be used for purposes of rational relaxation without crushing the loftier imaginative or reasoning faculties under a weight of commonplace moralizing and indolent representations of every-day life."

The Gilded Age, begun in February 1873 if we are to believe Albert Bigelow Paine, or in January if we are to trust a letter of April 7th by Warner, was completed in April. In the April 7th letter, written to Whitelaw Reid, Warner said, "Maybe it's a great piece of presumption, but Mark and I are writing a novel. . . . No one here, except our wives, knows anything of it. We conceived the design early in the winter, but were not able to get seriously at work on it till some time in January. . . . We have hatched the plot day by day, drawn out the characters, and written it so that we cannot exactly say which belongs to whom; though the different styles will show in the chapters." On the 16th of April Clemens wrote to Mrs. Fairbanks, "Ever since I arrived from England, several months ago, Chas. Dudley Warner & I have been belting away every day on a *partnership novel.* I have worked 6 days a week—good full days—& laid myself up, once. Have written many chapters twice, & some of them three times—have thrown away 300 clean pages of MS. & still there's havoc to be made when I enter on final polishing. Warner has been more fortunate—he won't lose 50 pages. . . . Every night for many weeks, Livy & Susie Warner have collected in my study to hear Warner & me read our day's work; & they have done a power of criticizing, but have always been anxious to be on hand at the reading & find out what has been happening to the dramatis personae since the previous evening.

They both pleaded so long & vigorously for Warner's heroine, that yesterday Warner agreed to spare her life & let her marry —he meant to kill her. I killed my heroine as dead as a mackerel yesterday (but Livy don't know it yet). . . ."

On April 26 Clemens wrote to his wife Livy, who was in Elmira for a brief visit, "I have finished trimming & revamping all my MS, & to-day we began the work of critically reading the book, line by line, & numbering the chapters & working them in together in their appropriate places. It is perfectly fascinating work. All of the first eleven chapters are mine, & when I came to read them right straight along without breaking, I got really interested; & when I got to Sellers' eye-water & his clock & his fireless stove & his turnip dinner, I could hardly read for laughing. The turnip dinner is powerful good—& is satisfactory now. . . . We both think this is going to be no slouch of a novel, as Solomon said to the Hebrew children."

When the book was published Clemens was in England and was being sought out as the famous author of *The Innocents Abroad* and *Roughing It*, as well as of numerous sketches and stories. The novel appeared in England at about the same time that it appeared in America. On December 11, 1873 Mark Twain wrote a preface to the London edition, which he signed:

"In America nearly every man has his dream, his pet scheme, whereby he is to advance himself socially or pecuniarily. It is this all-pervading speculativeness which we have tried to illustrate in 'The Gilded Age.' It is a characteristic which is both bad and good, for both the individual and the nation. Good, because it allows neither to stand still, but drives both for ever on, toward some point or other which is ahead, not behind nor at one side. Bad, because the chosen point is often badly chosen, and then the individual is wrecked; the aggregation of such cases affects the nation, and so is bad for the nation. Still, it is a trait which it is of course better for a people to have and sometimes suffer from than to be without.

"We have also touched upon one sad feature, and it is one which we found little pleasure in handling. That is the shameful corruption which lately crept into our politics, and in a handful of years has spread until the pollution has affected some portion of every State and every Territory in the Union.

"But I have a great strong faith in a noble future for my country. A vast majority of the people are straightforward and honest; and this late state of things is stirring them to action. If it would only keep on stirring them until it became the habit of their lives to attend to the politics of the country personally, and put only their very best men into positions of trust and authority! That day will come.

"Our improvement has already begun. Mr. Tweed (whom Great Britain furnished to us), after laughing at our laws and courts for a good while, has at last been sentenced to thirteen years' imprisonment, with hard labor. It is simply bliss to think of it. It will be at least two years before any governor will dare to pardon him out, too. A great New York judge, who continued a vile, a shameless career, season after season, defying the legislature and sneering at the newspapers, was brought low at last, stripped of his dignities, and by public sentence debarred from ever again holding any office of honor or profit in the State. Another such judge (furnished to us by Great Britain) had the grace to break his heart and die in the palace built with his robberies when he saw the same blow preparing for his own head and sure to fall upon it."

The Gilded Age is in many respects *a roman à clef* and it was widely recognized as such in contemporary reviews. The *New York World* wrote: "Senator Dilworthy will be as readily recognized as though his true name had been used. . . . So, too, the great Mr. Braham, New York's most successful criminal lawyer, is as palpable to the reader . . . as he is to the frequenters of our criminal courts." The *New York Evening Mail* wrote: "The murder trial in New York makes some hard hits, and Mr. Braham's speech will be easily identified. . . . The authors evidently meant, when they drew a character from life, that he should recognize himself. They have in some instances made sure of this by using the real name of the man intended, and in other cases the modifications made in the proper names of the persons described are so slight that nobody can mistake the originals. Thus we have Jeff Thompson, without any mask at all, as the engineer who of all others was the man to make a preliminary survey for a railroad, it being the principal business of the preliminary survey to make the road seem certain to pass through every town, and intersect every big plantation, within thirty miles of its probable route. We have Mr. Duff Brown too, whom every Western man will recognize simply by substituting for Brown another color." The Boston *Saturday Evening Gazette* noted that Senators Cameron and Nye might recognize themselves in the novel, as Senators Pomeroy and Harlan surely would. The Gazette also noted that Credit Mobilier, Back Pay, and other schemes and scandals were depicted with "photographic accuracy." The Springfield, Mass., *Union* reported: "The melancholy developments of political venality at Washington, last winter, with their exhibitions of religious hypocrisy and general corruption, are, with slight changes in the names of the parties concerned, fully shown up in a light mercilessly clear. That 'Christian statesman,' Senator Pomeroy [of Kansas], is one of the leading characters of the book. The character and methods of the Washington female lobbyists are fully illustrated in the career of Laura Hawkins. This lady finally kills her paramour, and her trial, acquittal and attempt to enter the lecture field are worked up from the Laura Fair case [of San Francisco], and the emotional insanity farces for which New York courtrooms have been famous. The reader of this book will say, how astonishing, absurd and sensational are its transitions and situations, and yet his memory will tell him that the most startling developments of the story are but slightly veiled reproductions of events that have been in the newspapers within a year."

The critical reception of *The Gilded Age* was not, on the whole, the kind that warms the cockles of an author's heart, or of his two hearts, as in this instance. There was a good deal of the usual uncritical praise in the small-town papers, and there was praise here and there in the large cities, but the authors were disconcerted by the general view that the experiment in joint authorship had failed. Clemens was gloomy, almost bitter, about the book's reception. Six years later he wrote to Howells, "I am justified in being afraid of the general press, because it killed the 'Gilded Age' before you had a chance to point out that there were merits in that book. The sale ceased almost *utterly* until the adverse criticisms were forgotten—then began again, & has kept smoothly on." Perhaps Clemens was still unaware that Howells had not much liked the book.

Down to near the close of his life Clemens remained sensitive about the critical reception of *The Gilded Age*. On September 27, 1907, his secretary, Isobel Lyon, wrote in her notebook that after dinner Clemens had been pacing his living room in Dublin, New Hampshire, when she remarked that in reading *The Gilded Age* that afternoon she had been "impressed by the fact that it was notably the work of two minds." Clemens had then talked about the novel. In 1933 Miss Lyon, consulting her notebook, recalled the gist of his remarks. "He said it was probably the end of 1872, when he had been in Hartford only a short time, that he suggested to Warner that they write a novel together. He said he did it because he had a fresh great reputation and he had a fear that he must not stand alone; so *The Gilded Age* was written and published. The first review of it in a Chicago paper was a hostile one. It said he was living on his reputation, and getting some one else to do his work. Mr. Clemens was in a serious mood; he went on to say it was all a mistake; he thought it was for the best, but it made discomfort all around, for Warner felt that the adverse criticism was for him."

Miss Lyon seems to imply that the Chicago review was the first review of the novel but her punctuation has the sentence state that it was merely the first Chicago review. It is impossible to know her precise meaning. Perhaps Clemens had in mind the review in the Chicago *Tribune* of April 5, 1874, which was by no means the first review of the book. On that day the *Tribune* quoted a comment from the St. Louis *Democrat:* "The secret is out. It is confidently asserted that *The Gilded Age* is a gigantic practical joke. It is declared that, wishing to test the credulity of the public, these two notorious wits had the book prepared by

several obscure newspaper local reporters. The covenant was
solemnly made that the joke was to be kept a profound secret
till 300,000 copies of the work were sold . . ." This comment
does not exactly match Clemens's description of it, or rather
Miss Lyon's recollection of Clemens's description. In 1907 Clemens had implied that he had been charged with getting Warner to
do his work for him, but the *Tribune,* if that was the paper he
had in mind, had charged both him and Warner with getting
others to do their work for them. Clemens's memory was no-
toriously unreliable at times, as can be illustrated in his recollections of the New York *Daily Graphic* review of *The Gilded
Age.* When he was dictating a chapter of his autobiography in
July 1906 he said:

"I believe that the trade of critic in literature, music and the
drama is the most degraded of all trades and that it has no real
value—certainly no large value. When Charles Dudley Warner
and I were about to bring out *The Gilded Age* the editor of the
Daily Graphic persuaded me to let him have an advance copy,
he giving me his word of honor that no notice of it should
appear in his paper until after the *Atlantic Monthly* notice should
have appeared. This reptile published a review of the book within
three days afterward. I could not really complain, because he
had only given me his word of honor as security. I ought to have
required of him something substantial. I believe his notice did
not deal mainly with the merit of the book or the lack of it but
with my moral attitude toward the public. It was charged that
I had used my reputation to play a swindle upon the public—
that Mr. Warner had written as much as half of the book and
that I had used my name to float it and give it currency—a currency which it could not have acquired without my name—and
that this conduct of mine was a grave fraud upon the people.
The *Graphic* was not an authority upon any subject whatever.
It had a sort of distinction in that it was the first and only
illustrated daily newspaper that the world had seen; but it was
without character, it was poorly and cheaply edited, its opinion
of a book or of any other work of art was of no consequence.
Everybody knew this, yet all the critics in America, one after

the other, copied the *Graphic's* criticism, merely changing the phraseology, and left me under that charge of dishonest conduct. Even the great Chicago *Tribune*, the most important journal in the Middle West, was not able to invent anything fresh but adopted the view of the humble *Daily Graphic*, dishonesty charge and all. However, let it go. It is the will of God that we must have critics and missionaries and congressmen and humorists, and we must bear the burden."

The *Daily Graphic* review was entirely different from what Clemens recalled it to be. Inasmuch as it has not been reprinted, to my knowledge, I include it here.

" 'The Gilded Age' is the title of the long expected novel written by Mark Twain and Charles Dudley Warner, and published by the American Publishing Company of Hartford, Ct. It is many months since this book was announced, and from the reputation of its authors it was anticipated that the book would be one of remarkable interest and merit. It is necessary to say that these expectations have been signally disappointed. Regarded either as a novel or an exponent of the wit and humor of the two authors, 'The Gilded Age' is a failure. It is simply a rather incoherent series of sketches, from which the characteristic fun of Mr. Clemens and the subtle humor of Mr. Warner have been, for the most part, eliminated. The reader can hardly fail to adopt the only theory of the manner in which the book was written, which will account for its peculiarities. According to this theory, each of the authors wrote alternate chapters of the work without any previous consultation. They then met and pieced those chapters together so as to form a story with some degree of connection between its parts. This theory easily explains the reason why characters introduced in one part of the book abruptly vanish in another, and why men who at their first introduction to us possess certain characteristics entirely lose them a little later. It explains, in short, why the book is so fragmentary in its character, and fully accounts for the wonderful weakness of the plot. We are inclined to think that Mark Twain originally intended that they story should be made as incoherent and exasperating as possible, by way of a joke, but that he was finally overruled, and a book that would otherwise have been a capital burlesque was fashioned into a semblance of a serious novel. But what will chiefly disappoint the readers of 'The Gilded Age' is the lack of that abundance of humor which we had the right to anticipate. It is probable that Mr. Warner revised Mark Twain's chapters, and saying to himself, 'This man's humor is far too wild and coarse,' toned them down till they had lost the characteristic mark of their authorship. And similarly it is probable that Mark revised Mr. Warner's chapters, and calling the good 'gosh' of New England worship to witness that Warner's humor was far too delicate and subtle, translated it into a plainness of speech adapted to the comprehension of the dullest idiot. And so it has come to pass that the two most brilliant humorists in America—with the exception of 'John Paul'—have written a book in which we look almost in vain for the traces of either's pen. Nevertheless, it is obvious that neither could altogether smother the other in a book of so many octavo pages. There are here and there a few glimpses of Warner's wit, and occasionally we find one of Mark's paragraphs which the destroyer has not wholly tamed. There is also much legitimate satire in the book; and the characters of Senator Dilworthy, the 'Christian statesman'; of 'Brother Balaam,' the pious occupant of a berth in the Interior Department; and of Mr. Braham, the eminent criminal lawyer of this city, are admirably drawn. In isolated passages the book is frequently clever and amusing. It is as a whole that it will be recognized as a rather dreary failure. There are illustrations without number scattered through its pages, but they are fearfully and wonderfully bad. There is neither humor nor artistic merit in any one of them, and in a second edition they ought without any exception to be ruthlessly struck out."

It was a biting, snide, harsh review and it went overboard in stressing the novel's flaws and was ungenerous and unfair regarding its virtues, especially those contributed by Clemens, such as the characters of Sellers and Laura Hawkins and the Missouri setting. It verged on idiocy when it put Warner in Clemens's class as a humorist. Warner's vein of humor was small and somewhat thin and at times it was very uncertain; and he had turned out two or three slim volumes as compared with the large and powerful and broad-scaled *The Innocents Abroad* and *Roughing It.* Strictly speaking he was not even a humorist. Idiocy was capped by lunacy when the review set John Paul (Charles H. Webb) above both Clemens and Warner. Clemens ought to have discounted the review by three-quarters, except for its strictures on the novel's illustrations. The illustrations were indeed bad, designed as they were for a subscription audience.

But intemperate though it was, the review was probably sincere, and it did not make the moral accusations against Clemens which the latter much later recalled that it had made. It did not set the style for reviews of the novel, and the Chicago *Tribune* did not echo it in essentials, "dishonesty charge and all." *The Gilded Age*—or part of it—was Clemens's first novel, and we can appreciate his sensitivity to the *Graphic's* hard approach, especially because we can imagine that he may have felt defensive about the idea of joint authorship once it was too late to abandon it. It may be true that the editor of the *Graphic* broke his word to Clemens that he would not print a review until after the *Atlantic* had printed one; I have no way of checking Clemens's memory in this detail. The *Atlantic* did not review the book, probably because Howells, the editor, had a mixed reaction to it. Howells read an advance copy at the end of 1873 and wrote to Warner: "Up to the time old Hawkins dies your novel is of the greatest promise—I read it with joy—but after that it fails to assimilate the crude material with which it is fed, and becomes a confirmed dyspeptic at last. Still it is always entertaining; and it kept me up till twelve last night, though I needed sleep. I was particularly sorry to have Sellers degenerate as he did, and none of the characters quite fulfill their early promise."

Clemens's strong reaction to the *Graphic* is an interesting one and suggests that there was more to his relationship with the paper than meets the eye. A study of the files of the *Graphic* illuminates the relationship. The *Graphic's* first issue was Tuesday, March 4, 1873. In the issue of March 12 there appeared a letter to the editor, headlined MARK TWAIN WANTS "THE DAILY GRAPHIC." It was dated Hartford, March 8. "If I enclosed a check to 'Publishers Graphic' the cashier might not consider it good commercial literature, but, perhaps, you won't mind taking the chances on it yourself. I would like to have the paper sent—six dollars' worth—to the lady who bore me, viz.: Mrs. Jane Clemens, Fredonia, N.Y. Very truly yours, Mark Twain. P. S. After all, it isn't worth while to bother you with this check. If it should prove worthless, it will occur to the publishers not to send the paper."

Two days later the *Graphic* printed a letter headed A LETTER FROM MARK TWAIN, prefacing it with, "The following letter from Mark Twain shows what our most eminent and popular humorist thinks of our enterprise." The letter was dated Hartford, March 13. "It is a marvellous paper—and the strangest marvel is that it seems to keep on going, like a substantial reality, instead of flaming a moment and then fading out, like an enthusiast's distempered dream. Every day when the carrier leaves it at the door, I think that that one doubtless contains the obituary (illustrated), and that he will collect his money now and come no more; but it does not result so, and I am one who is not sorry. Indeed, the pictures grow finer and clearer and softer, which is a surprising thing, and must be as gratifying to you as it is to me, I should think. I hope you will be able to keep it going all the time, for I don't care much about reading (unless it be some tranquillizing tract or other), but I do like to look at pictures, and the illustrated weeklies do not come to me as often as I need them. And then there is another thing—a national matter. We thought we invented the steamboat: England claimed priority and flooded the world with testimony. We thought we invented the magnetic telegraph: England claimed priority again, and gave all the credit to her Wheatstone. We thought we invented Old Probabilities—and now she comes forward with her old 'original Jacobs' in that line, and says he died some years ago and left no successor. But I don't think she has ever invented an illustrated daily newspaper. I do believe we have 'got her' at last, as the clergy say. And if it is so, let us keep her reminded of it in a friendly way—and pretty constantly. Yours truly, Samuel L. Clemens."

It is clear from this letter that Clemens at one time admired the *Graphic*, and that the *Graphic* was proud to be admired by him and that it regarded him, as did most newspapers, as highly newsworthy. It is doubtful that Clemens at that time believed that the *Graphic* "was without character" or that it was "poorly and cheaply edited" or that "its opinion of a book or of any other work of art was of no consequence." The *Graphic* was well edited, was printed on good paper, was expertly illustrated, and provided a variety of news and opinion. Its tone was lively and skeptical and it was recognized at once as a remarkable innovation. It is possible that Clemens thought highly of the paper and that for this reason he was stung by its sharp review. If he believed in 1906 that the *Graphic's* opinion of a book was of no consequence, how is it that his memory told him that "all the critics in America, one after the other, copied the *Graphic's* criticism"? Mark Twain may have felt that the *Graphic* had let their promising new relationship down. On the other hand the *Graphic* may have honestly felt that Mark Twain had let the cause of American humor down in the joint authorship project.

It was to the *Graphic* that Mark Twain publicly revealed the joint project. Learning that he was preparing to visit England, the *Graphic* asked him for a farewell statement to America. Clemens responded with a long and characteristically droll letter, which he closed with: "During the last two months my next-door neighbor, Chas. Dudley Warner, has dropped his 'Back-Log Studies,' & he & I have written a bulky novel in partnership. He has worked up the fiction & I have hurled in the facts. I consider it one of the most astonishing novels that ever was written. Night after night I sit up reading it over & over again & crying. It will be published early in the fall, with plenty of pictures. Do you consider this an advertisement?—& if so, do you charge for such things, when a man is your friend & is an orphan?

"Drooping now, under the solemn peacefulness, the general

stagnation, the profound lethargy that broods over the land, I am Yrs truly . . ." He wrote the letter April 17. The *Graphic* devoted more than a half of one of its large pages on April 22, reproducing Clemens's handwriting. The next day the *Graphic* printed a description of Mark Twain as an editor, which it copied from the *Globe,* a monthly magazine published in Buffalo, N.Y. The item described Clemens's habits in the offices of the Buffalo *Express.* Then there was a long silence, due perhaps to the fact that Clemens was out of the country. The silence was broken by the *Graphic's* review, which appeared at a time when Clemens was again in England.

On January 15, 1874, the *Graphic* reprinted a letter by Clemens, with the preface, "The London *Post* prints as 'a specimen of transatlantic puffery' this hit by Mark Twain at the custom the English have of insisting upon the presence of some person of rank at popular gatherings." The letter is perhaps worth reviving and preserving here as part of the record of Clemens's relationship with the *Graphic.*

"Now that my lecturing engagement is drawing to its close, I find that there is one attraction which I forgot to provide, and that is the attendance of some great member of the Government to give distinction to my entertainment. Strictly speaking, I did not really forget this or underrate its importance, but the truth was, I was afraid of it. I was afraid of it for the reason that those great personages have so many calls upon their time that they cannot well spare the time to sit out an entertainment, and I knew that if one of them were to leave his box and retire while I was lecturing it would seriously embarrass me. I find, however, that many people think I ought not to allow this lack to exist longer; therefore I feel compelled to reveal a thing which I had intended to keep a secret. I early applied to a party in the East End, who is in the same line of business as Madame Tussaud, and he agreed to lend me a couple of kings and some nobility, and he said that they would sit out my lecture, and not only sit it out, but that they wouldn't even leave the place when it was done, but would just stay where they were, perfectly infatuated, and wait for more. So I made a bargain with him at once, and was going to ask the newspapers to mention, in the usual column, that on such an evening His Majesty King Henry VIII would honor my entertainment with his presence, and that on such and such an evening His Majesty William the Conqueror would be present, and that on the succeeding evening Moses and Aaron would be there, and so on. I felt encouraged now; an attendance like that would make my entertainment all that could be desired, and besides I would not be embarrassed by their going away before my lecture was over. But now misfortune came. In attempting to move Henry VIII to my lecture hall the porter fell down stairs and utterly smashed him all to pieces; in the course of moving William the Conqueror something let go, and all the sawdust burst out of him, and he collapsed and withered away to nothing before my eyes. Then we collared some dukes, but they were so seedy and decayed that nobody would ever have believed in their rank, and so I gave them up, with almost a broken heart. In my trouble I had nothing in the world left to depend on now but just Moses and Aaron, and I confess to you that it was all I could do to keep the tears back when I came to examine those two images and found that that man, in his unapproachable ignorance, had been exhibiting in Whitechapel for Moses and Aaron what any educated person could see at a glance, by the ligature, were only the Siamese Twins. You see now, sir, that I have done all that a man could do to supply a complained of lack, and if I have failed I think I ought to be pitied, not blamed. I wish I could get a king just only for a little while, and I would take good care of him and send him home and pay for the cab myself."

On January 27, as if to buttress its opinion of *The Gilded Age,* the *Graphic* announced that the London *Athenaeum* had not praised the novel, and it quoted the final sentence of the *Athenaeum's* review: "We think it just possible that the authors, one or both, may have it in them to produce a story which we may read without fatigue and without constant jars to our taste, while it shall have no lack of humour; but we cannot say that in *The Gilded Age* they have reached this desirable consummation."

We can disagree with this judgment of *The Gilded Age* and still sympathize with its tone of disappointment. Clemens's great gifts were obvious in *The Innocents Abroad* and in *Roughing It*, and they were sufficiently displayed to make *The Gilded Age* a remarkable first novel, despite Warner's material and chapters. But it is not surprising that the merits of the novel—Clemens's merits—should have been obscured when the novel appeared. The Warner material distracts; often, as in the interminable love-and-flowers relationship between Philip Sterling and Ruth Bolton, it detracts. Also distracting, no doubt, was the contemporary reader's frustration in not knowing who created and who wrote what, a frustration shared by most of today's readers. Furthermore, Mark Twain's gifts were not as well understood or appreciated then as they are now.

When we remove Warner's material and chapters we tighten and strengthen a novel that often wanders and drags, a novel that is too long for its content and treatment. And we allow Mark Twain to hold the stage alone. He holds it commandingly. His material has a good deal more "bite" than Warner's. The novel no longer has the conventional happy ending which Warner appended to it. Now the story is all of a piece, all of one tone and style, one kind of wit and humor and pathos and tragedy. In *The Adventures of Colonel Sellers*, with its wonderful chapters on backwoods and river life, and with its caustic portraits of Washington and congressional society, Mark Twain holds the stage richly, uniquely and sometimes brilliantly. Which should hardly surprise us at this late date.

Princeton, New Jersey
June 1964

THE TRAVEL BOOKS
AND TRAVELS

Mark Twain wrote five travel books, three of foreign travel—*The Innocents Abroad* (1869), *A Tramp Abroad* (1880) and *Following the Equator* (1897),—and two of domestic travel—*Roughing It* (1872) and *Life on the Mississippi* (1883)—or not quite two, inasmuch as one-fifth of *Roughing It* is concerned with his experiences in the Sandwich Islands. Three of his travel books are widely read and admired today: *The Innocents Abroad*, *Roughing It* and *Life on the Mississippi*. The other two are just as widely neglected, for reasons which we shall presently examine. Elsewhere, in discussing his novels, I have suggested that few great novelists have had so inauspicious a beginning as a novelist as he had. The same can hardly be said of him as a writer of travel books—witness the great success, both financial and artistic, of his first full-length book, which was also his first travel book, *The Innocents Abroad*. I have also suggested that in a number of cases Clemens wrote a novel after a great expenditure of creative energy on a travel book, with the result that these novels suffered from the drop in temperature. In some respects Clemens was a novelist *manqué*. This cannot be said of him as a writer of travel books. In the latter respect we are dealing with what may be called the essential, rock-bottom Clemens, Clemens as humorist and creative journalist.

He was a fresh, youthful, excited traveler in *The Innocents Abroad*, which accounts in large measure for the book's bounce, humor, insight and verbal felicity. He was even more youthful and excited on his Western travels, described in *Roughing It*, although the latter was much more an exercise in recall than the former was. He was more wide-eyed, more exuberant, more open to experience in his Western years than he was subsequently, and he successfully projected his impressions and experiences when he wrote the Western book. In the first half (speaking approximately) of *Life on the Mississippi*, which he composed as a unit some years before he composed the second half, he went back still further in his life and again captured, with extreme vividness and authenticity, the excitement of his youth and of his early love of travel, this time as a pilot on the great river. Perhaps the finest of his travel writing is to be found in this first half, in which he probed farthest back into his life.

After *Roughing It* and after the publication of "Old Times on the Mississippi," those first nostalgic chapters of what was to become *Life on the Mississippi*, he undertook to gather materials for and to write *A Tramp Abroad*. Now, as in *The Innocents Abroad*, he was writing about concurrent, not recalled, time; but by now he was tired of travel and he forced himself to do it as a professional duty in order to produce a book to increase or at least sustain the income which he found had become so necessary to offset his considerable and still burgeoning domestic expenses. When he revisited the Mississippi in order to gather materials with which to complete *Life on the Mississippi*, he again was to write about concurrent time and out of professional duty and again he was a tired traveler. It is therefore no surprise that the second half of the river book lags far behind the first in every respect: suspense, narrative power, poetry, importance of subject matter, perception, style. *Following the Equator* was the most dutiful of his travel books. More than any of the others it was written for professional, not inner, reasons. Also, by now the process of travel threatened to overwhelm him. And he was sixty and burdened by debts. Once again, when he wrote *Following the Equator*, he was writing about concurrent time.

The suggestion I am making is that as he probed farther back in his life he wrote with greater harmony, illumination, power and style. Also, that as he grew more bored and tired as a traveler his travel writings showed the result, first in the lesser experiences which he derived from travel, second in a dulled critical sense in regard to what he was composing, and third in a kind of desperation to fill up space to meet the requirements of subscription publishing.

His travels began early, in his eighteenth year, when, telling his mother he was going up to St. Louis to earn a little money, he went *through* St. Louis to New York, where the Crystal Palace Fair was in progress in the hot months of 1853. It must have been quite an experience for the Missouri boy, who had been working for his brother Orion on the Hannibal *Journal*, to make his way from his lodgings on Duane Street up to Sixth Avenue and 42nd Street, to where Bryant Park now stands, and to stare at the progress of nations as displayed there, at an admission price of fifty cents. We can imagine young Clemens, full-throated, strong-nosed, keen-eyed, with his long, thick, carelessly barbered reddish hair and his country clothes, making his way uptown in that mob of urbanites, going from the sticky heat, the smells and the noise of downtown to the country flavors of 42nd Street and the site of the reservoir which drew its water from the Croton Aqueduct, where more than half a century later he was to observe the great building of the public library go up, he then white-haired, absorbed in dictating his autobiography, and tending to avoid the publicity which almost anywhere in the world surrounded the soubriquet of Mark Twain and the person to whom that name belonged.

"The visitors to the Palace average 6,000 daily—double the population of Hannibal," he wrote to his sister Pamela Moffett at two o'clock one morning. He would get up at six and be at work at seven. Where did he spend his evenings? "Where do you suppose, with a free printers' library containing more than 4,000 volumes within a quarter of a mile of me, and nobody at home to talk to?" There was not only the future, as represented by the Palace, in that metropolis of more than a century ago, but also the national past. "I saw a large company of soldiers of 1812 the other day, with a '76 veteran scattered here and there in the ranks." In an October 1853 letter to Pamela he called the city an "abominable place" but it intrigued him. "It is as hard on my conscience to leave New York, as it was easy to leave Hannibal."

Later, in 1867, he would write to the *Alta California* of San Francisco what a hard place New York was to live in, how it caught and tore and ripped and spewed out one's time, how noisy and distracting and death to peace of mind it was. Which did not prevent him, in his later years, from cheerfully taking up residence in it. One gathers from his early letters that he was alert, industrious and curious. His letters are informative but without the vein of humor which was later to characterize him. One imagines, however, that his conversation must have contained it amply, flavored by his southwestern drawl and country manners.

He worked in New York at the printing trade (on Cliff Street) then in Philadelphia (where he was aware, certainly, of the giant footsteps of another printer who had been there before him), made a brief trip to Washington and returned to Missouri after an absence of almost fifteen months. He may have had his qualms about being out in the great world but if he did he kept them out of his letters to his family. He was then, as he was later, a good traveler, a fellow who slept and ate well almost anywhere and who did not easily succumb to depression. However, he liked his comforts, particularly in the years of his success, and among them he ranked companionship very high. He rarely traveled without a friend if he could help it and he believed that a good guide was indispensable to his happiness. But this was in his affluent years. As a young man of eighteen he took up his trade in St. Louis for a while, then joined Orion in Keokuk, Iowa for a two-year printing stint on another of Orion's ill-fated ventures. When he tired of life in Keokuk under the melancholy and restrictive influence of Orion, ten years his senior, he was at no loss to decide how to make his fortune. He would go to the headwaters of the Amazon, collect coca and return home rich. The inspiration had come from reading William Lewis Herndon's volume about his explorations of the valley of that mighty river.

It pained him to tell Orion of his plans, for he knew he would receive only arguments, sincerely offered—for Orion was not easily capable of insincerity—yet difficult to deflect without hurting Orion's feelings. In a letter to his brother Henry he wrote: "But you know what Orion is. When he gets a notion into his head, and more especially if it is an erroneous one, the Devil can't get it out again." He was always an outspoken critic of Orion, at times to Orion himself. He had confided his Amazon plans to his mother. She advised him to handle the matter as he had handled an earlier one, the trip to New York. She reminded him of how diplomatic he had been with *her*. Why not tell Orion that he was going as far as New York—or whatever the port was going to be?

He went to Cincinnati and worked at his trade until April 1857 (he was not yet twenty-two), then took a boat down the Mississippi to New Orleans, ready to sail for South America and the Amazon. The only trouble was, as he explained much later in his autobiography, "When I got to New Orleans I inquired about ships leaving for Pará and discovered that there weren't any and learned that there probably wouldn't be any during that century." There was only one thing to do: to make his fortune by piloting; and so he persuaded a reluctant Horace Bixby to take him on as a cub and to teach him the sinuous, treacherous, shifting day life and night life of that other great river, the Mississippi.

He was taught the river and in the process he learned a cross-section of American life he could hardly have studied elsewhere. He got to know shoals, bars and towheads; towns and hamlets by the score; men by the hundred who would teem in his memory, types found on the river and in the river's basin; and he got to know the cosmopolis of New Orleans, with its foreign flavor. The river commingled American types as California does today. He learned the taste of independence and high pay, both of which were the rewards of Mississippi piloting. But the real fortune he made was not yet evident. It consisted of the optimism of his best years and of a keen sense of the American condition, qualities of mind and character which were to determine the output of his genius. (Not to mention the vast volume of American talk which his almost phonographic ear was exposed to.)

He would have continued on the river indefinitely, perhaps,

for piloting and the river were the loves of his life, but the Civil War put a period on piloting on the river. Clemens, after a two-week stint in the Confederate Army in Missouri (during which he was exhausted by continual retreating, as he claimed later), decided to sit out the war. Orion, whose luck and destiny would be as bleak as Sam's would be bright, had recently been appointed Secretary of Nevada Territory, and so Clemens accompanied him on a stagecoach journey to Nevada. The brothers took the stage at St. Joseph July 26, 1861, and it was only after five and a half years of roaming in Nevada, California and the Sandwich (Hawaiian) Islands, with a trip across the Isthmus to New York, before Clemens saw St. Louis and Hannibal again. When he began the trip he guessed that it would last about three months. He was an unknown former printer and former river pilot with an uncertain future. At the trip's conclusion his fame as an eccentric humorist, established to some degree in the West, was already beginning to spread eastward.

These were the years later to be recorded in *Roughing It*, the determining years of literary apprenticeship, of gathering materials, of learning the trades of newspaper correspondence and lecturing. No longer a printer and a pilot, Clemens became an amateur miner and scribbler, meanwhile observing and memorizing the life of the silver-mining frontier and that of the Sandwich Islands as he had observed and memorized the life of the river and its basin. Prospecting and mining became a passion which died, but the writing, beginning with letters to the Virginia City *Territorial Enterprise* signed "Josh," grew to the proportions of regular correspondence under the name of "Mark Twain." Clemens was a reporter in San Francisco, a correspondent in Hawaii for the Sacramento *Union*, a successful Pacific Coast lecturer and the author of the Jumping Frog story. In those years he was steadily approaching the threshold of fame. By 1867 he had almost gained the fortune which he had lost by not collecting coca along the Amazon. He had made it by giving up printing as a trade in favor of journalism, and dialect humor in favor of the plain, deeper humor which had already established his fame as "the wild humorist of the Pacific slope." He was now ready to blow upon the embers of his destiny and to light a great conflagration in the literary skies of his native land.

Shortly before sailing from San Francisco for New York December 15, 1866 the thirty-one-year-old Clemens had got the notion to go around the world and write a series of newspaper letters as he went, letters which would pay his way, serve as raw material for possible lectures, and perhaps even as the basis of a book. By the time he sailed his idea was more than a notion: a prominent San Francisco newspaper, the *Daily Alta California*, had agreed to print his letters at $20 each. It was no great risk for the *Alta California* to take, for Clemens was by now known to be one of the best correspondents available, with a brilliant and idiomatic descriptive gift in addition to what was even rarer, an apparently inexhaustible store of humor, a usually benign humor which when the need was felt could transform itself into an awesome invective, all with a flavor uniquely American.

Clemens's letters began at once, at sea, and continued from New York. In New York, having learned of the *Quaker City* excursion to the Holy Land, he abruptly changed his plans and prepared to join it. The excursion was well suited to his genius and became the basis of his extraordinary first book of travel, *The Innocents Abroad*. The excursion lasted from June 8 to November 19, 1867, and the immediate result for Clemens was some fifty letters to the *Alta California*, half a dozen to the *New York Tribune* and one to the *New York Herald*.

A few years ago I acquired rather accidentally an unpublished letter by Clemens without an envelope and with only "New York, June 8, 2 A.M." to identify where and when it had been written. It was addressed to a "Dear John." I remembered that the *Quaker City* had sailed from New York at 2 P.M. on June 8, 1867. The contents of the letter revealed that it had been written the same day. It was probably the last letter Clemens wrote before leaving the United States on the excursion which was forever to change his life and fortunes. He left the country as a young man of promise. When he returned five months later much of the promise had been fulfilled. It was on the *Quaker City* excursion that Clemens met his future wife's brother and saw for the first time a miniature portrait of her, which at once fascinated him. The letter is therefore interesting for several external reasons as well as for its contents, its free use of language and for what it reveals about Clemens's activities just before he sailed.

"Dear John—

"D—n it I have intended all along to write you the night before sailing, but here it is within 12 hours of leaving & I have not been to bed or packed my trunk yet. But I went to dinner at 3 P.M. with 'Private Miles o'Riley' and Jno Russell Young, Managing Editor of the Tribune (I am going to write for that— I find the Weekly has 200,000 circulation)—drank wine; dined from 6 to 9 at Jno Murphy's (*God* made *him*, you know, and Mrs. M. too,)—drank several breeds of wine there, naturally enough; dined again from 9 till 12 at Mr. Slote's, (my ship-mate's,) whom the same God made that made Jno Murphy— & mind you I say that such men as they are, are almighty scarce —you can shut your eyes & go forth at random in a strange land & pick out a son of a bitch a great deal easier;—drank much wine there, too. So I am only just getting over it now. Mr. Mac-Crellish & I are to take Christmas dinner at Jno Murphy's.

"Now I feel good—I feel *d—d* good—& I could write a good correspondence—can, anyway, as soon as I get out of this most dismal town. *You'll see.* Got an offer to-day for 3-months course of lectures next winter—$100 a night & no bother & no expense. How's that?

"John, I'll write from Paris. God be with you.

"Yrs fraternally   Mark."

The "Dear John" of the letter was very probably John Mc-Comb, one of the editors of the *Alta California*. It was McComb who encouraged Clemens to give his first lecture, which was delivered in San Francisco on October 2, 1866 and the subject of which was the Sandwich Islands. When Clemens asked the proprietors of the *Alta California* to pay his fare of $1250 on the *Quaker City* they did not believe it would be a profitable ar-

rangement for the paper. It was McComb who convinced them
to invest in Mark Twain. Later, when the proprietors planned
to publish Clemens's letters in book form against his will, it was
McComb who again came to his support by urging them not to
publish. Miles O'Reilly was the pseudonym of Charles Graham
Halpine. Halpine, born in Ireland, came to the United States
in 1851 and became a brigadier-general in the Union Army.
He wrote a humorous book about Civil War events, *The Life and
Adventures . . . of Private Miles O'Reilly*, which was published in 1864. John Murphy was chief of the New York bureau
of the *Alta California*. It was he who handed over to Clemens,
probably at 42 John Street, the *Alta California* office, a check for
$1250. The "Mr. Slote" of the letter was Dan Slote, Clemens's
shipmate on the *Quaker City*. (The *Quaker City*, by the way,
was a vessel of 1800 tons operating on steam and on auxiliary
sails.) Clemens described Slote in a letter to his mother and
sister. "I have got a splendid, immoral, tobacco-smoking, wine-
drinking, godless roommate who is as good and true and right-
minded a man as ever lived—a man whose blameless conduct
and example will always be an eloquent sermon to all who shall
come within their influence." Slote is the "Dan" of *The Innocents Abroad*. In later years Slote manufactured Clemens's
patented scrapbook and Clemens eventually came to the conclusion that Slote had been something less than strictly honest
with him in his royalty statements. "Mr. MacCrellish" was
Frederick MacCrellish, the chief proprietor of the *Alta California* (the newspaper was owned by Frederick MacCrellish &
Co.). In his autobiography Clemens belabored MacCrellish in
his best style of invective. It is not surprising that Clemens received an offer for a series of lectures just before sailing. In addition to having made a name for himself as a lecturer on the
Pacific Coast, on May 6, 1867 he had given a very successful
lecture on the Sandwich Islands at Cooper Institute in New York.

As a majestic, revered old man, living on comfortable terms
with his fictitious name, Clemens let his memory wander over
the important events of his life. When it came to the *Alta California* letters and the writing of *The Innocents Abroad* it curi-

ously betrayed him. It seemed to him, as he wrote in his autobiography, that he had used only "several" of the letters, "ten or twelve, perhaps." He said he had found "they were newspaper matter, not book matter." And he imagined himself in San Francisco, a bright, healthy young man, writing *The Innocents Abroad* in sixty days, largely at night. "I could have added a fortnight's labor with the pen and gotten along without the letters altogether."

A comparison of the letters with the book shows how mistaken he was. Without them he would have had no book at all, for his notebooks were only jottings and could not have supported the weight of fact and description of the book. They were excellent letters and he used them wholesale, improving diction and grammar, occasionally toning down slang, eliminating references which were too locally Californian, and in general giving the material a more polished look, yet without trying to "write up" to Eastern readers. Sometimes he merely rearranged the order of the letters. For example, in the letters he presented Pompeii before Naples; in the book he reversed the order. In many cases he stepped away from the foreground by changing "I" to "we," adding to the effect of modesty as well as of breadth of experience. With his basic materials secure, he could relax, expand and invent. His main additions were comic sequences, dialogue and such American color as his vituperation on the name Tahoe.

He was angry when he recalled the *Alta California* letters as an old man. While writing the first ten chapters of the volume in Washington he learned from a Western friend that the *Alta California* proprietors had copyrighted the letters and were planning to issue them in book form. This news sent him to San Francisco to persuade the proprietors to relinquish book rights in the letters. He never forgave them for the fright they had caused him. Recollecting his youth, it seemed to him that he was boundlessly strong in those halcyon days and could accomplish anything, even the writing of *The Innocents Abroad* in sixty nights with only the smallest help from the letters. The truth was that much of his work in San Francisco was of an editorial nature and that the true brilliance of his achievement was the writing of the letters under the difficulties of travel. The *Alta California* letters are important in Clemens's literary career as none of his other newspaper letters are. The *Enterprise* letters, the *Union* letters, the *Tribune* letters and the *Sun* letters all figure in his biography, but nowhere nearly as prominently as the *Alta California* ones.

The Innocents Abroad was composed in the first half of 1868 and was issued by the American Publishing Company of Hartford in July 1869. Clemens was now in his thirty-fourth year. Between the completion of the manuscript and its publication he traveled extensively on a lecture tour and also successfully courted his future wife, Olivia Langdon, becoming engaged to her February 4, 1869. *The Innocents Abroad* was a great success. The United States had been on the receiving end of a procession of sour-eyed visitors from Europe and had got the wincing habit as a result. Now it was time to return the compliment with a flourish. Clemens had the apprenticeship and the background for the task. Above all, he had the appetite and the skill.

The prose of *The Innocents Abroad* sings. It is not Melville's supercharged, somewhat feverish, rhetorical kind of singing but the singing of over-arching good health and spirits. Clemens was delighted to join the excursion, to send the letters, to write up the book; and he evidenced his delight in his improvisations, his very funny inventions. Hadn't the *New York Herald* called him editorially "that most amusing American genius"? And wasn't he still in his early thirties and bursting with health? We quickly sense the euphoria of this gifted writer whose mind has been stimulated by strange, colorful scenes and who is brimful of his awakened and still unfolding powers, powers which reveal themselves in the fresh, tireless language energy of the book, in the broad and sophisticated vocabulary and in the easy ability to achieve many kinds of effect. Much of the pleasure we derive from the book stems from his sheer gift of gab—the gift of gab of itinerant preachers, healers, salvation-mongers, circus barkers, minstrel men. In those middle years of the last century, when rhetoric was an old standby in politics and when schools all had their elocution courses, the gift of gab was perhaps rated more highly than it is today, although the language exuberance of a Thomas Wolfe and a Billy Graham, together with their popular success, reveals that even in this day of semantic skepticism it has its rooters. Clemens probably did not consider such matters, for his was a rather naive genius, but the effect and the result were nevertheless present in his work. Nor can we overlook the book's technical skill—for example the subtle shifts of tense from past to present to give sudden vividness to scene and description, or the wise, sly avoidance of much use of the first-person pronoun, suggesting that the author's opinions and reactions are typical.

Clemens's fellow excursionists had much to do with the creation of the book. They constituted a microcosm of American humanity on European and Asiatic and African soil and gave the author a chance to satirize traveling Americans while he was satirizing such time-encrusted cultures as those of Italy and Egypt. His association with that assemblage of some sixty persons no doubt was partly responsible for the sudden flowering of his literary ideas—through the ferment of study, language, character and manners which he could share and observe. The journalistic atmosphere of San Francisco influenced the tone and content of the book as it did those of the letters. It helped give the book its fresh view of older cultures. The mood of the country at large also profoundly affected the book, which refreshed readers saddened by war and eager to escape into the apparently ludicrous world abroad. *The Innocents Abroad* is a charming title but its accuracy is open to some inspection. How innocent could a group of Americans be a scant two years after a fratricidal war? Perhaps it is more likely that many members of the group were going to seek innocence, not in Europe but in the Holy Land. Some were traveling as pilgrims. Wasn't the voyage touted as the Holy Land excursion and wasn't the steam-propelled sidewheeler named the *Quaker City*? In not mentioning the Civil War in his book Clemens was being faithful to his slim relations with it; but he was also noting and adhering to the mood of the nation as he knew it. Of course, he was not obliged to mention it in a book about a Holy Land excursion; but then he was not obliged to expatiate on Lake Tahoe, on the advantages of life in the United States, and on a quaint stay in the Benton House back home.

The five years from 1865 to Clemens's marriage in February 1870 were the miraculous years of his life. They set the tone and structure of it. In them he found his mature style, left journalism for literature, embraced fame and affluence, transferred the scene of his actual activity from the West to the East, and married the woman who was to have so great an influence on his life and work.

After his marriage in 1870 Clemens settled in Buffalo and wrote humorous sketches for the Buffalo *Express* (of which he had become part owner) and for a New York monthly magazine, *The Galaxy*. But before long his publisher, Bliss, urged him to follow up the phenomenal success of *The Innocents Abroad* with a book about his Western experiences, to be called *Roughing It*. Clemens was willing; the book, however, was not. He seemed to have forgotten the details of the overland stage trip and feared he had lost touch with the slang and idiom of its time and place. In a letter to Orion he said he could remember nothing at all; could Orion recollect the route and any of the incidents? Orion sent a memorandum book but the notes were meager and the frontier book clearly showed it had no intention of easily relenting. There were other matters pressing Clemens— deaths in the family, the uncongeniality of Buffalo to a man of his interests and temperament, and the considerable outgo of money for domestic expenses. He did not remain in Buffalo long, deciding in favor of Hartford, then a literary center. In the meantime he spent the summer of 1871 at Quarry Farm outside Elmira, struggling to give life to Bliss's notion. He had no newspapers to lean on for the early chapters, and the events were a decade old. He did have his writings for the Virginia City *Territorial Enterprise* and the Sacramento *Union* but they were of no direct help in starting the book. He made progress, however, while enduring a kind of stage fright.

Then one day he received a visit from Joe Goodman, editor of the *Enterprise*, who had given Clemens the job of city editor in the absence on leave of Dan de Quille. Goodman read the early chapters at Clemens's request and said, why they were excellent. It was all the mercurial Clemens needed, and soon he was crying that *The Innocents Abroad* would have to get up early in the morning to beat *Roughing It*, and that the latter would straightway sell 100,000 copies—no, a million. He persuaded Goodman to stay a month and they talked and talked of those old times which to Clemens had seemed so faded but which now took on great vividness.

He completed the volume in the autumn of 1871 and it was issued the following February, not as a trade but as a subscription book. *The Innocents Abroad* had also been sold on the subscription plan. *Roughing It* was the first book written after his marriage and his settling in the East. (One discounts "Mark Twain's Burlesque Autobiography," published in 1871, on the grounds that it was too slim to be truly called a book.) Like *The Innocents Abroad*, *Roughing It* was greeted with friendly and favorable reviews. Mark Twain was becoming a national figure. The literary elect, however, were largely myopic regarding his great qualities.

Roughing It is an invaluable social history of the silver-mining days, for even if its facts are sometimes open to question the essential truth of its portrait is not. Its language is looser, thinner, freer and more idiomatic than that of *The Innocents Abroad*. If the greater variety of scenes of *The Innocents Abroad* is part of the latter's charm, the more poetic vein and the tone of a great fable are to the advantage of *Roughing It*. Clemens was able to regard certain of his experiences in such a way that they took on infinitely greater scope and resonance than the other actors in them would have dreamed they could possess. His special dimension was always his great, earthy humor, often cast in a vernacular style that does not easily date. In *Roughing It* he made no mention of his piloting days, probably because he had already determined to reserve them for a river book. When at the conclusion of the volume he spoke of the "seven years of vicissitudes" of his Western travels he was probably alluding half-poetically to the magical, Biblical number seven, for, as we have noted, the travels lasted five and a half years. On the other hand he may simply have been in error. Such errors did not seem to trouble his olympian, cigar-smoking calm. As an example of his easy relations with facts, we note that in Chapter 74 he states that the crater of Vesuvius is 300 feet deep, whereas two chapters later he says it is 1,000 feet deep. The Sandwich Islands chapters are as fine as any in the book. Their concreteness and vividness is due in large measure to the fact that he amply utilized his Sandwich Islands journalistic correspondence, as he had utilized his *Quaker City* correspondence earlier. For certain parts of the volume he had clippings of the *Enterprise* to aid him, as we have seen.

The sales of the Western book were considerable—40,000 copies in the first three months—but they fell far behind those of *The Innocents Abroad*. The latter sold 100,000 copies in its first three years; it took *Roughing It* a decade to reach that figure. When the first royalty check arrived Clemens did not forget Orion's memorandum book. For its use he sent his brother $1,000.)

In the winter of 1871–72 Mark Twain went on another domestic lecture tour. The following August he sailed alone for England with the intention of collecting material for a book on that country. But the warm welcome he received and the extensive socializing he enjoyed put an end to note-taking for the project, which he abandoned. In the middle of November he left for home. In April 1873 he brought his family to England. In November he escorted them home, returning alone almost immediately for a lecture tour and remaining until the middle of January. For the next three years he did not travel much.

In May 1877 he went to Bermuda with his friend Reverend Joseph Twichell, jotting in a notebook that it was "the first actual pleasure trip" he had ever taken. Meanwhile the complexity and expense of his Hartford way of life were beginning to tax his strength and optimism. In a letter to his mother written in

February 1878 he said: "Life has come to be a very serious matter with me. I have a badgered, harassed feeling a good part of my time. It comes mainly of business responsibilities and annoyances, and the persecution of kindly letters from well meaning strangers—to whom I must be rudely silent or else put in the biggest half of my time bothering over answers. There are other things also that help to consume my time and defeat my projects. Well, the consequence is, I cannot write a book at home. This cuts my income down. Therefore, I have about made up my mind to take my tribe and fly to some little corner of Europe and budge no more until I shall have completed one of the half dozen books that lie begun, up stairs." And in one of the notebooks of that time we find this jotting: "To go abroad has something of the same sense that death brings—'I am no longer of ye; what ye say of me is now of no consequence—but of how much consequence when I am with ye and of ye.' I know you will refrain from saying harsh things *because* they cannot hurt me, since I am out of reach and cannot hear them. This is why we say no harsh things of the dead."

Clemens and his family sailed for Germany April 11, 1878. He went to Europe with the plan of taking a walking tour with Twichell which would be the basis of a new book of travels. While waiting for Twichell, Clemens and his family settled down in Germany, where they continued their assiduous study of the German language, begun in the Hartford house. Twichell arrived early in August and he and Clemens set out for the Black Forest. Twichell remained in Europe, as Mark Twain's guest, for about six weeks, after which the Clemens family went down to Italy, staying three weeks in Venice, a week in Florence and a fortnight in Rome. Then they went to Munich, where Clemens began working on *A Tramp Abroad*, writing and destroying much in the winter of 1878-79. He could not seem to work up enthusiasm for the book as a whole, although he wrote many sections which pleased him. The Clemenses tried Paris at the end of February 1879. They encountered a cold wet winter and Clemens's work on the book continued heavy and plaguing. As usual, he found himself indulging in much social life. The summer arrived; it too was cold. The Clemenses made their way to London via the Low Countries but London was no respite; it was as cold and wet as Paris had been. They sailed for home August 23, 1879.

Work on *A Tramp Abroad*, continued at home, seemed at times like a nightmare and Clemens was infinitely relieved when the task was done. The book was published the middle of March 1880. It was fairly well received. Howells praised it, which was music to Clemens. In later years Brander Matthews pronounced it superior to *The Innocents Abroad*, a judgment with which few readers would agree today.

The Innocents Abroad reflected the author's joy in writing it. *A Tramp Abroad* reflected his labors and uncertainty. It's a pity that he allowed himself to mar the book by self-indulgently inserting much boring material. His critical faculties seemed to be on vacation, his artistic conscience to be dozing more than usual; or perhaps he was pressed by the need to fill up space to meet the requirements of a large subscription book and was too tired or bored to meet them creatively. Because of the insertions the book is at times unpleasant to read. They account for the fact that for many years it has been out of print, as has also been the case with *Following the Equator*. *A Tramp Abroad* needs to be relieved of its useless freight by skilful abridging and editing. There are many fine things in it, enough to make a good book, but at present they are often obscured by debris. Perhaps Clemens had to some extent and temporarily written himself out. Within a decade he had written in detail about his experiences in Europe and the Near East, in the West and the Sandwich Islands, and in the Mississippi basin; in addition he had written *Tom Sawyer*, the river idyll, the work of nostalgia harking back to his Hannibal years. Thus he had substantially drawn upon all the basic themes and materials of his creative life.

What was required to make *A Tramp Abroad* work was that Clemens should go to Europe unencumbered by family, free to be fresh and impulsive, and committed to writing letters for a newspaper, preferably a Western one; free from the need to write long letters to Howells complaining about the book's lack of progress; free from the need to try to impress Howells in one way or another (an inner need and expressed not without charm); free from the badgering he had been undergoing in Hartford, badgering which he himself in the last analysis was largely responsible for. *A Tramp Abroad* lacks the tension, the fire, the brilliant detail, the vocabulary, the energy and the invective of the earlier book. But in terms of stretches of sustained humor, of heights of humor, of sustained virtuoso performance, *The Innocents Abroad* does not come near it. There is nothing in the earlier book as inspired as "The Awful German Language," which is an appendix of *A Tramp Abroad*, or as funny as the ascent of the Riffelberg. My tastes are low, for the ascent of the Riffelberg makes me laugh aloud, with its boiling of thermometers, barometers and guides.

If these are harsh strictures, let us add that they are made in the context of Mark Twain's performance as a whole. It was not a question of his faculties being on the wane. *A Tramp Abroad* was essentially a failure of stance. In *The Innocents Abroad* the text is serious; the embroidery is enlivened by jokes. In *A Tramp Abroad* the text itself is often a series of jokes. An example of bad taste and of straining for comic effect is Harris's Official Report, with its hodgepodge of exotic, impossible words strewn over it. (The figure of Harris, by the way, is based to some extent on Twichell.) Clemens seems to have had some suspicion that he was being less than funny, if one can judge by the stridency of the report. In the concluding chapter he wrote: "I had not enjoyed a pleasure abroad which seemed to me to compare with the pleasure I felt in seeing New York harbor again." We can believe him. Perhaps it was no accident that in his long career he composed not one first-rate book on foreign soil.

The January 1875 issue of the *Atlantic* was no ordinary issue, for in addition to containing two poems by Longfellow, an essay on Weimar by Bayard Taylor, and an essay on "The Americanized European" by Oliver Wendell Holmes, it contained the opening of *Roderick Hudson,* by Henry James, and the first installment of "Old Times on the Mississippi," by Mark Twain. Many years later Howells recalled that the *Atlantic* had hoped to increase its sales because of the Mississippi sketches, which appeared in seven issues of the magazine, but that the lax observance of copyright in those days had frustrated its hopes. According to his testimony, the *New York Times* and the St. Louis *Democrat* benefited from the advance copies of the magazine which they regularly received by reprinting the Mississippi sketches and placing them on the market before the magazine was on the stands. These two papers pretty well covered the nation, Howells said, and they, if anybody, benefited from the sketches for which the *Atlantic* had paid $20 a page, high rates for the magazine at that time.

However, perhaps Howells's memory betrayed him, for it seems reasonable to assume that if the magazine had looked forward to a substantial increase in sales it would have displayed the Mississippi sketches prominently. The first page of the issue opened with the *Roderick Hudson* installment, and almost all of the other contributions began with a full page. There was a full page for Taylor; for "Wilhelmina," by Constance Fenimore Woolson; and even one for the anonymous "Touching Visitants from a Higher Life." When it came to the Mark Twain contribution a middle or half-page beginning (on page 69) sufficed—a precedent that was followed in the subsequent issues—which recalls the fact that at those subdued Boston dinners where Clemens was so sought after as a speaker, for some time he was not thought worthy enough to sit on the dais with the literary giants: Whittier, Bryant, Longfellow and the others. The English sensed his greatness before the Boston savants did, with the exception always of Howells.

The seven installments of "Old Times on the Mississippi" were each the equivalent of two chapters of the book which appeared several years later, and specifically were Chapters 4 to 17 of the book. They did not entirely comprise the first half of the book (the recollected half), for Chapters 1 to 3 were written later, as were 18 and 19 (Clemens's relations with the pilot Brown), 20 (the explosion of the *Pennsylvania* and the death of his younger brother Henry), and a short chapter, 21, headed "A Section of My Biography." The text of the installments was almost identical with that of the book. Clemens was a great believer in economizing work.

The appearance of the installments renewed in him an old desire to go down the river to collect material for a book. On November 27, 1871 he had written to his wife: "This [*Roughing It*] is a better book than the Innocents, and *much* better written. If the subject were less hackneyed it would be a great success. But when I come to write the Mississippi book, *then* look out! I will spend two months on the river and take notes, and I bet you I will make a standard work." As usual he disliked traveling alone. Because neither Howells nor Osgood (now Clemens's publisher) nor John Hay was free to accompany him, he postponed revisiting the river. It was not until April 17, 1882 that he finally set out for a journey of six weeks. He went to St. Louis, down the river to New Orleans and up the river to St. Paul. He was accompanied by Osgood and a male stenographer. Many details of the trip are given in *Life on the Mississippi*, which he completed that summer and autumn at Quarry Farm and in Hartford. He had his troubles in finishing the book but many of them stemmed from his resentment of deadlines. He felt he had one on this book and he finally broke it. It is doubtful that he had resented deadlines to such an extent during his newspaper days. His resentment of them now seemed to be related to his distinction between "newspaper matter" and "book matter," between journalism and literature. He suppressed Chapter 48 of the manuscript, which was set up in type and cancelled in the proofs, probably because he feared it would offend Southern readers. The key paragraph reads: "In one thing the average Northerner seems to be a step in advance of the average Southerner, in that he bands himself with his timid fellows to support the law, (at least in the matter of murder), protect judges, juries, and witnesses, and also to secure all citizens from personal danger and from obloquy or social ostracism on account of opinion, political or religious; whereas the average

Southerners do not band themselves together in these high interests, but leave them to look out for themselves unsupported; the
results being unpunished murder, against the popular approval,
and the decay and destruction of independent thought and action in politics."

Life on the Mississippi was published in May 1883. "Upon the
whole," wrote Howells after his friend's death in 1910, "I have
the notion that Clemens thought this his greatest book." A long,
sustained calm and profound reservoir of power supplanted the
ebullience of *The Innocents Abroad*. In the river book humor
for the most part was subdued. Clemens was so absorbed in
writing about the life of the river basin which he understood
and loved that he readily dispensed with jokes, burlesques and
gimmicks. Unfortunately his wayward artistic conscience allowed him to include in the river book the raft chapter of a work
in progress, which he was never to restore to its rightful owner,
Huckleberry Finn; it was the novel's loss, not the river book's.
The latter is a period piece of an aspect of the nation's youth
which could not have been done better by another hand. Clemens owed the river years much. They had given him two great
disciplines from which he had benefited as a writer: close observation and memory practice. He repaid the debt by creating a
masterpiece.

He liked to claim that he had a bad memory, just as he liked
to say that he was lazy. But no one with a bad memory could
have learned the every-changing river as he had learned it, nor
learned the countless lectures and speeches which he gave in
his lifetime, almost all of them carefully memorized, and which
he could repeat years later like a trained actor with a large
repertoire. He would amuse himself at times by describing contrived or public parts of himself as genuine and indispensable.
His daughter Clara in her book about him tells how his famous
drawl was sometimes missing in the privacy of their home. As
for his laziness, the sheer mass of his writings, not to mention
his lectures, private letters, unpublished manuscripts, business
activities, vast socializing and travels belie his claim. He was
not only a great writer, he was also a man of the world. He had

been out in the world, the world that does not know society, and he had also been in society. He was more various and more ambiguous than either of the worlds he had known. Howells illumined that side of him in a vivid sentence. "He glimmered at you from the narrow slits of fine blue-greenish eyes, under branching brows, which with age grew more and more like a sort of plumage, and he was apt to smile into your face with a subtle but amiable perception, and yet with a sort of remote absence; you were all there for him, but he was not all there for you." And Kipling wrote to an American correspondent, "How is the godlike Clemens?" Such descriptions recall Gorky's description of Tolstoy, the godlike creature (like some Pan) sitting under the lime tree.

Life on the Mississippi enlarged Mark Twain's reputation, especially in Europe, as an author who was a good deal more than just an inspired wit or buffoon. Thomas Hardy remarked to Howells at a dinner in England, "Why don't people understand that Mark Twain is not merely a great humorist? He's a very remarkable fellow in a very different way." And he went on to praise the Mississippi book.

The winter of 1884–85 Clemens spent platforming with George Washington Cable. Clemens hated the rigors and banalities of lecturing, and Cable's presence tranquilized the experience a good deal for him, although on occasion he was very critical of Cable in his letters to his wife. Then came *Huckleberry Finn* and *A Connecticut Yankee*, together with that business mania, that mania for acquiring sudden riches, which brought disaster to him and his family and which occasioned his famous lecture tour around the world at sixty to pay off his load of debts and occasioned also his last travel book, *Following the Equator*. In August 1890 Clemens went to Keokuk, Iowa to see his dying mother. The following spring he closed the manorial Hartford house and took his family to Europe in order to live a quieter and less expensive life. He and his wife Livy were suffering from rheumatism; the Paige typesetter bubble was threatening to burst; and his publishing house was in serious financial trouble. The Clemenses sailed on June 6, 1891 for France. Not long afterward Clemens wrote to his business manager that he intended to write another travel book and would take a year or two to collect the materials for it. Then followed a long and hectic period of hopes, despairs and troubles, punctuated by frequent transatlantic crossings by Clemens for business, not professional, reasons. He accomplished little sustained work during this time.

The winter of 1891–92 was spent in Berlin. The following spring was spent in the south of France. Then the Clemenses tried Venice, Berlin again, and finally a villa on a hill near Florence. In the summer of 1892 Clemens visited the United States for less than two weeks. On his return to Europe he and his family lived in Nauheim, moving at the end of September to the Florence villa. On March 22, 1893 he returned to his homeland for two months, returning to Europe in May. In June the Clemenses closed the villa and went up to Germany for the baths. On August 29th he left Europe again for the United States, this time staying away from his family for seven months. He made his headquarters in New York, where he met H. H. Rogers, the financier who was to be of great help to him in his business troubles, and where as always he enjoyed being lionized. He went to Europe in March 1894, spent about three weeks with his family, and was back in New York by the middle of April.

On April 18th his publishing house, Charles L. Webster & Co., failed. In May he returned to Europe for a summer in southern France. By the end of the year the Paige typesetter affair, in which he had invested heavily, ended in a fiasco. On February 23, 1895 he sailed for New York, returning to Europe the end of March. It was then he decided to make his lecture tour around the world. In May the Clemenses embarked for the United States, Mrs. Clemens and her children having been abroad continuously for four years. In July Clemens, his wife, and his daughter Clara left Elmira for the trip around the world, arriving in Vancouver August 16th, sailing for Australia August 23rd, and arriving in England the middle of the following July. Clemens was alone in London when he was handed a cable informing him of the unexpected death of his favorite child, Susy. Livy and Clara were on the seas, hurrying to Susy's bedside. Susy died of spinal meningitis on August 18th. Clemens's cup was running over.

A little later the Clemenses settled down in a house in Tedworth Square, London, where he wrote *Following the Equator.* On October 26, 1896 he remarked in his notebook, "Wrote the first chapter of the book today." On April 13th he jotted, "I finished my book today," and on May 18th he wrote, "Finished the book *again.* Addition of 30,000 words." In January he had written to Twichell, "I am working, but it is for the sake of the work—the 'surcease of sorrow' that is found there. I work all the days, and trouble vanishes away when I use that magic. This book will not long stand between it and me, now; but that is no matter, I have many unwritten books to fly to for my preservation; the interval between the finishing of this one and the beginning of the next will not be more than one hour, at most."

Following the Equator was published in September 1897. Together with the lecture tour, it enabled Clemens to pay his debts to the last cent. The miracle is that it got done at all, considering the circumstances of its composition. A book to be good must have an inspiration, a compulsion, of its own. In this case the lecture tour was the chief spirit and the book merely a poor, tight-lipped, disjointed, wandering, aching record of it. It is strange how the feeling of weariness and age can make its way into prose—by a grayness, by a loss of lilt in phrasing and of daring in invention, by a sputtering in choice of words, a falling off of metaphor, a tendency to meander, a turning of energy inward. It is kinder to say no more, except that there were good things in it, more than enough to witness that a giant had breathed upon it, and to add that if it had been carefully pruned it would have found a higher place among his works than it did. Chapter 51 of the manuscript was suppressed at the request of Mrs. Clemens "on the ground that the first part is not delicate and that the last part is indelicate," as Clemens explained to a friend. Presumably Mrs. Clemens objected to the sentences which read, "It was embarrassing to stay, and it was embarrassing to try to go. On the whole, I thought I would try to go," and which came after the statement that Clemens had drunk nine cups of coffee. Also one presumes that she objected to the use of the word "guts" at the chapter's conclusion.

Because we think of Mark Twain as *the* American author above all others we do not readily imagine him spending years away from his country. We easily recall Herman Melville's voyages, or images of Henry James in London, of Hawthorne in Rome, of Washington Irving in Spain. When Clemens comes to mind it is usually the Mississippi we think of or Nevada or Hartford, Elmira, New York. He crossed the Atlantic twenty-seven times and spent more than a decade away from his homeland. On the whole he was a conventional traveler who treasured his comforts and was content to go where others had gone before. One suspects that he went to California mainly because of its proximity to Nevada and that he liked San Francisco largely because he could pursue his trade there while enjoying a society which by the standards of his childhood and youth was very cosmopolitan. As far as I know he did not visit Monterey (the old Pacific capital), the missions, Sutter's fort, the village of Los Angeles. Unlike Robert Louis Stevenson, he had no desire whatever to exile himself to a primitive place like Samoa. (The claim that Samoa was perfect for his precarious health was partially a wish on Stevenson's part; the fact is he died there suddenly at the age of forty-four despite the benevolence of the climate.) Nor did Clemens care to undertake the sort of travel which Washington Irving undertook when he made his trip to the Great Plains in those early days of American exploration. When it came to travel abroad, Clemens was even more conventional. He made no effort to penetrate into Africa. He did not bother to record his week in Spain near the end of the Holy Land excursion. In later years, despite many visits to Europe, he did not go to Spain, Greece, Russia or any of the other places where travel was likely to be uncomfortable. He liked the well-padded trails: England, Germany, Switzerland, Austria, Italy.

His journey around the world was not the last of his travels. There was the summer of 1897 in Switzerland; a long stretch in Vienna; the summer of 1899 in Sweden; then London. On January 8, 1900 Clemens wrote to his friend, H. H. Rogers, "I am tired to death of this everlasting exile." The summer of that year was spent outside London. In the first week of October the Clemens family finally left for their homeland. Clemens said to a reporter: "If I ever get ashore I am going to break both of my legs so I can't get away again."

In 1902 he went to Missouri to accept an honorary doctorate. In October 1903 he took his family to Italy for Livy's health (she died there), returning July 1904. Early in 1907 he went to Bermuda. In June of that same year he went to Oxford to accept a coveted doctorate. In 1908 he went to Bermuda again; also in 1909; again in 1910. On April 12, 1910 he left Bermuda for the last time. He died April 21st of that year.

His views on travel were set down in an interview which he granted to a reporter for the *New York World* in London on October 6, 1900. The interview appeared in the *World* on October 14th. I quote the relevant passages.

"Is it true that you have resolved never to leave the United States again?"

"Not a word of truth in it. Perhaps we may spend the rest of our days at home. I don't know and no consideration on earth could induce me to give a pledge about that or anything else. That is another of my rules of life. I never give pledges or promises about things of that sort. If I felt myself under the constraint of a pledge the situation would become so irksome to me that only on that account alone I would be irresistibly compelled to come away again. No—as far as I am able to speak about a subject on which other people have the controlling voice more or less—I propose to stay the winter in New York, and then go back to Hartford in the spring."

"But do you really think that such an indefatigable traveller as you have been can settle down at home? Won't you feel restless?"

"An indefatigable traveller! That's where I am misunderstood. Now I have made thirty-four long journeys in my life, and thirty-two of them were made under the spur of absolute compulsion. I mean it—under nothing but sheer compulsion. There always was an imperative reason. I had to gather material for books or sketches, I had to stump around lecturing to make money, or I had to go abroad for the health or the education of my family. For love of travel—never any of these thirty-two journeys. There is no man living who cares less about seeing new places and peoples than I. You are surprised—but it's the gospel truth. I had a surfeit of it.

"When I started out, in 1867, for a six months' tour in the *Quaker City* I was a voracious sightseer. With nearly all the rest of that gang I said to myself: 'This is the opportunity of my life—never again shall I have the chance, the time or the money to see the Old World.' We lived up to that idea. We went in for seeing everything that was to be seen. In a city of inexhaustible treasures like Rome we got up at six in the morning and throughout the whole day, in rain or shine, we made a perpetual procession through picture galleries, churches, museums, palaces—looking at things which for the most part did not interest us one cent but which we thought we had to see. And we saw them. If our meals interfered with our seeing any old thing our meals were put aside. At nine or ten at night we returned to our hotel, our brains and our bodies reeling with fatigue and utter exhaustion. My head used to ache, my eyes to swim, but I would not succumb to the terrible temptation to throw myself on the bed, as if I did so I could not rise from it again before morning. I had to resist because we had to see something else by moonlight or because there was no moon or some other foolish reason. The only rest we had was when we went a short voyage from one port to another in the Mediterranean, and then I slept all the time. What was the result of this insensate sightseeing? Why, that I was so fagged that I lost the capacity to appreciate most of what I saw or to carry away any coherent idea of it. Since then only hard necessity has ever driven me to travelling. When I went around the world, five years ago, it was because I wanted money to pay off debts that were a nuisance to me—they burdened my conscience. People say that it was to relieve my creditors. Not at all. It was far more to relieve Clemens than creditors. I could not be happy until I got rid of that debt. I have never recovered from the *Quaker City* surfeit of sightseeing, and don't think there is any reasonable prospect of my doing so now."

Princeton, New Jersey
February 1966

THE ESSAYS

Mark Twain's characteristics as an essayist may perhaps best be gauged by comparing him with other essayists, particularly with those who did not make their reputations chiefly as essayists but who rather wrote essays as part of a broader, motley career. These I think of as amateur essayists. Clemens was certainly an amateur in the essay form, in the best sense of the word, as he was also an amateur in almost every other literary form he used, with the exception of humor. Like the great pendulum in San Francisco, which visually proves that the earth rotates (and confounds one's attempts to understand it), his genius, pervading his essays, tries to prove that it is human, while often crippling one's hopes of comprehending it. Humor, like quicksilver, is elusive. It is like the snaky tumble-polished agate shedding its skin with the light's every refraction. It is an Apache tear, now transparent, now opaque, now dark indeed, almost black, now an emerging, crisping, lighthearted tea color. It seems to reside in the very center of the human drama and perhaps for this reason, like the restless particles whose life is so ghostly within the atom, to surpass our understanding. How rare the best kind is, which Clemens was apparently inexhaustible in, may be seen in a survey of modern world literature. His humor performs the subtlest of functions, it humanizes. It reaches down into the bomb-cellars where man huddles, tear-stained, fearful. This posture of huddling, of waiting, is of course old with man. It reaches back, back in time. . . . Mark Twain's humor leavens; it annoints; it lulls dissension; through the sound of our common laughter it hints to us of our origin and destiny, our brotherhood, our vale of tears.

Several years ago I edited an unorthodox college textbook called *Essays of the Masters*. It did not focus on the history or the development or the "form" of the essay and did not concentrate on the professional essayists at all—and by "professional" I mean those writers like Lamb and de Quincey and, in modern times, Mencken and E. B. White, who find their best and fullest expression in the essay medium. What it did instead was to show how the large creative minds, which produced the novels, plays and poems of the past century and a half, put the essay to their use. Professional essayists commonly project their personalities directly onto paper. The flavor of their personalities is an important stock of their trade. Whereas in their major works the writers of my textbook generally project their personalities in disguised form; for example, Clemens projected his through the voice and character of Huck Finn. You are left to make out what you can about the authors when you read novels like *The Magic Mountain* or *The Counterfeiters* or *The Castle*, and although in the long run the impression of personality is overwhelming, still it is tantalizingly indirect. Curiosity being what it is, we want a more direct view and a more intimate sampling. The hope to satisfy this desire was one of the chief inspirations for the making of the textbook. Leafing through the book now helps me to differentiate Mark Twain's qualities as an essayist.

Here is Henry James on Turgeniev, displaying a cultivated mind and sensibility, with subtlety of insight and phrase, beauty and rightness of tone, and sound personal and literary judgments. There is no humor and only a little wit but the sparkle of good will, good mind and enthusiasm is very winning. Here is Somerset Maugham in *A Summing Up*, a piece dry, shrewd, intelligent, frank, written with precision and without flourish or humor; the interest is in the sharpness of insight and language. Here is Tolstoy's "On Art," without humor, didactic, stubborn, dogmatic, whose tone reminds one of current Soviet discussions on the nature and function of the writer in Russia. A little humor could lighten the discussion, endow it with perspective, relieve it of its close air, make it more palatable. But this is Tolstoy in his later phase and humor would probably seem frivolous to him. Mark Twain also had a later and dogmatic phase but it was not without humor except in the avowedly didactic pieces like "What Is Man?" Here is Thomas Hardy with "The Profitable Reading of

Fiction," sometimes dull, prosaic, sometimes heavily hifalutin, as when he writes "efficacious for renovation" when he means "beneficial." He could have learned something from Clemens. Here is Shaw's witty, persuasive, expansive, brilliant review of Chesterton's book on Shaw. Here is Dickens on "New York," with an exuberant piece of observation, full of dry humor or some tone just suggestive of humor, and full of enormous vitality and felicity, colorful, pungent, manly, greatly gifted and greatly sustained. Clemens could learn from Dickens, as of course he did. And here is Heine's "London and the English," an extremely energetic essay, its independence and perception, its clarity of mind and lively fancy evidencing a great spirit and sounding quite modern. Which reminds one that Mark Twain's language dates so much less than that of most of his English and American contemporaries; he is so vital in his idiom. His texture, however, seems rather coarse when compared with Shaw's or Hawthorne's or James's. I suppose this is at least partly due to his colloquial tone, the very thing which makes his language live. Many of his essays sound like dictated utterances.

Clemens as an essayist? A man of strong opinions. Self-educated and surprisingly well-read, especially in history. His journalistic apprenticeship often shows in his work. Bold, direct, impatient, restless. A traveler who claims to loathe travel, yet who endures a great deal of it and gives the impression of enjoying it. Like James fascinated by the innocent and ignorant American among the tradition-encrusted Europeans. An optimist by physiology and a pessimist by sustained observation of "the damned human race." Like Voltaire, a self-appointed correction officer for the species. (Some of Voltaire's *Philosophical Dictionary* sounds as if it had been written by Mark Twain, especially the section on "fatalism": determinism or a variant of it.) A haloed clown. A dogmatic, saddened, weary tragedian. A nightwatch man patrolling with his smoking torch the dark streets of sham, cant and oppression. A bloodhound sniffing out injustice. A Bessemer oven blasting at it. A knight-errant cantering to the aid of unfranchised holocausting damsels in distress.

A linx-eyed observer of his own foibles, also of the foibles of the race. A competent journalist who like every professional enjoys the exercise of his skill. An amateur literary man in every sense, including love of the vocation. A dogged researcher into the Case of Adam and Eve. A stout defender of Satan on the ground that Satan is the original underdog. ("I have no special regard for Satan; but I can at least claim that I have no prejudice against him. It may even be that I lean a little his way, on account of his not having a fair show. All religions issue bibles against him, and say the most injurious things about him, but we never hear *his* side.") The man with the unruly mop and the assassin's drawl telling the nations how to behave. The printer's devil from Hannibal sounding off to the globe and, like Ambrose Bierce, finding it, in the end, mostly rotten, inherited as it is by man. No ivory tower man, no Humor for Humor's sake man, not even a Cigar for Cigar's sake man. At times a deliberate censor of his work, withholding it from public view through paying too much homage to the power of public opinion. Sometimes, extending himself beyond the sphere of his competence, as in the Shakespeare essay, very human, which is to say very foolish. A man of moods and whims. He detests the French, derides the Italians, adores the English and covertly respects the Germans and the Austrians while overtly ridiculing their language and certain of their institutions, such as student dueling. He deplores dueling yet uses sarcasm on the French because they do not duel bloodily enough, not as bloodily as the Austrians. A republican, he waxes warm through contact with the English nobility and the Viennese court, warm enough to neutralize some of the acid of his thought and prose and to set down statements, as in "The Memorable Assassination," which show his perspective to have blown away in the winds of monarchical excitement. In short he is masculine, personal, sarcastic, tender and nostalgic. He is also sometimes funny.

So much for a long view. Close-ups show probably more-interesting features. "Two Mark Twain Editorials," for example, is an early witness of both his strong and his weak sides. The first editorial is wry, clever, in a sound vein. The second is bombastic, flowery, emotional, the big bass drum effect. It is a pulpit style, and all that is missing from the pulpit is the acknowledgment that the orator knew the deceased, a fact which for some reason Clemens is reticent about, perhaps because he considers it too personal for a newspaper. Yet his having known Burlingame and having been generously helped by him at a crucial moment in his career (see "My Début as a Literary Person") have a bearing on the emotional style of the eulogy. That he is a beautifully descriptive writer, fertile and energetic, and essentially a noble writer despite his fondness for jokes, pranks, hoaxes, tall tales and guffaws, is made clear by "Queen Victoria's Jubilee." In "War Prayer" he speaks with the mind and tongue of one of the old prophets, only he includes himself among the sinners and has compassion for them. The essays which I like best are those that are outrageously funny, like "Letters to Satan," and those that are outraged—by politics, human stupidity, human cruelty, vested interest.

For deep thinking in an orderly, intellectual way I do not go to Mark Twain, nor for closely reasoned textual or biographical analysis in the way of James or Thomas Mann. As for intellectual consistency, Clemens is often without it. There are passages in "Saint Joan of Arc," for example, which can be used to confute the chief arguments in "What Is Man?"—that influence is merely external, that there is no free choice, that motives boil down to selfishness. Even an early and minor piece, "Disgraceful Persecution of a Boy," illuminates him clearly, showing how ferocious, deadly, inspired his sarcasms can be, and evidencing the fertility of his mind, his humanitarianism and his extraordinary tendency to identify with all kinds of people instead of feeling separate from them.

I have been flitting about with a purpose (I hope), in an effort to call his full figure to mind, not merely the image of a man writing at a desk but of one who like Dickens went out and met his large public and enthralled them. His public did not simply read him, they saw him and they felt they knew him as a friend. In few instances in modern literature has there been so little "distance" between an author and his audience. This fact

profoundly influenced his writing. If one wishes to read the essays as his contemporaries read them one ought to keep in mind
the vitality of his public image. He was an extraordinary figure,
impressive not only to his countrymen but to many people
abroad, and not only as a novelist and sage but as a platform
figure as well. The following contemporary account (signed
"R.C.B.," it appeared in *The Critic* of April 25, 1896) affords a
striking view of him on the Australian lecture circuit that time
when he was circling the globe in a determined and finally successful effort to pay off his debts. It is well worth reviving here:

"As a lecturer—or rather, story-teller, for the author objects
to be called a lecturer—Mark Twain is, and has proved himself
to be, in his opening Australian "At Homes," a decided success.
Like Charles Dickens, he relies entirely on his old books for the
pabulum of his discourses, but, unlike the author of *Pickwick*,
he does not read long extracts from the books. He takes some
of his best stories—"The Jumping Frog," *Huck Finn*, the
difficulties of the German language, *par exemple*—and re-tells
them, with many subtle additions of humor and some fresh observations, in the most irresistibly amusing manner. He is in no
sense a disappointment as a humorist. He starts his audience
laughing in the very first sentence he utters, and for two hours
keeps them in a continual roar. The only serious moments occur
when, with the unutterable pathos of which the true humorist
alone is capable, he interpolates a few pathetic touches which
almost make the tears mingle with the smiles. Every story he
tells serves the purpose of illustrating a moral, and, although, for
the most part, he talks in low, slow, conversational tones, at
times he rises to real bursts of eloquence—not the polished,
grandiloquent eloquence of the average American speaker, but
the eloquence conveyed in simple words and phrases, and
prompted by some deep and sincerely felt sentiment. The author has the power of seeming to jest at his serious side, just as
in his books; but there is no mistaking the seriousness with which,
for example, he is moved by the remembrance of the iniquities
perpetrated on liberty in the old slavery days amid which Huck
Finn and Jim the slave lived. He makes the most unexpected

anecdotes point the most unexpected morals, but it is the recital of the old, familiar stories without any moral attaching to them which pleases most, coming as they do warm from the brain of the man who invented them.

"Mark Twain steals unobtrusively on to the platform, dressed in the regulation evening-clothes, with the trouser-pockets cut high up, into which he occasionally dives both hands. He bows with a quiet dignity to the roaring cheers which greet him at every "At Home." Then, with natural, unaffected gesture, and with scarcely any prelude, he gets under weigh with his first story. He is a picturesque figure on the stage. His long, shaggy, white hair surmounts a face full of intellectual fire. The eyes, arched with bushy brows, and which seem to be closed most of the time while he is speaking, flash out now and then from their deep sockets with a genial, kindly, pathetic look, and the face is deeply drawn with the furrows accumulated during an existence of sixty years. He talks in short sentences, with a peculiar smack of the lips at the end of each. His language is just that of his books, full of the quaintest Americanisms, and showing an utter disregard for the polished diction of most lecturers. "It was not" is always " 'twarn't" with Mark Twain, and "mighty fine" and "my kingdom" and "they done it" and "catched," and various other purely trans-atlantic words and phrases, crop up profusely during his talk. He speaks slowly, lazily, and wearily, as a man dropping off to sleep, rarely raising his voice above a conversational tone; but it has that characteristic nasal sound which penetrates to the back of the largest building. His figure is rather slight, not above middle height, and the whole man suggests an utter lack of physical energy. As a matter of fact, Mark Twain detests exercise, and the attraction must be very strong to induce him to go very far out of doors. With the exception of an occasional curious trot, as when recounting his buck-jumping experiences, Mark Twain stands perfectly still in one place during the whole of the time he is talking to the audience. He rarely moves his arms, unless it is to adjust his spectacles or to show by action how a certain thing was done. His characteristic attitude is to stand quite still, with the right arm across the abdomen and the left resting on it and supporting his chin. In this way he talks on for nearly two hours; and, while the audience is laughing uproariously, he never by any chance relapses into a smile. To have read Mark Twain is a delight, but to have seen and heard him is a joy not readily to be forgotten."

"The Sandwich Islands" letters appeared in the *New York Tribune* of January 6 and 9, 1873. They were dated January 3 and 6 from Hartford and were occasioned by the death of King Kamehameha, with the consequent renewed interest in the fate of the islands, which were subsequently renamed the Hawaiian Islands. I located the letters by a fluke, after several vain attempts. Knowing from experience the unreliability of Twain's bibliographer, Merle Johnson, I had about assumed that he was again in error regarding dates and perhaps even the name of the newspaper. There was no sign of the letters in the two issues of the *Tribune* which he listed as source. Then one day, while working at the New York Historical Society, I requested the issues again, and to my surprise received a bound volume I had not seen before. It was a variant edition of the run of those two days and contained the letters. Johnson had probably seen scrapbook copies of them. The letters were shortly afterwards reprinted in an edition of the weekly *Tribune*, from the same type, and in 1920, according to Johnson, were included in *The Sandwich Islands*, a volume of thirty-nine pages, the edition being "strictly limited to thirty copies." I suffered remorse for having murdered Johnson several times in my daydreams.

"A Memorable Midnight Experience" is part of an aborted book on the English people and their institutions. Clemens sailed alone for England in August 1872 with the intention of collecting material for the book. The warm welcome he received, together with a good deal of socializing, ended note-taking for the project, and the project was abandoned. The idea had been to strike a satirical or at least an ironic note but Clemens was disinclined to sustain the attempt. The essay was written in 1872 and first appeared in *Sketches, No. 1* in 1874. Vivid, it is permeated by his love affair with the romantic past, which was later to find fictional expression in such works as *Huckleberry Finn*, the *Connecticut Yankee* and *Joan of Arc*. He writes: "It was a derisive reminder that we were a part of this present sordid, plodding, commonplace time, and not august relics of a bygone age. . . ."

In 1891–92, while he and his family were in Europe, Clemens published half a dozen travel letters in the *New York Sun*. One, "Playing Courier," which was the third in the series, I included in a collection of his short stories, for it is far and away too fanciful to be considered non-fiction. The other five, in the order of their appearance in the *Sun*, are "Aix, the Paradise of the Rheumatics," "At the Shrine of St. Wagner," "Marienbad, a Health Factory," "Switzerland, the Cradle of Liberty," and "The German Chicago." The first letter appeared in the *Sun* of November 8, 1891, and the last in the issue of April 3, 1892. The letters also appeared in the *Illustrated London News*, sometimes with minor variations in the text. Clemens at first believed that the six letters could make a small book, then thought better of the idea and embarked on a trip down the Rhône, minus family, in the hope of turning the journey into literature and thus filling out the desired book. The Rhône journey was made in September. It resulted in "Down the Rhône," which was published posthumously. Clemens filled 174 pages of notes before the pleasure of the trip made note-taking seem altogether beside the point. Small wonder—he had spent three months in travel and sightseeing, and what with the worrisome matters occurring back home in the States, he had every justification for dreaming, smoking, forgetting. Besides, the journey lacked incidents and colorful characters; for an experienced journalist there was simply not enough copy. After ten days of it Clemens rejoined his family.

Clemens was a masterful writer of travel pieces—vivid, precise, breathing his curiosity, vitality, play and opinions into many of the places and people he encountered. He had a wonderful copiousness of thought and language and was one of the most natural writers we have had. His "voice" was always his own, easily, gracefully reflecting ideas and feelings. He was, as is well

known, also an uneven writer. The "Aix" piece is well controlled, but the "Marienbad" one wanders—there is a good deal
of landscape, a few anecdotes, a Goethe poem, and little of the
feeling of the health resort. But the letters as a group are excellent, and very fresh from a tired man of fifty-six, who often
sounds as enthusiastic and as playful as in those halcyon days of
The Innocents Abroad. The "Switzerland" essay witnesses his
continuing delight in portraying his countryman in Europe as a
thick-head, a democratic shover of men, atwitter with the work-
aday aspects of life. "The Cholera Epidemic in Hamburg,"
written in 1892, according to Paine, for some reason was not
published during the author's lifetime.

One of Clemens's favorite roles is that of Mark the Dragon-
Killer. In the Harriet Shelley episode the unfortunate dragon is
Edward Dowden, Irish Shakespeare scholar, also the official
biographer of Shelley under the patronage of Lady Shelley,
Mary Godwin's daughter-in-law and detractor and suppressor of
Harriet. Mrs. Louise Schutz Boas, the author of the very recent
Harriet Shelley (1962) asserts that Dowden's Victorian morality compelled him to disparage Harriet in order to make a purer
portrait of Shelley. She also states, "The letters between these
two gentlemen [Dowden and Richard Garnett, Lady Shelley's
coadjutor] trying to be gentlemanly in their denigration of Harriet make an amusing study in self-justification, Victorian smug-
ness, and determined prejudice." Clemens read the Dowden
biography, concluded that it was a character assassination of
Harriet, and proceeded, in three issues of the *North American
Review* of 1894, to assassinate Dowden in every possible department—style, logic, innuendo, guesswork, evidence, scholarship,
decency, sanity: the whole spectrum of the Dragon's armor.

He had the will, the motive and the genius to make an astound-
ing performance of it. Clemens was rarely in danger of verbal
constipation, but now his literary sluices were wide open. Not,
however, at the expense of organization, logic or cool-headed-
ness. He did not stammer, or go blind with rage, or slam into
dead ends. Instead, he proceeded with forensic skill and the
passion of a knight-errant. The flow of energy, the tenaciousness

of mind, the untiring stream of language are quite amazing. He is writing about people long dead, yet he is as excited and angered as if Bysshe and Harriet are still alive, or as if Harriet is a dead relative, or perhaps a girl he once loved. Fortifying his anger is his Victorian idealization of woman, family and the home. Bysshe had promised to be a husband to Harriet and had turned out to be something of a rake, at least in Mark Twain's view. Therefore he is a scoundrel. Clemens is too worked up to stop to consider Shelley's views on marriage and to attempt to see the institution with the poet's eyes. Having stern notions of his own, he is not averse to roundly condemning the young poet for failing to live up to them. Clemens was no ethical relativist. He was deadly on the subject of the French, for example, because of their different approach to the world of sex. One wonders what Dowden's reaction was to this shower of brimstone, this descent from Vesuvius.

Another Dragon was Paul Bourget, French man of letters. Bourget's mistake was that he published *Outre-Mer*, a critical journal of his visit to the United States in 1893. As Paine has well said, "Clemens could criticize his own nation freely enough, but he could hardly be patient under the strictures of a Frenchman, especially upon American women." Once again there is hell to pay. This moralizing humorist, who early was known as "the moralist of the Main," is sometimes a cramped American moralist, a Protestant, even a Presbyterian, moralist, and nothing gives him more refined pleasure than taking digs at the French. A countryman of Bourget's, Max O'Rell (nom-de-plume of Paul Blouet), offered a clumsy defense of Bourget in the pages of the *North American Review*, in which the attack had occurred. Whereupon Clemens belabored O'Rell with a shillelagh. Clemens's rejoinder is not successful. It is coy and unclear in its pretense that O'Rell's reply is by Bourget, and this device guts much of its strength. The rejoinder, however, did not require much strength to badly wound O'Rell. Clemens gives the impression that the rejoinder will appear in the *North American Review*. It did not appear there. It made its first appearance in *Tom Sawyer, Detective* in 1896.

"Concerning the Jews" was first published in *Harper's Magazine* in September 1899. Clemens wrote to his friend H. H. Rogers, the financier, "The Jew article is my 'gem of the ocean.' I have taken a world of pleasure in writing it & doctoring it & fussing at it. Neither Jew nor Christian will approve of it, but people who are neither Jews *nor* Christians will, for they are in a condition to know the truth when they see it." Clemens was a great admirer of the Jews. He once wrote to his friend and pastor, Joseph Twichell, "The difference between the brain of the average Christian and that of the average Jew—certainly in Europe—is about the difference between a tadpole's and an archbishop's. It is a marvelous race; by long odds the most marvelous race the world has produced, I suppose."

The essay elicited an interesting reply from M. S. Levy, a rabbi, which appeared in the *Overland Monthly*. Responding to Twain's statement, "In the United States he [the Jew] was created free in the beginning—he did not need to help, of course," which implied that the Jew in America did not help in the struggle against England, Levy listed names of Jews who had fought in the war. He also mentioned those who had given large sums to the cause, among them Hyam Salomon ($300,000, "an immense fortune for those days") and Manuel Mordecai Noah (£20,000). He went on to cite Jewish patriots of the Civil War. Mark Twain wrote in his essay, "The Jew is a money-getter," and spoke of "all his fat wealth." To which Levy retorted, "Money-getters? The Vanderbilts, the Goulds, Astors, Havemeyers, Rockefellers, Mackays, Huntingtons, Armours, Carnegies, Sloanes, Whitneys, are not Jews, and yet they control and possess more than twenty-five per cent of all the circulated wealth of the United States. They seem to be all right as 'money-getters,' and little have they done for humanity. Baron de Hirsh was a 'money-getter,' and 'fat in wealth,' but he gave his millions to suffering human kind irrespective of creed. Nathan Strauss, of New York, saved infant mortality by twenty-five per cent by his sterilized milk societies. Baroness de Hirsh, a Jewess, gives fifty millions to charity in her lifetime." And so on. Possibly Clemens added the postscript to his essay partly as a result of the

Levy reply. The statistics of the postscript, however, are not taken from the Levy article.

"What is Man?" is the ultimate, the perfect, expression of the least attractive side of Mark Twain—his dreary penchant for determinism, which he seized upon with the fanaticism of one who believes he has at last found *the* light. How is it that this noteworthy product of the freetrading, freewheeling Mississippi and the western frontier took to his mind with such ardor a system of thought which denies the possibility of individual choice, which asserts that all is predestined, that man is a machine, and that we are all slaves of the great chain of circumstance? To these views Clemens added others—that God is indifferent to man's fate if not hostile to it; that man is the butt of nature's practical joke; that his fate is to be born of woman and to suffer evil, sin and disease until a blessed death releases him from bondage—and he fictionalized all of them, with great skill, in "The Mysterious Stranger," a long short story. In the present essay, however, as also in "The Turning-point of My Life," he tries to sledgehammer them into the reader's head.

The best thing about this side of Mark Twain is that he himself had serious doubts about it underneath the burning faith, which is why he couldn't speak suavely, coolly, gracefully and humorously on the subject. His style is strident with italics, his language dull when he touches upon this awful wisdom, this fixed idea. Fortunately, there is a distinction to be made between his preachment and his practice. For example, he condemned the Italian anarchist who assassinated the Empress of Austria, and did not excuse the crime on the ground that its perpetrator had no choice but to commit it. It is interesting to speculate how he would have reacted to twentieth-century science, in which the principle of indeterminacy of quantum physics has lent support to the doctrine of free will, the opposite of his favorite doctrine. This principle asserts that the behavior of particles within the atom is not determinable except in terms of broad statistics and probability.

Another quixotic aspect of Clemens is his support of the Baconian authorship of the Shakespeare works. As strict argument, "Is Shakespeare Dead?" is often difficult to take seriously, it wanders so from the point, with its claimants, recollections of Ealer and the river, its remarks on Satan, and so on. Its main "evidence" is the statements by the several lawyers on the legal knowledge in the plays. It is curious that Clemens does not see that all the arguments in favor of a great, systematic legal knowledge in the plays prove nothing about the so-called legal training of the author of the plays—that it is surmising of the very sort that he, Clemens, objects to. A skilled dialectician, using the kind of "evidence" that Clemens here finds acceptable, could no doubt prove that Clemens could not have written most of his books, having been too uneducated, too etcetera, to have done so; he could probably prove that they were written by William Dean Howells, whose natural modesty prevented him from owning up to the authorship of so vast an array of works as to embarrass his colleagues and his time.

Clemens's seventieth-birthday speech is possibly the finest he ever made. It exemplifies an uncanny knack which in him was developed to the point of genius. A thing sounds absurdly exaggerated, then as an afterthought you see sound reality in it, and finally wisdom. His humor often seems to spring from a sense of the incongruity of life, of man's estate, and to rise from the depths as if certain that the bottom is a great joke, or a laugh, or a sarcasm. At other times it is the humor of the surface, inspired slapstick. One is aware in this speech of the breadth of his experience. He seemed to have a genius for partaking of the world, and for being allowed to partake of it. Franz Kafka, the Jew, the alien, sensed his time in an altogether different way; he sensed the moral discontinuity of it and had to flesh out his visions with fantastic, incoherent shapes. Whereas Clemens, like Tolstoy and Balzac, had the breadth of popular experience to rely on.

"The Memorable Assassination" has as its subject Amelie Eugenie Elizabeth, consort of Francis Joseph, emperor of Austria and king of Hungary. She was stabbed in Geneva on September 10, 1898 and died within a few hours. Mark Twain was living near Vienna when he received the news from Countess Wydenbouck-Esterhazy. He went to the capital and watched the funeral ceremonies from the new Krantz Hotel, which faced the Capuchin church where the royal dead lay buried. He sent the essay to H. H. Rogers to offer to the magazines, then recalled it for reasons not clear. It was not published until posthumously. It is one of his perceptive pieces. Some of it is excited chatter, making him seem like a court-dazzled American. The stir of the moment and of his surroundings have engulfed his better judgment. He writes about the funeral crowd being dispersed by soldiers: "It was all so swift, noiseless, exact—like a beautifully ordered machine." Yes, and deadly when one thinks of the repressions of the Empire. Kafka could have enlightened Clemens, although he was only a boy of fifteen at the time. Clemens relates the rumor that the assassin may have been prompted by "the criminal militarism which is impoverishing Europe and driving the starving poor mad" (a militarism which was to find fruit in the First World War), yet fails to see the irony of the square's being filled exclusively by the military. Clemens writes, "dull clothes would have marred the radiant spectacle." Would they? Ought there to be a radiant spectacle at a time of national mourning? Or a spectacle of men at arms? The spectacle was pure barbarism, a pluming of males on the occasion of the killing of a woman. Clemens misses much, although he is cool enough to use field glasses the better to collect material. Perhaps he saw the essay's shortcomings afterwards and for this reason did not publish it.

My daughter Susy, four and a half, a blonde with explosive brown eyes, hearing I was going to the library the other day, asked, "Are you going to meet Mark Twain?"

"Well, not exactly."

"Is he nice?"

"Very."

"Why does he have a mustache?"

"To warm his nose."

"Really really?"

"No, he really has it to hide his upper lip."

"Why?"

"He likes his upper lip to be like a garden, with grass growing all over it and partly covering his mouth. That way everything's toasty."

"Are you and Mark Twain writing a book?"

"*I'm* writing a book."

"Why?"

"Because he's lazy."

"You mean he doesn't help?"

"Well . . . I guess he helps—a little."

Princeton, New Jersey
September 1962

THE AUTOBIOGRAPHY

IN MY OPINION Mark Twain's autobiography is a classic of American letters, to be ranked with the autobiographies of Benjamin Franklin and Henry Adams. I think that it will be regarded as such over the years. The final work of one of our country's most beloved authors, it is the product of one of those nineteenth-century giants whom we of this century are slow in replacing. It has the marks of greatness in it—style, scope, imagination, laughter, tragedy.

It is the product of a highly original yet representative mind and it brings back the tone and flavor of an America which was young and optimistic, a homespun, provincial America but an America with greatness in its heart. Thoreau's America may have contained many lives of quiet desperation. Mark Twain's decidedly did not. The midwestern and western frontiers were not the America of Concord and Boston. The difference between these places accounted, in the autobiographical context, for the difference between Mark Twain and Henry Adams, and in the literary one between Mark Twain and Henry James.

It must be said at once that now for the first time the material of the present volume* is being presented as autobiography, and in the sequence which one would reasonably expect from autobiography. And for the first time the whole manuscript is being used as the source, not parts or selections of it. Also, the present volume contains from 30,000 to 40,000 words which have never before seen print. Mark Twain left a manuscript of unwieldy proportions, which included whole small books, such as *Is Shakespeare Dead?* He had thrown them into the grab bag which he thought of as his autobiography. Leaving such books out, we have a more reasonable manuscript. Bernard DeVoto has reckoned that Albert Bigelow Paine used about half of the latter manuscript in his edition of the autobiography (1924) and

* *The Autobiography of Mark Twain*, Harper, 1959.

that he himself used about half the remainder in *his* edition
(1940).

To put it briefly, Paine either did not envision the possibility
of a true autobiography or did not care to undertake to make
one. The same can be said of DeVoto. Both said in their introductions that what they were presenting was not really autobiography but a kind of table-talk.

When Mark Twain died in 1910 he was widely regarded as the
most prominent and characteristic American writer of his generation. He had a large and devoted public, and this public had
some reason to expect from him, as a posthumous publication,
an autobiography which was the equal if not the superior of any
yet written in the United States. It had been known for some
time that he was writing such a book, and a number of chapters
had appeared in twenty-five installments of the *North American
Review* of 1906 and 1907. But his public was disappointed, for
Mark Twain had some curious notions about writing an autobiography, notions which kept changing over the years except
in one respect: they became ever more curious.

He began with composing sections by hand and ended with a
series of autobiographical dictations. As early as the 70's he was
writing fragments. Around 1873 he wrote a brief autobiographical sketch for Charles Dudley Warner; in 1877 he
recalled the early days in Florida, Missouri; in 1885, on the death
of General Grant, he dictated a series of recollections of his
meetings with the General; in 1890 he set down the Paige type-
setting machine episode, that fiasco of his middle years, and his
memories of his mother; in 1897–98, while in Vienna, he wrote
the brilliant chapters on the early days spent on his uncle's
farm; in 1899 he composed an autobiographical sketch for the
use of his nephew, Samuel Moffett, on the basis of which Moffett wrote a biographical essay for the Uniform Edition of Mark
Twain's works, issued in the same year; in 1904 he wrote the
notes on the Villa Quarto and the memory of John Hay while
living on the outskirts of Florence; and in 1906 he undertook
the sustained series of dictations which added so greatly to the
autobiography's bulk.

The task alternately irked and pleased him. In 1877, at the age

of forty-two, he had resolved to begin his autobiography at
once, in a formal way. "I did begin it," he wrote in 1904, "but the
resolve melted away and disappeared in a week and I threw my
beginning away. Since then, about every three or four years I
have made other beginnings and thrown them away. Once I
tried the experiment of a diary, intending to inflate that into an
autobiography when its accumulation should furnish enough
material, but that experiment lasted only a week; it took me half
of every night to set down the history of the day, and at the
week's end I did not like the result.

"Within the last eight or ten years I have made several attempts to do the autobiography in one way or another with a
pen, but the result was not satisfactory; it was too literary. . . .

"With a pen in the hand the narrative stream is a canal; it
moves slowly, smoothly, decorously, sleepily, it has no blemish
except that it is all blemish. It is too literary, too prim, too nice;
the gait and style and movement are not suited to narrative. That
canal stream is always reflecting; it is its nature, it can't help it.
Its slick shiny surface is interested in everything it passes along
the banks—cows, foliage, flowers, everything. And so it wastes
a lot of time in reflection."

Later he experimented with newspaper clippings. "I shall
scatter through this Autobiography newspaper clippings without end. When I do not copy them into the text it means that I
do not make them a part of the Autobiography—at least not of
the earlier editions. I put them in on the theory that if they are
not interesting in the earlier editions, a time will come when it
may be well enough to insert them for the reason that age is
quite likely to make them interesting although in their youth
they may lack that quality."

He was not afraid to wander. "In this autobiography it is my
purpose to wander whenever I please and come back when I
get ready." Once he thought he had found the "right" way.
"Finally in Florence, in 1904, I hit upon the right way to do an
Autobiography: Start it at no particular time of your life; wander at your free will all over your life; talk only about the thing
which interests you for the moment; drop it the moment its

interest threatens to pale, and turn your talk upon the new and more interesting thing that has intruded itself into your mind meantime. . . .

"And so, I have found the right plan. It makes my labor amusement—mere amusement, play, pastime, and wholly effortless."

But early in 1906 he was having difficulties. "The difficulties of it grow upon me all the time. For instance, the idea of blocking out a consecutive series of events which have happened to me, or which I imagine have happened to me—I can see that that is impossible for me. The only thing possible for me is to talk about the thing that something suggests at the moment—something in the middle of my life, perhaps, or something that happened only a few months ago. It is my purpose to extend these notes to 600,000 words, and possibly more. But that is going to take a long time—a long time."

At other times he was quite proud of what he was composing.

"I intend that this autobiography shall become a model for all future autobiographies when it is published, after my death, and I also intend that it shall be read and admired a good many centuries because of its form and method—a form and method whereby the past and the present are constantly brought face to face, resulting in contrasts which newly fire up the interest all along like contact of flint with steel. Moreover, this autobiography of mine does not select from my life its showy episodes, but deals merely in the common experiences which go to make up the life of the average human being, and the narrative must interest the average human being because these episodes are of a sort which he is familiar with in his own life and in which he sees his own life reflected and set down in print. The usual, conventional autobiographer seems to particularly hunt out those occasions in his career when he came into contact with celebrated persons, whereas his contacts with the uncelebrated were just as interesting to him and would be to his reader, and were vastly more numerous than his collisions with the famous.

"Howells was here yesterday afternoon and I told him the whole scheme of this autobiography and its apparently systemless system—only apparently systemless, for it is not that. It is a deliberate system and the law of the system is that I shall talk about the matter which for the moment interests me, and cast it aside and talk about something else the moment its interest for me is exhausted. It is a system which follows no charted course and is not going to follow any such course. It is a system which is a complete and purposed jumble—a course which begins nowhere, follows no specified route, and can never reach an end while I am alive, for the reason that if I should talk to the stenographer two hours a day for a hundred years I should still never be able to set down a tenth part of the things which have interested me in my lifetime. I told Howells that this autobiography of mine would live a couple of thousand years without any effort and would then take a fresh start and live the rest of the time.

"He said he believed it would and asked me if I meant to make a library of it.

"I said that that was my design but that if I should live long enough the set of volumes could not be contained merely in a city, it would require a state, and that there would not be any multibillionaire alive, perhaps, at any time during its existence who would be able to buy a full set, except on the installment plan.

"Howells applauded, and was full of praises and indorsement, which was wise in him and judicious. If he had manifested a different spirit I would have thrown him out of the window. I like criticism, but it must be my way."

And in a similar vein:

"This Autobiography of mine differs from other autobiographies—differs from *all* other autobiographies, except Benvenuto's, perhaps. The conventional biography of all the ages is an open window. The autobiographer sits there and examines and discusses the people that go by—not all of them, but the notorious ones, the famous ones; those that wear fine uniforms, and crowns when it is not raining; and very great poets and great statesmen—illustrious people with whom he has had the high privilege of coming in contact. He likes to toss a wave of recognition to these with his hand as they go by and he likes to notice that the others are seeing him do this, and admiring. He likes to let on that in discussing these occasional people that wear the good clothes he is only interested in interesting his reader and is in a measure unconscious of himself.

"But this Autobiography of mine is not that kind of autobiography. This Autobiography of mine is a mirror and I am looking at myself in it all the time. Incidentally I notice the people that pass along at my back—I get glimpses of them in the mirror— and whenever they say or do anything that can help advertise me and flatter me and raise me in my own estimation I set these things down in my Autobiography. I rejoice when a king or a duke comes my way and makes himself useful to this Autobiography, but they are rare customers, with wide intervals between. I can use them with good effect as lighthouses and monuments along my way, but for real business I depend upon the common herd."

And in March of 1907, while on vacation in Bermuda, he recorded still another objective of the autobiography. "I do not need to stay here any longer, for I have completed the only work that was remaining for me to do in this life and that I could not possibly afford to leave uncompleted—my Autobiography. Although that is not finished, and will not be finished until I die, the object which I had in view in compiling it is accomplished: that object was to distribute it through my existing books and give each of them a new copyright of twenty-eight years, and thus defeat the copyright statute's cold intention to rob them and starve my daughters. I have dictated four or five hundred thousand words of autobiography already and if I should die tomorrow this mass of literature would be quite sufficient for the object which I had in view in manufacturing it."

In his autobiography Mark Twain let out most of the stops in whatever disciplines he had managed to maintain during his writing career. Bernard DeVoto believed that Twain's failure to write a coherent autobiography was due to a certain dread. "When he invoked Hannibal [that is, his early years] he found there not only the idyll of boyhood but anxiety, violence, supernatural horror, and an uncrystallized but enveloping dread.

Much of his fiction, most of his masterpiece [*Huckleberry Finn*], flows from that phantasy-bound anxiety.

"I think that the impulse to write his autobiography was in part an impulse to examine and understand that dread. And I think that the impulse was arrested short of genuine self-revelation because the dread was so central in him that he could approach it only symbolically, by way of fiction."

But one does not need to rely on such a theory in order to account for Mark Twain's difficulties with his autobiography. His mind, rich in memory and nostalgia, kept seeking anecdotal forms of recollection, forms which did not easily suit the chronological organization of the classic autobiography. And it was a case of the story teller irked by "facts," the dross which inhibited fancy. If the facts were sometimes the losers, that worried Mark Twain not at all. "I don't believe these details are right but I don't care a rap. They will do just as well as the facts," he once wrote in his autobiography. In this respect he had good company, even the meticulous Henry Adams. Speaking of a journey to Washington with his father as a twelve-year-old in 1850, Adams wrote in his own autobiography, "The journey was meant as education, and as education it served the purpose of fixing in memory the stage of a boy's thought in 1850. . . . This was the journey he remembered. The actual journey may have been quite different, but the actual journey has no interest for education. The memory was all that mattered. . . ."

Mark Twain's life was a long and rich one; it seemed to him an inexhaustible mine of recollection. The associations streamed out from it in a million directions and it was his quixotic hope to capture most of them with the irony and humor and storytelling gift which were his own way of regarding the human drama. He was staggered by the size of the task and justly so. The real question is whether he actually failed, as has been generally believed. It is true that he did not use a comprehensive, a strategic approach, that he kept winning tactical battles at the cost of winning a war. But many works of art are approached in such a way, works which reach a great culmination. Perhaps

if he had lived a few years longer he would have found a sufficient perspective to organize the autobiography and edit out
of it all the irrelevant materials which his odd methods of composition had allowed to sneak in. The fact is that the greatness
is *there*. You can edit the trivia out but you cannot edit the
greatness in. One of the ironies of art is that it is possible to win
a war and lose the battles, and that it is more tragic to lose the
battles than the war. Formal neatness and comprehensive sweep:
and dead or dying details. The details in Mark Twain's autobiography are intensely alive, those which are part of the true
birth.

Mark Twain was trying to amuse himself: that was his chief
aim during the dictations. (It was during the dictations, near
the end of his life, that he let most of the trivia in. And the
trivia is always set apart; there is no case of a brilliant section
which contains it. Everything is distinctly of a piece: the good
is good, the bad is clearly bad.) He had produced his share of
work in the world; he had outlived most of the people he cared
for; the world was in a bad way and he was not averse to leaving it. And so he reminisced, and by so doing he amused himself—reminisced on his own terms, not on the world's, not
according to some theory of autobiographical composition.

It was in 1906 that Albert Bigelow Paine began to have an
influence on the autobiography. Meeting Clemens at a dinner in
New York, he asked if he might visit him soon. At their next
meeting he proposed to write the official biography of him and
Mark Twain agreed. As a result, Clemens undertook a series of
autobiographical dictations, to be used partly by Paine as the
basis of the biography and to be published in and for themselves at an appropriate time. The word "appropriate" in this
connection turned out to have a surprisingly flexible meaning.
At first it was Mark Twain's intention to publish no part of his
autobiography until a century after his death; then, shortly afterward, he set about publishing numerous chapters of it in the
North American Review. In some parts of the typescript he indicated marginally that they were to wait for fifty years after his

death; in others seventy-five; and in several places five hundred years after the year of composition. Some of these injunctions have been adhered to by his heirs and executors; others, for good reasons, have not.

The dictations were begun in Clemens's New York home at 21 Fifth Avenue, were continued for a while near Dublin, New Hampshire, then in New York again and eventually in Redding, Connecticut, in Stormfield, Twain's last home. They went on fairly continuously for two years, then intermittently for another two, and were ended by Clemens's death in the spring of 1910. The dictations, although rarely the equal of certain of the reminiscences Mark Twain composed earlier, by hand, are nevertheless invaluable for a complete account of his life, and in many instances they are excellent.

Paine had the unhappy choice of publishing the autobiography as he found it or of regarding it as raw material and bringing it to a more or less finished state. I say unhappy because he faced a very special dilemma. What he found was a manuscript of unwieldy size, consisting of a series of extended notes—a bundle of things relevant and inspired mixed with items irrelevant and dull; all in so disorganized a condition as to be bewildering, although the sections and fragments in themselves were thematically, stylistically and factually complete. If Paine had published the manuscript as he found it he would have been charged with lack of an understanding of his whole responsibility; if he had edited the manuscript he would probably have been criticized even more strongly. He decided to leave the responsibility with Mark Twain, except for the omissions he made whenever the spirit moved him, usually in the interest of "propriety" as he understood it, often failing to warn the reader that something had been left out.

Paine had another choice to make. Mark Twain had requested him to publish the autobiography not in chronological order but in the sequence in which it was written and dictated. What an extraordinary idea! As though the stream of composition time were in some mysterious way more revealing than that of autobiographical time! To gauge Paine's problem adequately one must keep in mind the fact that Mark Twain had approached his autobiography from all directions simultaneously. Paine offered no details of the manner or wording of Mark Twain's request, nor did he suggest whether it was written or given orally, or whether made at the beginning of their relationship or near the end. And so we are unable to judge how much earnestness there was behind it. He merely noted: "The various divisions and chapters of this work, in accordance with the author's wish, are arranged in the order in which they were written, regardless of the chronology of events." Ought Paine to have taken Mark Twain's wish regarding sequence so literally? It was a delicate problem, but by no means either the first or the last of its kind to be presented to a literary executor. At any rate Paine adhered to Mark Twain's wishes, and as a result it is impossible to call to memory another autobiography by a major writer which made its debut so inauspiciously and in so confusing a manner.

The shortcomings of the two volumes were plain. The autobiography of 1924 was incomplete, raw, badly arranged. It was a grab bag, a repository for anything and everything; its chief flaw was that it correctly reflected Clemens's notions and methods. Beginning with fragments composed by hand as early as 1870, it ranged over sublime and ridiculous chapters down to dictations of April 1906. Much of it was embarrassing: fragmentary notations on news stories of the day, exchanges of letters, opinions of the moment. Parts, such as the reminiscences of the uncle's farm, were among the best things Mark Twain had ever written, and cried out to be saved. But it was difficult to save such an inauspicious edition, and the good things in it began to be forgotten with the bad. In time there were literate readers, and admirers of Mark Twain, who barely realized that he had tried his hand at an autobiography. Paine's hope of issuing more volumes in the autobiographical series was doomed, and his desire to fulfill Mark Twain's request by ending the work with the latter's account of the death of his daughter Jean was frustrated.

Reviewing the two volumes, Carl Van Doren wrote in the

Saturday Review of Literature, "Are there still further candors to be expected? Or was Mark Twain really so cautious that the occasional objurgations of this book seemed to him untempered violence? These questions ought to be answered one way or the other, and not slurred over as they have here been by Mr. Paine." He spoke of the work as being "casual and repetitious and disorderly" but added that it was "far from being a damp fizzle." He asked insistently, "Is there more of it somewhere?" Richard Aldington attacked Clemens as not being very funny or much of a writer, and spoke of "the tedium of these desultory disconnected pages" in a review in the *Spectator*. Mark Twain's friend, Brander Matthews, liked the book as the expression of a great and wise man, yet wrote, "There is here no consecutive record of a career, but only tumultuous recollections, poured forth as the spirit moved him. . . . It begins anywhere; it doesn't end at all; it has no skeleton and no adroit adjustment of members; it ranges through the Cosmos and arrives at Chaos; it is compounded of unrelated fragments; it is haphazard and helter-skelter; it is casual and fortuitous . . ."

The best review was written by Mark Van Doren for *The Nation*. Van Doren warned that the book would be disappointing to anyone who "expected a consecutive or otherwise ordered account" of Mark Twain's life. "How much order anyone had a right to expect from the mind of this man is a question; but the fact remains that the book as it now appears is a jumble of things some of which are consequential and some of which are not. . . . Unpublished articles and other scraps on hand were shoveled in to make the manuscript 'complete.' The sections were arranged in the order of their composition, not in the order of the events related. . . . But the Autobiography, shapeless and disappointing as it is, must still be called a great book. Perhaps by very reason of its imperfections it reveals, in the plainest and most naked way, the quality of Mark Twain's literary sinew." After comparing Clemens with Fielding, Shakespeare and Rabelais, Van Doren wrote, "He shares with those men their vast riches in the mine that is so indispensable to a writer of the first rank, the mine of eloquence. This is shown

here not only in numerous paragraphs and pages which mount
to the top pitch of expression, not only in eulogies and diatribes
which sweep the reader from his bearings, but more convinc-
ingly yet in the evidence everywhere that Mark Twain's interest
in the arts of language was unbounded."

Sixteen years after the appearance of Paine's edition, Bernard
DeVoto issued *Mark Twain in Eruption,* which brought to the
public a large new portion of the autobiographical typescript.
DeVoto did not like Paine's edition, which he called shapeless
and annoying. He did not emulate Paine's technique of "sampling" the contents of the autobiography but instead depended
on "omitting trivialities and joining together things that belonged together." He did not hesitate to select, rearrange and
edit. The organization of his volume was thematic. But the
book he issued was supplementary to and conditioned by the
edition of his predecessor; consequently it was as incomplete
as Paine's two volumes.

Speaking of the order which he gave his volume, DeVoto said,
"It is a loose order but it is the tightest one that can be given
the Autobiography; and occasionally I have chosen to let the
original order stand, at some cost in incoherence." But DeVoto
was in error. His thematic order was an imposed one and could
not accurately be called the tightest which can be given the
autobiography, the essence of whose internal order is time. The
tightest order of any work is the order functional to it, inherent
in it, the order which is in harmony with its subject.

DeVoto worked only with the unpublished parts of the typescript and as he did so he had occasion to make omissions. "I
have left out what seems to me irrelevant or uninteresting," he
wrote; yet later in his introduction he admitted that he left out
certain passages because they contained matter which was "fantastic and injurious." He added that he had omitted other passages "because the exaggeration gets so far into phantasy that it
becomes a trivial rage." I have been able to examine the passages
in question and have reached the conclusion—not an unexpected
one—that the wise course is to let Mark Twain have his say in
these matters of high emotion.

In some of the omissions DeVoto was no doubt influenced by opinions which he could not ignore, such as those of the Estate and of the surviving daughter; but in others, such as the suppression of the concluding observations relating to the Bret Harte matter, he exercised a kind of judgment which can be questioned. The remarks which I have included on temperament are all publishable and important, without involving the sensibilities of living persons, now or in 1940; they were among the remarks DeVoto omitted. "I have left out nothing that seemed to me important, and I assume responsibility for the omissions as well as for what is printed," DeVoto wrote. In fact, he did leave out matter which he considered important; and the full responsibility for omissions was not his if in his role of editor he was deferring to the wishes of others.

But aside from such peculiarities as I have mentioned, DeVoto's was a good volume, and the judgment and ability of its editor were clearly superior to those of Paine. It had clarity and organization. It resurrected forgotten chapters from the pages of the *North American Review*. It revealed new facets of Mark Twain which until 1940 had been observable only by scholars. It deserved the good press it received. The tone of its reception may perhaps be exemplified by Clifton Fadiman's review in *The New Yorker*. "It seems Mark Twain, scared to death of what Mrs. Grundy would say, left a whole pile of manuscripts to be issued at intervals after his death. Some of these odds and ends were published in Albert Bigelow Paine's edition of the Autobiography, about as disappointing a book as ever came from the pen of a first-rate writer. Out of a part of the remainder, that sagacious Resurrection Man, Bernard DeVoto, has carpentered a book which may add little to Mark Twain's literary stature but a good deal to our understanding of his split temperament. . . . All in all, a valuable book, readable for itself and indispensable for the new light it throws on the author. Mr. DeVoto's industry, taste and knowledge of his subject have combined to produce a volume in which Mark Twain's voice speaks unmistakably, though from the grave."

By now the reader will have surmised what my own plan
has been. Working with the autobiographical manuscript as a
whole, both unpublished and published parts, I weeded out a
variety of material. I did this for several reasons: in order to
make a wieldy volume which would meet certain requirements
of the general reader (for whom this book is designed); in order
to unburden the excellent parts of the dated, dull, trivial and
journalese sections of the work; and in order to concentrate
less on opinion and second-hand recollection and more on the
more truly autobiographical, the more purely literary and the
more characteristically humorous material. My volume is to a
high degree anecdotal, but I believe this to be a virtue rather
than a defect, in that it correctly represents the creative slant
of Mark Twain's mind.

From the published parts I have omitted such matter as the
lengthy notes on the Grant memoirs, the beauties of the German
language, the Morris incident, much of Susy's biography, various comments on the news or correspondence of the day, elongated remarks on Theodore Roosevelt, Andrew Carnegie, the
plutocracy and so on. From the unpublished parts I have
omitted material on the San Francisco earthquake, which I believe to be under par (besides, Mark Twain did not experience
the quake personally), on a mining friend's literary effort, on
spontaneous oratory, on the supremacy of the house fly (both
of these pieces being rather strained, in my opinion), on simpli-
fied spelling, on palmistry, and other matters. I do not believe
that it would do justice to Mark Twain's literary reputation to
publish these sections.

Unlike DeVoto, I do not assume responsibility for all of the
omissions. Had the authority been mine I would have included
in this edition the dictations of five days—June 19, June 20,
June 22, June 23 and June 25 of 1906. But I would not have put
them into the body of the autobiography, for they are more
essayistic than autobiographical; I would have made an appendix
of them. Mark Twain's surviving daughter, Mrs. Jacques
Samossoud, who has the authority and the responsibility, has

decided that it would serve no good purpose to publish the chapters at this time. It was also DeVoto's desire to publish them but he did not do so because Mrs. Samossoud (then Mrs. Gabrilowitsch) requested him not to. Three of the chapters have penciled on their title pages, "Edited, for publication in *Mark Twain in Eruption,* but omitted at the request of Mme. Gabrilowitsch." It was these especially which I had in mind when I said earlier that DeVoto omitted matter which he considered important, and that he did not, as he claimed, have full responsibility for the omissions.

In a letter to William Dean Howells, Mark Twain wrote: "Tomorrow I mean to dictate a chapter which will get my heirs and assigns burned alive if they venture to print it this side of A.D. 2006—which I judge they won't. There'll be lots of such chapters if I live 3 or 4 years longer. The edition of A.D. 2006 will make a stir when it comes out. I shall be hovering around taking notice, along with other dead pals. You are invited." He was referring, apparently, to the first of the five chapters mentioned above. On the title pages of two of the chapters is a penned note in his hand: "Not to be exposed to any eye until the edition of A.D. 2406. S. L. C." In his biography of Mark Twain, published in 1912, Paine offered sample tidbits of the chapters (Vol. III, pages 1354–57). If read superficially the chapters seem savagely irreverent, but they are the work of a profoundly religious man. They are attacks on orthodoxy, cant and sham in religion, and are an indication of the boldness and strength of Mark Twain's mind. He discusses, among other things, the character of God, the defects of bibles, the immaculate conception, the evil influence of the Bible, his belief that the present God and religion will not endure, and his belief that Christ did not prove that he was God.

I have considered it an essential part of my task as an editor of the autobiography to hold judgment in abeyance and to bring into the light of publication as much of what Mark Twain wrote as possible, without doing injury to his literary reputation. For this reason I have tried to fill various omissions. I have found forgotten important material in the pages of the *North*

American Review—pages on bowling, pool, bad pool tables, "Quaker," Redpath, Dean Sage. (I also found there material which I did not think worth reprinting.) It was necessary to hunt in the *North American Review* because the manuscript and typescript of the autobiography as they now exist at the university library at Berkeley are incomplete, whole chapters and sections of material which were published in the magazine and in Paine's edition being no longer among the papers. I have put into its correct place in the autobiography the final chapter, the death of Jean, now published as part of the autobiography for the first time. I have included material from the unpublished typescript which struck me as being too important to leave out (in this too I have disagreed with DeVoto). Examples are the experiments in phrenology and the village phrenologist (Chapter 13), the recollections concerning Louisa Wright (Chapter 16), the remarks on the significance of repetition in humor (Chapter 28), the further ruminations on Webster (in Chapter 49), the remarks on the effrontery of amateur literary efforts (Chapter 58), the comments on man which are the concluding section of the remarks on Bret Harte (Chapter 63), the illness of Mark Twain's wife (Chapters 67–70), the receiving of honorary degrees (Chapter 73), the final comments on Mrs. Aldrich (in Chapter 76), and the remarks on baldness and cleanliness in man (Chapter 78). I have also included the pages on the death of Mrs. Clemens (Chapter 71), written immediately after the event. These are filed separately from the autobiographical typescript among the Mark Twain papers in Berkeley, but I believe them to have been intended as part of the autobiography. Mark Twain described the deaths of Susy and of Jean and included the detailed notes on his wife's illness in his autobiography, and it is likely that he desired to include the death of his wife also. Finally, I have picked up many corrections of the text by Mark Twain which my predecessors overlooked, and have put whole paragraphs and pages back in their rightful places, which were either suppressed or forgotten. These are too numerous to list here, but important examples are the anecdote about Dr. McDowell in Chapter 3, the unflattering comments on the actor Raymond in Chapter 5, the anecdote in dialect about the venerable lady in Chapter 6, the anecdote about Orion in the bathtub in Chapter 43 and also the one about Billy Nye in the same chapter.

Having prepared such a manuscript as I have just described, I then arranged it in a chronological sequence. Strict chronology was undesirable; it would have too often interrupted the flow of Mark Twain's thoughts and style, for he liked to range here and there in time, according to his narrating habits. But then strict chronology is to be found only in biographical statistics, not in autobiographies. The advantages of the chronological arrangement are self-evident.

The original typescript contains many summarizing titles, which Paine carefully published. I have agreed with DeVoto that they are boring and unnecessary. The division into chapters is mine. In the earlier editions the dates of composition were printed prominently. I have regarded these as of minor importance and have indicated such dates only when the context required them and then only in footnotes. Finally, I edited the manuscript for consistency and, following DeVoto's practice, modernized the use of commas by deleting hundreds of them. It is probably a pity to take liberties with Mark Twain's commas, but the practice in this instance is not without some justification. There is no definitive text; there is only a typescript in most cases, often in more than one draft. We do not know whether, in his dictations, Twain specified punctuation. The probability is that he did not. The punctuation is not stable. It is true one can argue that the punctuation has some authority, inasmuch as he corrected at least some of the pages; but even here it has many inconsistencies. Furthermore, sections of the original manuscript and typescript are missing, as I have already said, and we must depend on Paine's published version and on the pages of the *North American Review* to know what they contained, and these are not authoritative sources as far as punctuation goes. An interesting sidelight on this problem occurs in the margin of a typescript page. "*Private:* Discard the stupid Harper rule for once: don't put a comma after 'old'—I can't *have* it! S L C"

The notation is in Clemens's hand. He was referring to a phrase—
"beyond that old safe frontier."

In a very few instances I have inserted a connective sentence
such as "But to go back a bit" or have brought in a sentence or
two from the autobiographical sketch which Mark Twain wrote
for his nephew Sam Moffett, or I have deleted a sentence which
was repetitive under the new arrangement; otherwise the language is Mark Twain's. I have worked in the belief that the
main facts and outlines of his life are sufficiently known to the
reader to preclude the insertion of biographical data either in
the form of connective paragraphs or of footnotes.

In a tradition established by Paine, I should like to inform the
reader that not everything that Mark Twain says in this book
is gospel fact. He may have thought it was the fact, or he may
have invented or forgotten. Contemporary documents such as
diaries and letters lead one to be wary of accepting as gospel
all that Mark Twain says here, although on the whole, and in
the profoundest sense, in the poetic and psychological sense, it
is true. In particular, his attacks on persons ought to be read
with caution as well as with delight.

New York
September 1958

MARK TWAIN AND THE RUSSIANS

AN EXCHANGE OF VIEWS

O<small>N</small> AUGUST 18, 1959, the Moscow *Literary Gazette*, known in the Soviet Union as *Literaturnaya Gazeta*, published a criticism of my edition of *The Autobiography of Mark Twain*. This criticism came to my attention in the fourth week of September. The gist of it was that America has an official line on Mark Twain, that the nation tries to suppress or forget him, that his editors have followed the line carefully and that I have been the worst offender in this respect.

Since I had been dealing with materials in my own language and had had access to the original manuscripts and typescripts, and since my volume had enjoyed a certain critical success in my own country (all these facts were available to the Russian critic), it seemed to me that the writer's self-confidence was presumptuous. Still, I was encountering the official Soviet literary line regarding America (the *Literary Gazette* is the official newspaper of the Union of Writers in the U.S.S.R.) and so I was not entirely surprised by the content of the criticism or by its harsh and self-righteous tone.

Normally I do not reply to criticisms of my books. This particular one, however, offered a special and complex challenge. It was obviously "protected"; it struck through me at the society of which I am a part; and it seemed to discount the possibility of free literary endeavor in my country. Consequently I decided to take some action to bring my views to the attention of those readers who had been exposed to the article defaming me. It seemed a quixotic enough hope, in view of the fact that no rebuttal by an American in the *Literary Gazette* was on record.

I did not think I stood much chance of receiving favorable treatment from the editors of the *Literary Gazette*. But Premier Khrushchev had recently made his visit to the United States and was in an expansive mood and so I applied directly to him. On October 13th I sent him a two-sentence letter in which I said in part, "In the interest of cultural relations between our two nations, will you please ask the *Literary Gazette* to open its pages to me for a reply?"

Being uncertain what it cost to send an airmail letter to Moscow, I had to experience the embarrassment of taking my letter to the post office, where I hoped the clerk would not notice the name on the envelope. He did notice it, however. "What? Khrushchev? Are you crazy?" he exclaimed. I couldn't blame him.

I did not hear from Khrushchev but on November 16th I received a letter from the foreign editor of the *Literary Gazette*. The letter, dated November 9th, was brief: "We received your letter and although we have no reason to change our opinion about your book, we shall gladly open our pages to you for a statement on the subject." On November 17th I wrote and airmailed my reply, with the notation that the reply had to be published as a whole or not at all.

An invitation to an American to reply to an attack in a Soviet literary journal—in this case the official literary journal—was so unusual that it merited front-page stories in the *New York Times* and the *New York Herald Tribune* of November 18th. The *Tribune* ran an editorial on the subject and the *New York Post* published a "closeup" of the exchange. The AP and the UPI sent the story and its sequel over their national wires. All of which was not a commentary on me but on the nature of relations between the Soviet Union and the United States.

The *Literary Gazette* published my reply in its issue of December 12th, together with a new criticism by its correspondent, the new criticism being almost twice the length of my reply. Again the controversy made news in the United States. The second criticism was notably different in tone from the first. Its tone could almost be described as reasonable. Far from being impersonal, the article was couched in the form of an open letter to me. It even contained remarks complimentary to me. I promptly airmailed a reply to this second criticism and exactly eight weeks later received an airmail reply from the foreign editor of the *Literary Gazette* with the following explanation: "It seems that you and Mr. Bereznitsky expressed your views about Mark Twain and his works in full. That is why we do not consider it necessary to continue this discussion any longer."

Because of the interest which the controversy has aroused in the United States and because the documents in the case have not been seen here, it seems worth making them available to the public, particularly when Mark Twain is enjoying a revival of popularity at home. The timing is especially apt, for 1960 contains two significant dates in the history of Mark Twain literature: the 50th anniversary of his death (April 21) and the 125th anniversary of his birth (November 30).

These recent criticisms in the *Literary Gazette* are not isolated ones, nor are they new. The attacks follow an old Soviet line on Mark Twain, which consists in general of this: Mark Twain is of primary significance as a social and political observer; the objects of his criticism are chiefly aspects of the American scene; and the United States officially and unofficially suppresses or distorts his criticism of itself. This notion of America's being a monolithic structure, with control stemming from the top, strikes most Americans as a curious one.

Even more curious, perhaps, is the way in which Soviet literary spokesmen view us as if we were a mirror image of themselves, and this despite their protestation that we are so different from them. *They* live under an official line and under censorship; *they* are primarily social and political critics; and it follows that we closely resemble them. One wonders what the mass of Soviet readers think. Can they digest the official line? And are they as humorless as their literary spokesmen often give the impression of being? I like to believe that they are not, and that Mark Twain's great popularity among them is an indication not so much that the official line has been getting through as that

Mark Twain has. That he is very popular among them is indicated by some recent statistics published in the *Literary Gazette*. There have been 250 printings of Twain's works in 25 languages of the Soviet Union, with a distribution of about 11,000,000 copies. A twelve-volume edition of his collected works is now being prepared.

Mark Twain is primarily a humorist. If he had never possessed his humorous gift, if he had only written his social criticisms, he would not now be read by millions of Russian readers and it would be useless for Soviet literary spokesmen to point to him as the great critic of democratic morals. He is also a writer of fiction. It was through these two gifts that he made the reputation which is so well sustained fifty years after his death. His American readers on the whole have no difficulty in comprehending this fact and I like to think that most Russian readers have the same common sense, that they read him basically not for the lessons he teaches of the inherent "evils" of the nation across the Iron Curtain but because he enlarges their lives imaginatively through a flow of pleasure. Great humor, being so rare, is a very exportable commodity. When blended with wisdom and humanitarianism it is irresistible.

If one were exposed only to the official Soviet view one might think that Mark Twain spent most of his time in attacking aspects of his own country. If he did not write much concerning his love of his country it was not only because professed patriotism embarrassed him, it was also and chiefly because love of his country was implicit in all he wrote. He was, after all, *the* American writer close to the native soil; and the American writer who in *The Innocents Abroad* forever put out of fashion the literary habit of fawning on Europe while finding no worth back home. In both of these respects, by the way, he resembles Dostoyevsky, just as his opposite number, Henry James, resembles Turgeniev the Francophile. Among the great American writers of his period he was the most representative, at a time when it was already fashionable to expatriate oneself in Europe.

From the way official Soviet critics sometimes speak of him, one might imagine that if he were alive today he would be delighted to take up permanent residence in Moscow. If he were unpredictable enough to do such a thing he would soon complain of the quality of the borsht there. It is not the sort of borsht they served up in Missouri or Nevada or California in his day—or even in Connecticut and New York. And he would be instructed forcefully that criticizing Moscow borsht is forbidden in the Soviet Union—a lesson which Boris Pasternak recently learned to his sorrow.

Mark Twain is useful to the Soviet spokesmen—and to most Americans as well—as a critic of certain aspects of American life. What the spokesmen fail to acknowledge is that his criticism of America was a department of a larger criticism, his criticism of man, and that under that heading he would now be criticizing the Russian form of government as well as various lapses in the American way of life.

The fact is that Americans are better prepared to admire and value self-criticism than the citizens of a nation which still remains an autocracy. Democracy for all its shortcomings prizes self-criticism as it cannot be prized in an autocracy, inasmuch as democracy flourishes under self-criticism, whereas an autocracy dies by it.

New York
January 23, 1960

POSTSCRIPT

On returning home from Bermuda on March 18, I found in my mail a curious item, an appendage to my affair with the *Literary Gazette* which assumed the form of a treasurer's check for $49 drawn on the Morgan Guaranty Trust Company of New York by order of the Bank for Foreign Trade of the U.S.S.R. in Moscow. Under the amount of the check there was an explanation: "B/O Redaktzia Literaturnoi Gazety—Author's Fee." Both *The New York Times* and *The New York Herald Tribune* published stories about this check on March 20, for it is well known that literary dollars rarely leave the Soviet Union.

I made the following statement to the *New York Times:* "It is an interesting experience to be paid for defending myself against an attack and for attacking a critic of the *Literary Gazette.* In the United States it is not the custom to pay for letters to the editor. Whether it is the custom to do so in the Soviet Union I do not know but I heartily approve of the practice in this instance. I appreciate the desire of the *Literary Gazette* to show its good will toward me as a representative of American writers and editors in this cultural exchange."

As the newspapers reported, I shall spend the $49 on paperback editions of the works of contemporary writers whom I think the Russians are not too familiar with, and shall send the books to the *Literary Gazette.*

New York
March 20, 1960

Mark Twain on the Bed of Procrustes*

Shortly before the opening of the American exhibit in Moscow, the correspondents of the *Literary Gazette* who were getting acquainted with its proposed exposition were amazed to notice that among the books selected for display at the exhibit there were neither any new editions of the works of Mark Twain nor any interesting new publications about his works. Obviously the organizers of the exhibit caught themselves in time, and recently on one of the bookshelves in the Sokolniki [Park] there stood *The Autobiography of Mark Twain,* newly edited in New York.

Still, that initial forgetfulness expresses fairly accurately the relationship of official America to its greatest writer. They try to forget him. And if they have to take notice of him anyway, then in that case everything possible is done to crop the great writer's hair, to deflower the blazing and furious colors of his satire, to eat away the socially unmasking resonance of Twain's

* From *Literaturnaya Gazeta,* Moscow, August 18, 1959, p. 4.

work and, in the last analysis, to make him up as a benevolent
and simple-minded scoffer. The new edition of the *Autobiography* is the logical fruit of these efforts at literary hairdressing.

Here before us is this beautifully published, weighty volume.
The dust jacket again and again invites us to note that "in the
present volume Mark Twain's autobiographical notes are fully
assembled for the first time."

But when you open "the present volume" and begin to famil-
iarize yourself with its contents, it becomes clear that both the
thunderous advertising preceding its appearance and the come-
on information supplied by the dust jacket—all that is no more
than a beautifully daubed-up label.

Unlike his two predecessors, the editor of the new edition,
Charles Neider, tried to observe the principle of the chronological sequence of events in his disposition of materials. But the
trouble is that the really autobiographical element occupies a
rather minor place in Twain's notes. To put all the wealth of
their content into the Procrustean bed of chronological sequence
is a task of incredible difficulty.

Procrustes, as is well known, either stretched his victim to the
desired length or else cut off those parts of the body which
seemed superfluous to him. Charles Neider uses both methods.
On the one hand, he actually introduces into the volume he has
edited several items which had no place in previous editions. On
the other hand, he excludes from it a large part of the material
which went into the editions of 1924 and especially of 1940;
moreover, the principle upon which he bases his selection is so
interesting that it is fitting to discuss it more fully.

Who does not know Twain's famous pronouncements about
American "democracy," his indignant notes about the predatory
wars which the United States carried on half a century ago, his
satirical sketches, cutting as a slap in the face, of the oil king,
Rockefeller, Senator Clark, General Wood, President Theodore
Roosevelt, and other knights and henchmen of American expan-
sionism. All these materials (except for an insignificant part
which came out in the 1924 edition) came out in the 1940 edition.
True, even then an effort was made to soften Twain's more

than unambiguous remarks about the bosses of political life in the America of his time. Bernard DeVoto, the editor of that edition, expressed, in part, a naive amazement that Mark Twain, who had once called himself "an unwashed son of labor," could not accept in Rockefeller and T. Roosevelt fellow "sons of labor." But the debunking voice of Mark Twain cuts through the most stifling editorial comments. In 1959 Charles Neider found the precautions of his predecessors insufficient, and he decided without superfluous ceremony to "shut Twain's trap," blotting out from his edition all the notes mentioned above. This is a supreme example of scholarly ill faith and of that very political tendentiousness whose pretended absence certain American men of letters so love to boast on occasion.

As to previously unpublished materials, Neider resolved to introduce into his edition Twain's meditations on baldness, on the value of hair-washing, on beginning writers, on phrenology, on honorary degrees, etc. It is naturally hard to say anything against the inclusion of these notes in *The Autobiography of Mark Twain*. But it is no less hard to come to terms with the idea that these few, inoffensive trifles are called upon to replace the brilliant, angry pages of the original, unprocessed Twain, which are many times superior to them in scope and significance. It is plain that the bitter prophecy which Twain made in the midst of work on his Autobiography in a letter to William Dean Howells is coming true:

"Tomorrow I mean to dictate a chapter which will get my heirs and assigns burned alive if they venture to print it this side of A.D. 2006—which I judge they won't. There'll be lots of such chapters if I live 3 or 4 years longer. The edition of A.D. 2006 will make a stir when it comes out. I shall be hovering around taking notice, along with other dead pals. You are invited."

Not very happy lines. And although there remains almost a half century till the time Twain mentioned, it would hardly have pleased him to watch how the editor of an eviscerated and washed-out edition of his Autobiography tries to put forth his crime as a virtue and does not burn alive for shame at that.

Literally, "virtue." This is how he expresses it: "My volume," writes Neider in his Introduction, "is to a high degree anecdotal, but I believe this to be a virtue rather than a defect, in that it correctly represents the creative slant of Mark Twain's mind."

An anecdote. Fine and dandy. And though this anecdote is far from young, it grows none the less sad for that, none the less exacerbating to the memory of the greatest American writer.

Y. BEREZNITSKY

(Translated by Robert L. Belknap)

[Reply] *

On August 18th the *Literary Gazette* published a rather severe criticism of the so-called American attitude toward Mark Twain, as well as of my editing of the recently published *Autobiography of Mark Twain*. I should like to say a few words about this criticism, which was signed by Y. Bereznitsky.

The criticism described "the relationship of official America to its greatest writer" by saying, "They try to forget him." I find it difficult to read this without a wry smile. For the fact is that "official" America does well to "forget" Mark Twain, inasmuch as our readers would make it quite hot for our officials if the latter dared to interfere either to make us remember or to forget any author. Far from forgetting Mark Twain, America—official and unofficial—is currently enjoying a fresh outburst of interest in him. One of the great successes of the last theatrical season in New York was the impersonation of Mark Twain by the young actor, Hal Holbrook, with an evening of readings from Twain's works. Holbrook is now touring the country with his impersonation and readings. A recent issue of the very popular *Life* magazine devoted an article to the subject of Holbrook and Twain. A new motion picture is currently being made of *Huckleberry Finn*. And numerous books by and about

* From *Literaturnaya Gazeta*, Moscow, December 12, 1959, p. 4.

Twain are appearing. One of these is a collection of Holbrook's readings, which will be published late in November. Another in the press is the voluminous correspondence between Mark Twain and his friend William Dean Howells.

The article went on to charge that if "official" America has to take notice of Mark Twain, then it does everything possible to suppress his social satire and "to make him up as a benevolent and simple-minded scoffer." The Russian writer is able, miraculously, to glimpse a political mechanism which no American is aware of. Is this goal of "official" America achieved through the Library of Congress? Congressional committees? The White House? The Supreme Court? The State Department? The F.B.I.? I am certain that American publishers—and anyone can become a publisher if he has the necessary funds: there is no license required, no fee, no examination—will be interested to learn that they are being supervised and suppressed after all.

The article also charged that my predecessors as editors of Mark Twain's autobiography took "precautions" through "stifling editorial comments," as well as other means, to follow the "official" line. Yet it carefully failed to state what every student of Mark Twain knows. The first editor, Albert Bigelow Paine, Twain's friend and literary executor, slavishly followed Twain's requests in the matter of the autobiography and by no means undertook "stifling editorial comments." On the other hand Bernard DeVoto, the second editor, broke Twain's own injunctions in publishing his edition, and did so at the request of and with the approval of the Mark Twain Estate. I too broke Twain's injunctions as expressed in his manuscripts. And so if anyone is to blame for the slowness with which the autobiography has been made public it is Mark Twain himself, who wanted it that way. The article also failed to state that far from suppressing anything, DeVoto freely published Mark Twain's "political" utterances of some thirty-five years previous: the attacks on Theodore Roosevelt, General Wood, Senator Clark, and others.

And now I must speak about my own edition. Mr. Bereznitsky wrote: "In 1959 Charles Neider found the precautions of

his predecessors insufficient, and he decided without superfluous
ceremony to 'shut Twain's trap,' blotting out from his edition
all the notes mentioned above. This is a supreme example of
scholarly ill faith and of that very political tendentiousness
whose pretended absence certain American men of letters so love
to boast on occasion." Yet the writer carefully failed to state
that my position was made clear in my introduction and that it
was simply this:

My intention was to make a volume designed for the general
reader, not the scholar, a volume culled from the autobiographical manuscript as a whole, published as well as unpublished
parts (for there were still sections unpublished). It was my hope
to unburden the excellent parts from the dated, dull, trivial, and
journalese sections of the work. And finally I hoped to concentrate less on opinion and second-hand recollection and more on
the truly autobiographical, the more purely literary and the
more characteristically humorous material. For me Mark Twain
is essentially a great fabulist and not a great maker of political
utterances. The reason that I omitted his attacks on the politicians
was that I found them dull and dated. Besides, anyone who
cared to look them up could easily do so by referring to the
earlier editions, as well as to various editions of his works. What
is more, I listed for my readers the contents of the previous editions, so that ready comparisons could be made and my own
omissions noted.

In my edition I included 30,000 to 40,000 words previously
unpublished. Mr. Bereznitsky made light of these, yet they are
more characteristically Mark Twain than his political utterances; and the fact is that through my efforts they are now
disseminated among a wide public and not lying in the drawers
of a library where only specialists might see them.

Finally, Mr. Bereznitsky wrote: "It is plain that the bitter
prophecy which Twain made in the midst of work on his Autobiography in a letter to William Dean Howells is coming true."
And then he quoted from the letter. I should like to quote the
letter again, for to do so is relevant to an illumination of Mr.
Bereznitsky's critical methods. "Tomorrow I mean to dictate

a chapter which will get my heirs and assigns burned alive if they venture to print it this side of A.D. 2006—which I judge they won't. There'll be lots of such chapters if I live 3 or 4 years longer. The edition of A.D. 2006 will make a stir when it comes out. I shall be hovering around taking notice, along with other dead pals. You are invited."

Now this letter referred to the first of five chapters which Twain dictated on the subject of religion. On the title pages of two of the chapters is a penned note in his hand: "Not to be exposed to any eye until the edition of A.D. 2406. S.L.C." The meaning is clear. Writing to Howells, Twain dared his heirs and assigns to print the chapters a century hence. But on his own manuscripts he specifically prohibited his heirs and assigns from publishing the chapters until *five* centuries hence.

It is unfortunate that Mr. Bereznitsky did not feel the scholar's responsibility to inform his readers that all of the above information was available in my introduction and that he quoted only from the letter. If he had played fair with his readers it would not then have been so easy for him to imagine an "official" America as the origin of Mark Twain "suppressions." Nor would it have been quite so easy for him to belabor DeVoto and especially myself, both of whom have deliberately broken the great writer's injunctions in the belief that it is a public service to do so, without in any way being a disservice to his memory.

CHARLES NEIDER

The Question Is Significantly More Profound *

A LETTER TO CHARLES NEIDER

Sir, the editor of the *Literary Gazette* has acquainted me with the letter in which you express disagreement with the content of my article, "Mark Twain on the Bed of Procrustes." I consider it my duty to answer you.

* From *Literaturnaya Gazeta*, Moscow, December 12, 1959, p. 4.

It was extraordinarily pleasant to me to learn that in America
there is now noted a "fresh outburst of interest in the writer."
I honestly believe that this outburst is not only long-lasting,
but even continuous. Of course, an "outburst," as you naturally
understand, can follow only a greater or lesser "extinction."
Probably another great American writer, Dreiser, had just this
tight period in mind when he observed in one of his articles,
"Those few authentically great thinkers whom America has
created—Poe, Whitman, Twain—are under a ban here." Probably also to this unfortunate period belongs the sadly renowned
pronouncement of Congressman Joseph Shannon (a fully official
figure, isn't he?), which called Twain "a forsaker of the interests of the South, a coward and a deserter," and demanded the
abolition of all celebrations connected with the name of that
writer.

You doubtless know that the best and the most popular of
Mark Twain's works, *The Adventures of Huckleberry Finn*,
was more than once fully subjected to "official" persecutions
and bans. I take the liberty of referring to your colleague, one
of the greatest contemporary American critics, Lionel Trilling.
In his introduction to the regular edition of the renowned novel,
which appeared under his editorship in 1948, Trilling wrote:

"*Huckleberry Finn* was once barred from certain libraries
and schools for its alleged subversion of morality. The author-
ities had in mind the book's endemic lying, the petty thefts, the
denigrations of respectability and religion, the bad language and
the bad grammar. We smile at that excessive care. . . ."

Lionel Trilling smiled, as I have mentioned, in 1948. I do not
know whether he continued smiling in the following year, 1949,
when the responsible "powers" crossed from the list of literature permitted for reading in the educational institutions of
New York City another work of Mark Twain, *A Connecticut
Yankee in King Arthur's Court*. And then a year or two later
the exclusion of that very *Huckleberry Finn* was demanded by
none other than the now deceased Senator McCarthy. When in
1957 the Board of Education of New York City crossed the
book about Huck from the books permitted for reading in ele-

mentary and junior schools of the city, the smile on the face of Mr. Trilling may well have changed into that very "grimace of loathing" with which you, in your own words, read my article. By the way, with just what expression did you watch the television version of *Huck Finn*, two years ago, in which, as the newspapers asserted, poor Jim was struck from the cast of characters? These same newspapers wrote, as I recall, that as a result, an "all-white entertainment" was made. I hope that the movie *Huckleberry Finn*, whose filming I learned of with pleasure from your letter, will not be like its televised forerunner.

It is true that you could smile and say that all these facts took place before the "outburst" you mentioned and that it is not worth while waving dead cats around, leaving Tom and Huck to occupy themselves with that. But right before me is the September issue of the English journal *Books and Bookmen*. It appeared six months after the publication of your book and it is apparently already in the period of the "outburst." On the thirty-second page under the general heading, "Banned," to my sincere sorrow, I saw the name of Twain's masterpiece in the strange company of *Lady Chatterley's Lover* and the works of Henry Miller. Poor Huck, again (for the how-manyth time!), had not been permitted in the New York schools.

The basis of your objections, as I recall, involved in your eyes an insufficiently respectful attitude on my part toward the work which was performed by you as editor of the third edition of *The Autobiography of Mark Twain*. No, you did great work— I would even say difficult work—as far as you are concerned. You quite successfully coped with this work as you wanted to. In your edition Twain actually appears as you are trying to present him. And you are trying to present him as a "great fabulist" (from your letter) or a master of "anecdote" (from your Introduction). But is the real Twain like that? Let us try to remember what he himself said about this. This citation is doubtless well known to you. I am taking it from your edition of his Autobiography:

". . . within the compass of these forty years wherein I have

been playing professional humorist before the public, I have
had for company seventy-eight other American humorists. . . .
Why have they perished? Because they were *merely humorists.*
[Here and in the later quotations the italics are mine. Y. B.]
Humorists of the 'mere' sort cannot survive. . . . I have always preached. That is the reason that I have lasted thirty
years. If the humor came of its own accord and uninvited I have
allowed it a place in my sermon, but I was not writing the sermon for the sake of the humor."

The sermons about which Twain writes are just what consti-
tute the social content of his work. This content is inseparable
from the humor, just as the humor is inseparable from it. And
you cut Twain's work in two and call the part which you don't
like "dated, dull, and trivial." Yes, in your Introduction you
listed just what you left out. "From the published parts I have
omitted such matter as the . . . Morris incident . . . elongated
remarks on Theodore Roosevelt, Andrew Carnegie, the plutocracy, and so on." If it were only a matter of remarks (or "attacks" as you call them in your letter) it might really not be
worth while building up a case. But in these "remarks" or "attacks" are expressed Twain's feelings, thoughts, interests; and
this all helps re-establish the writer's countenance, a goal, which
from my point of view, should also be sought by the autobiography of a great writer.

Still, on this issue you maintain another point of view: "I
hoped to concentrate less on opinion and second-hand recollection and more on the truly autobiographical . . . material." In
short, only *events* interest you. Although you scorn "opinion,"
I shall take the liberty of reminding you of Twain's opinion on
a question which interests you, which he expressed in the same
Autobiography. I must cite this passage from Paine's edition of
1924, since it is omitted from your edition. Speaking of the
Morris incident (she tried to have an audience with the President and was driven from the White House and was treated
coarsely by the police), Twain continues:

"There you have the facts. It is as I have said—for a number
of days they have occupied almost the entire attention of the

American nation. . . . It is this sort of thing which makes the right material for an autobiography." (You considered this material unfit for an autobiography. Y. B.) . . . "[A man's] life consists of his feelings and his interests, with here and there an incident apparently big or little to hang the feelings on."

I think you understand why I have offered this extensive quotation. Twain's political writings (it is hard for me to understand why you put the word "political" in quotation marks in your letter) are interesting not only because in them he "preaches," "proclaims," but also because they express his "feelings and his interests." Remember the words with which he begins his story of the annihilation by General Wood in the Philippines of six hundred men, women, and children of the Moro tribe (of course this passage is omitted from your edition):

"We will stop talking about my schoolmates of sixty years ago, for the present, and return to them later. They strongly interest me, and I am not going to leave them alone permanently. Strong as that interest is, it is for the moment pushed out of the way by an incident of to-day, which is still stronger."

That is what *interests* Twain. And it interests you to show that "Mark Twain was trying to amuse himself: that was his chief aim during the dictations." (Autobiography, Y. B.) But since it is quite, quite hard to prove that, you justify the numerous omissions and wilfulness in placing the materials by recourse to the fact that the volume was "designed for the general reader."

The composers of numerous "digests" which offer *David Copperfield* and *Anna Karenina* in a form fit for "digestion" are sick with the same disease: they consider that only the bare bones of events are fit to interest the simple reader, and "the feelings and interests" which are "based" upon them are not in his power to digest. But it seems to me that the logical inconsistency of that part of your letter would strike even "a simple writer"; throwing light on my "critical methods," you refer to Twain's "demands" and "prohibitions." You claim credit for yourself and DeVoto for having "deliberately broken the great writer's injunctions," and right next to this, when it is a question of "the slowness with which the Autobiography has been made public," or of still unpublished chapters, you again refer to these same "demands" and "prohibitions." After all, if in some cases you break Twain's injunctions, it is hardly worth while to take refuge in it.

I would be sorry if you took all the above as only my comments, or even attacks, on your book, or your method of editorial work. No, the question is significantly more profound, and the dispute is going on actually not between you and me, but between two opposed tendencies in literary scholarship. One of them, which you represent, and which appears to be if not official, then at least the governing one in American literary scholarship, tries to show the social content of the work of this or that writer as something petty, secondary, incidental, and sometimes simply nonexistent. The representatives of this tendency try to present the great democrat and lover of life, Walt Whitman, as "a poet of death" and a "conservative" (the collection of essays, *Leaves of Grass One Hundred Years Later*). The representatives of this tendency try to reduce the meaning of the plays of the greatest contemporary American playwright, Arthur Miller, to "the history of a personal disorder and not to social disorganization" (Joseph T. Shipley). Every representative of this tendency has ignored the work of Dreiser in the thirties, and *An American Tragedy* appears in their interpretation like a private occurrence in the life of a certain Clyde Griffiths. Understandably, no one will begin to assert that there are no representatives of other tendencies in literary criticism in America, tendencies trying to clarify the phenomenon of literature in all its integrity and complexity. In our press, for example, there has already been given a detailed evaluation of P. Foner's interesting book, *Mark Twain: Social Critic*.

In conclusion, I would like to make it known to you that of those thirty or forty thousand words which you first included in your edition, and toward which in your words I "behaved scornfully" (on what basis you reached that conclusion is a riddle to me), a significant part was published in our press (in the magazine *Crocodile*, with an edition of 1,200,000 copies, and in the Estonian newspaper, *Hammer and Sickle*) even before the appearance of your book, on the basis of the preliminary publication in *Harper's Magazine*. I mention this to show you how great is our interest in the work of Mark Twain, what joy every new publication of his text furnishes us, how dear to us are all the manifestations of his genius, and what incomprehension and protest is called from us by any attempt to narrow and present in an impoverished light his wonderful and many-faceted countenance.

I hope that the circumstance that I address this letter directly to you, and not through President Eisenhower, will not be taken by anyone as a display of my disrespect toward him, but merely as a reluctance to have recourse for the solution of unofficial literary disputes to the intermediation of highly placed official figures.

Sincerely yours,
YAN BEREZNITSKY

(Translated by Robert L. Belknap)

[Reply] *

Mr. Bereznitsky's chief argument in his criticism of August 18th was that I omitted in my edition of Mark Twain's autobiography parts which he, Mr. Bereznitsky, would like to see included; and that I did so in response either to an "official" line or to an "official" climate. Of course theoretically it is preferable to publish the whole of the autobiography in one comprehensive edition, but what is theoretically desirable is not always practical in a practical world, as Mr. Bereznitsky will no doubt admit. I am delighted to see in Mr. Bereznitsky's second criticism, of December 12th, a tacit admission that no official point of view regarding Mark Twain exists in America; also I am delighted to find that he recognizes the existence of a multitude of literary viewpoints in the United States.

* Airmailed to *Literaturnaya Gazeta*, Moscow, from New York, December 21, 1959. Publication declined.

Mr. Bereznitsky's complaint now consists of the fact that I
did the job differently from the way he would have done it. If
it is any comfort to him, I also did the job differently from the
way other Mark Twain scholars—American ones—would have
done it. Mr. Bereznitsky would naturally like me to see the
matter in his way, and to handle it in his way. But because of
different circumstances I see it differently. These circumstances
are both linguistic and aesthetic, and I should like to say a few
words concerning them.

Mr. Bereznitsky arrives at the conclusion, somewhat to my
astonishment, that it is only "events" which interest me in Mark
Twain's autobiography. This is certainly news to me, for
events are perhaps what I am least interested in in the autobiography. In the first place the "events" as Mark Twain states
them are not always accurate; in the second place Albert Bigelow Paine, in his three-volume biography of Twain, takes care
of the "events" quite well. What I am interested in primarily are
psychology, humor, emotions, reflections and reminiscences—
all those matters which cannot easily be referred to as didactic—
and I am interested in these because it happens that when he is
dealing with them Mark Twain is at his best as a stylist and
creator.

Despite these facts, Mr. Bereznitsky is unfortunately in error
to think that I knowingly slight the didactic side of Mark Twain
or wilfully underestimate the social content of his work. If De-
Voto had not published his 1940 volume, if the materials in it
had been lying in their pristine state awaiting an editor, I would
have been delighted to publish them; I would have seized on
them as valuable documents of a great writer. But DeVoto *had*
published them—less than twenty years previously; his book
had been widely distributed; and I could not see the wisdom,
under the circumstances, of repeating so soon after their publication material which does not strike me as being central to an
autobiography. As I understood it, my function as an editor was
to make publicly available as much of the unpublished autobiography as possible, as well as to select the finest sections of
it (from the aesthetic, not the social view) and arrange them all

in chronological order. I worked in the belief, which I still possess, that the material contained the possibility of an American classic, and I aimed at nothing less than a classic standard and form.

In our discussion it is well to remember that I regard an autobiography as capable of being a work of art, and that I come to it with certain aesthetic expectations, even requirements. It is true that I read autobiographies for other reasons also, especially if they are in translation: I want to know something about the person and his period. But in my own language I make demands which I do not make of works in translation. There is the whole question of language to be considered, and beyond that of style, beauty and form. The didactic Mark Twain, particularly the journalistic and didactic Mark Twain, frankly seems to me too often strident, or flat, or humorless—I am speaking chiefly of language. (I have no way of knowing how such passages come through in Russian translation.)

I suspect that many authors enjoy an undeserved rank in translation, and that this rule works generally in inverse proportion to the original beauty, depending of course to some extent on the talent of the translator. Great stylists can seem empty in translation, whereas third-rate writers can seem quite grand. For me—and there are many novelists and critics in America with the same orientation—there is a beauty of language, a nobility or harshness of language, which is closely bound to great work and that is inseparable from it. A thought or an emotion or a bit of psychology does not exist in itself but through and with the language which it forms and which forms it. The aesthetic element for me is a primary one when it comes to literature. I am content to believe that it is the first function and value of the artist to perceive and to create works of beauty—that is what he specializes in, from my view. There are few first-rate scientists who are also first-rate political thinkers or economists; and I believe that there are few literary artists who are such. I do not think the less of Mark Twain for his didactic works; I admire him for them. But just as his didactic works do not heighten for me the greatness of a book like *Huckleberry Finn*, so it is that the didactic parts of his autobiography do not for me heighten the more psychological, humorous and nostalgic parts.

Perhaps I should put the matter in another way. If, as it sometimes happens, the didactic parts are as fine stylistically as the others, then I accept them with the same whole-hearted delight as I accept the others. It seems to me that style, like a gesture or a facial expression, is a key to the profundity of a man's beliefs and emotions. If a writer like Dreiser is not capable of a great style that is another matter, of course; one judges him by his own scale—I am speaking always of the original language. Mark Twain *is* capable of a great style and I have selected those passages of his autobiography which I believe show him at his pitch of true stylistic greatness, which always turns out to be something larger than mere "style" as one might casually think of style—style the envelope rather than the true voice.

Among the finest didactic chapters of the autobiography are the five chapters on religion which my book unfortunately did not include, and which still await the first fine light of publication. It was painful to me to have to exclude them, but Mr. Bereznitsky will recall that in my introduction I placed the responsibility for their exclusion where it rightfully belongs, on Mark Twain's daughter. She has the legal right to keep them from being published, a right her father conferred on her in his will, and no person or agency in America can force her to publish them. I said in my introduction that unlike DeVoto I do not assume responsibility for all of the omissions. It was therefore incorrect of Mr. Bereznitsky to accuse me of an inconsistency: of "boasting" of having broken Mark Twain's injunctions on the one hand, while using those same injunctions as a defense. For my part, at this late date I would have broken every injunction, in the honest belief that that is what Mark Twain would also have done. Anyhow, it is Mr. Bereznitsky who is inconsistent, for I was making not a personal but a public point: I was saying that it is Mark Twain's injunctions, followed in some instances, not followed in others, which account for the slowness with which the autobiography has appeared, and not the "official" American line which Mr. Bereznitsky originally imagined to exist.

As for his comparison of my edition with digests of such books as *David Copperfield* and *Anna Karenina*, let me point out that this is hardly an accurate or fruitful comparison. These books are novels, not works of nonfiction; they were published during their authors' lifetime and under their authors' supervision; and they are both finished works. In the introduction to my edition I stated my belief that Mark Twain, had he lived longer, would have worked over the materials of his autobiography—I stress the fact that they are materials and not the finished product—until he had obtained a book which was unified and controlled. It seems to me pointless to accuse me of belonging to the "digest" school of editors when I am after all dealing not with a finished product but with more or less raw material for such a product. A better comparison would be, say, with the voluminous diaries of Tolstoy.

I would not like to leave the impression, however, that I am constantly in disagreement with Mr. Bereznitsky. Together with him I deplore the banning of *Huckleberry Finn* and any other of Mark Twain's books from the public schools of New York City; the silly comments by a former Congressman on matters he was not competent to judge, however inconspicuous that Congressman may have been in public life (as Shannon apparently was); the comments of the overconspicuous Senator McCarthy (who, by the way, before his death was the subject of a resolution of censure in the United States Senate, and the consequent object of ostracism, as a result of his notorious behavior); and similar instances of literary and cultural stupidity or blindness.

That the question of translation is a complex and difficult one is brought home to me as a result of our exchange of opinions. In response to Mr. Bereznitsky's charge that "official" America tries to "forget" Mark Twain, I said, "I find it difficult to read this without a wry smile." How sad it is that a mistranslation should have hurt his feelings. My "wry smile" became a "grimace of loathing." A wry smile—at least my wry smile, dear sirs—has no loathing in it and no grimace. It contains irony, but often also a certain sympathy. And my remarks that Mr. Bereznitsky "makes light of" the 30,000 to 40,000 words of the autobiography which I published for the first time became in translation "behaves with scorn." Again I am saddened, for I am sure that Mr. Bereznitsky was not scornful. "Makes light of" was my way of describing what he said about the new parts— "few, inoffensive trifles" is what he called them. It would be so much easier for this exchange if we were both using the same language, which for obvious reasons we cannot do.

In closing this communication I should like to say how happy I am to note the change in Mr. Bereznitsky's tone between his first and his second criticisms. The tone of the first was harsh and accusatory; the tone of the second shows a genuine effort to comprehend my point of view, and is not only friendly but at one point even highly complimentary. If we can understand each other better through this exchange of opinions—and I am sure we will—the exchange will have had some value beyond its immediate subject.

CHARLES NEIDER

ON MARK TWAIN
CENSORSHIP

THE CHAPTERS on religion from Mark Twain's autobiography were finally published in October 1963 in *The Hudson Review*, a literary quarterly issued in New York, after being suppressed for fifty-seven years, first by Clemens himself, then by Paine, and finally by Clemens's daughter Clara. Their publication in a more permanent form, either as a brochure or as part of *The Autobiography of Mark Twain*, has been and is still being discouraged. Why were the chapters suppressed, and in what manner? Why did Clara Clemens finally agree to their publication and, as a direct consequence, agree to the publication of another suppressed work, "Letters from the Earth," and to any and all still unpublished Mark Twain manuscripts? What was the public reaction, so feared by Clemens, Paine and Clara Clemens, to the publication of these two works? And why does the Mark Twain Estate still resist a more permanent publication of the chapters? It is the purpose of this essay to examine these and related questions and to present Clara Clemens's views in detail as she expressed them in letters to me. But first it may be relevant to describe the works in question.

The chapters on religion, which I entitled "Reflections on Religion" for their first publication, were composed in 1906. "Letters from the Earth" was composed in 1909. The "Reflections" are straight-forward opinion; the "Letters" are opinion in the disguise of fiction. The "Reflections" are bolder in statement and more extreme in the views espoused, also more detailed. They deal specifically with religion and its harmful effects; the "Letters" also deal with religion but in a more general way, and devote more energy to the question of the total and interesting foolishness of man. The "Reflections" contain withering remarks about Christian Science and Mary Baker Eddy; the "Letters" do not refer to either. Clara Clemens was a Christian Scientist. Although she did not mention the remarks to me as a reason for her suppression of the chapters on religion, she was undoubtedly offended by them and they probably influenced her decisions regarding the chapters. She had fewer personal reasons for suppressing the "Letters" but she suppressed them just as effectively as she suppressed the chapters. "Reflections" is about 9,000 words long, "Letters" is about 20,000 words.

Clemens dictated the "Reflections" in a rented house a couple of miles from Dublin, New Hampshire. This was the Upton House, located on a slope of Mt. Monadnock. With him during the summer of 1906 were his daughter Jean, a stenographer (Miss Josephine Hobby), and Paine. Clemens's wife had died two years previously in Florence, Italy. Clara Clemens lived at this time in a retreat under her physician's care in Norfolk, Conn. It was a pleasant summer environment outside of Dublin, although Paine found it somewhat spectral, perhaps because of a west wind that never seemed to relent. Clemens's mornings were chiefly devoted to dictating his autobiography. Paine, who lodged in the village for the summer, would drive up to the house each morning to be present for the session, sometimes returning in the afternoon to interview Clemens. Whenever the weather permitted, Clemens dictated while pacing a long colonnaded veranda open to the country views, or while sitting in a rocker. These are the veranda and rocker pictured in the famous series of seven photographs of Clemens which Paine, a former photographer, took that August and which Clemens inserted in his autobiography. On rainy days Clemens worked indoors, pacing constantly. After work there would be relaxation with music, usually Beethoven, Chopin or Schubert.

On Sunday, June 17, 1906, Clemens wrote to Howells, who was at Kittery Point, Maine, the letter which announced that tomorrow he intended to dictate a chapter of his autobiography which would get his heirs and assigns burned alive if they printed it "this side of 2006 A.D." The following day he began a dictation on a religious subject but almost immedi-

ately strayed to other topics. On the 19th he composed the first
of the chapters, about the character of God as revealed in the
Bible; on the 20th the second, about the defects of bibles and
containing remarks on the Immaculate Conception, which he
discussed as if it were identical with the Virgin Birth (apparently
he missed the point that the Immaculate Conception refers to the
conception of Mary and not to that of Jesus); on the 22nd and
23rd the third and fourth, about Russian pogroms, war, the evil
influence of the Bible on children, and the character of the "real"
God; and on the 25th he dictated the final chapter, about the human race and about man being a machine and not responsible for
his actions. The next day he went to New York for business reasons and wrote to Howells in the evening. "I have been dictating
some fearful things, for 4 successive mornings—for no eye but
yours to see until I have been dead a century—if then. But I got
them out of my system, where they had been festering for years
—& that was the main thing. I feel better, now." Some time
after writing this, Clemens changed his mind and enjoined his
heirs and assigns from publishing the chapters until five centuries
after 1906.

In his biography of Clemens, issued in 1912, Paine quoted from
the chapters but did not identify them. He offered a few fragments as musings or table talk and scattered them about, abridging, rewriting and rearranging. His edition of the autobiography
(*Mark Twain's Autobiography*, 1924) omitted the chapters, although he could have printed them if he had wished, inasmuch as
he was not only Clemens's literary executor but also the editor of
the Mark Twain Papers.

Clemens composed "Letters from the Earth" at Stormfield, his
house in Redding, Conn., in October and possibly also in November 1909. Clara Clemens had married early in October and was
not living at Stormfield now. Clemens's daughter Jean was there,
and Paine was an almost constant visitor, sometimes spending the
nights at Stormfield as well as the days, his room separated from
Clemens's only by a bathroom. In a letter of that time to his
friend Elizabeth Wallace, Clemens wrote, "This book ['Letters
from the Earth'] will never be published—in fact it couldn't be,

because it would be felony. . . . Paine enjoys it, but Paine is going to be damned one of these days, I suppose." Paine wrote in his biography regarding the "Letters," "Clemens allowed his exuberant fancy free rein, being under no restrictions as to the possibility of print or public offense. He enjoyed them himself, too, as he read them aloud, and we laughed ourselves weak over his bold imaginings." Paine noted in the biography, "Most of the ideas in this his last commentary on human absurdities were new only as to phrasing. He had exhausted the topic long ago, in one way or another; but it was one of the themes in which he never lost interest. Many subjects became stale to him at last; but the curious invention called man remained a novelty to him to the end." Paine in his biography quoted briefly from one of the letters but took care not to include the letters in any of the Mark Twain works which he edited and published after Clemens's death. Paine was a timid man in literary matters and as afraid as Clemens was of shocking the reading public. Furthermore he was slavish in his admiration of Clemens and did not easily stray from any publication line Clemens had set down.

"Letters from the Earth" consists of eleven letters from Satan to the archangels Michael and Gabriel. Satan, banished from heaven for 1,000 Earth-years, visits Earth to see how the new human-race experiment is coming along. From Satan's outlander point of view man is a microscopic, insane tissue of life. Satan writes about man's concept of heaven and about the concept's curiousness, and about sexual intercourse, which Clemens rarely explicitly and candidly discusses elsewhere in his work. The attack on the Christian ideal of heaven is in some respects like the attacks of Nietzsche and D. H. Lawrence. Letter 2 is a riproaring attack on man's hubris in his religious thinking, on his imaginative shortcomings, on his being a sheep to follow the teachings of the priesthood against his own instincts. Clemens cannot easily forgive man for his religious asininities. He regarded religion not, perhaps, as the opiate of the masses so much as the extreme form of wilful self-delusion and self-harm. What caused Clemens to be so bitter about religion? There is no simple answer to such a question. His loss of his wife and of his daughter Susy admittedly

embittered him. But very early in his career, when he first went
to Europe, he already showed signs of being anti-clerical. He
attacked the priests of Rome, well-fed and comfortable, in *The
Innocents Abroad*, and attacked the Roman Church again in *A
Connecticut Yankee*.

In the chapters on religion he had complained that man's concept of God is a shoddy one and stems from man's own shortcomings, and that man is presumptuous in thinking that he has
an inside track with God. He says these and similar things in
"Letters from the Earth" also. He speaks, with Satan's voice, of
curiosities in the Bible and waxes hot as though the Bible were
written yesterday, blaming man for his anthropocentric view.
He makes full use of the effects of anachronism, applying nineteenth-century knowledge as a sword against the ignorance and
fatuousness of Biblical man, who assumes he is God's darling,
nub and navel of the universe. Clemens sometimes seems to suggest a double God: the God of the Bible, who is man's creation
in his efforts to rationalize history; and the God of modern man,
who identifies God with the irrationalism of nature and with
nature's unconcern with the welfare of man. Clemens combines
these two concepts for his own dramatic purposes. At times he
is furious not so much with man as with the God-Nature which
he believes torments man. His well-known inclination to help
the underdog causes him to view God as the prime bully and
man as the prime victim. On occasion his arguments become tedious in their monomania. The reader, for instance, grants that
man embodied in his early portrait of God many of the bar-
barisms of nature. Clemens knows that the reader knows this; he
also knows that many men before him ridiculed the notion of
the Bible as fundamentalistically sound, as well as the notion of
an anthropomorphic God, yet he is swept along by the stream
of his argument for its own sake.

Clemens, for his own purposes, read the Bible as a literalist,
then accused man of stupidity in being a fundamentalist. Certain
churchmen, reacting to the "Reflections," said he was ignorant
of nineteenth-century Biblical studies, which had largely outmoded or at least modified fundamentalism, and that therefore

his attacks were anachronistic, misguided, and motivated purely by personal bitterness. But three things can be said in his defense. In the first place, the world did not lack for fundamentalists in 1906, despite the Biblical studies referred to, and these fundamentalists were by no means all Roman Catholic. In the second place, there had been long ages when fundamentalism was unmodified by scientific Biblical studies, and Clemens was addressing himself to those times just as firmly as to his own. The point was that he was concerning himself with the follies of man the superstitious animal as a whole in all ages; he was not limiting himself to Hebrew-Christian man. He was not about to admit that, because of the Biblical studies, man had suddenly seen the light and had shed his tribal superstitions. Clemens was using the Hebrew-Christian Bible as his text because he was more familiar with it than with other bibles but he was not limiting his remarks to it, he was not singling out for his invective any special sect of the human race. The whole human race, from beginning to end, was his subject, and this was what the churchmen did not understand when they reacted to the publication of the "Reflections." However, Clemens may have made a tactical error in sticking too close to the text and by involving himself too specifically (and too sarcastically) in details of theory and practice. Perhaps the churchmen were right to misread him. His view was cosmic but his application of it was not. As if to correct this deficiency, he wrote, months before his death, "Letters from the Earth," in which sarcasm gave way (in many but by no means all instances) to irony, and in which the cosmic view was embodied in the figure of Satan, with his incomparably greater perspective, in time and space, than man's. If in real life Clemens was at times the devil's advocate, in this piece of fiction Satan was Clemens's advocate for the reason that any of the other angels would not have been shrewd and biting enough in his observations. Clemens, in pain with increasing frequency because of the angina condition which was soon to give him the ultimate peace he longed for, was now making statements on religion from an olympian height but at the price of having to mute them with the guises of fiction.

Common to both the "Reflections" and the "Letters" is Clem-

ens's insistence on injecting his deterministic views, which he
seems to have deduced from the omnipotence and omniscience of
God. But he is not doctrinaire in his determinism, and he is often
more poetic than logical and he implies contradictory things. He
implies that God is more sinful than man, while at the same time
implying that man is free of sin because God is responsible for
sin. Or he implies that Christianity is responsible for sin because
it causes man to act counter to his instincts, an idea which recalls Nietzsche, as we have already noted. He also implies that
man is not free of sin because the God who is responsible for sin
is man's creation. He sometimes seems to say that there are no
elect among mankind, that all are equally doomed to unhappi-
ness, that the nature of the human condition is reprobation, that
we are all reprobates but not true reprobates because essentially we are innocent (our nature having been foreordained, we
cannot be blamed for being unable to act counter to it), we are
only reprobates in the judgment of a vengeful, small-minded,
unfair God. In Clemens's view God is far from dead as far as man
is concerned. Although God may not presently be interested in
man's condition he long ago foreordained the circumstances
guaranteed to make man suffer. Clemens believes that man's
suffering ends in death, Clemens is too indignant about the un-
fairness of Hell and similar places to believe that it and they
exist. At times he seems to believe that man's sole escape from
God is by death, at other times he seems to believe that there is
no God, or at least no God in the way that man has been able to
imagine him, that there are only the vast reaches of the inorganic
world, blazing endlessly and with a purpose beyond man's understanding, interspersed on rare occasions with a bit of suffering,
quenchable life.

"Letters from the Earth" is the title piece of an extremely uneven anthology of Mark Twain gleanings, edited by Bernard
DeVoto in 1939, suppressed by Clara Clemens, and finally published in September 1962, after DeVoto's death and two months
prior to Clara Clemens's death. It is about twenty-eight per cent
of the anthology. Parts of the book, such as the extracts from
"Methuselah's Diary" and the "Extract from Eve's Diary," are

failures without qualification. Other parts are successful, among them "The Lowest Animal," with its unsparing view of man's vanity, weakness and cruelty. DeVoto's editorial notes are often long-winded and coy and his persistent habit of referring to Clemens as "Mark," a habit to which even Clemens's own daughter, Clara, was not immune, is rather dreary. The use of "Mark" is meant to exhibit affection for a lovable old character, one supposes, but DeVoto did not know Clemens personally and in any case was not entitled to such a liberty. William Dean Howells, who knew Clemens well, never called him anything but Clemens. Howells said he couldn't bring himself to call Clemens "Mark", it would have sounded false. DeVoto's successor as editor of the Mark Twain Papers, Dixon Wecter, had the addiction too. It seemed to have been irresistably contagious at one time and is by no means wholly out of fashion yet. It smacks of cultism and is irritating when one doesn't at a particular moment share DeVoto's desire for intimacy with the personality of Clemens but wishes at that moment only to understand and enjoy Clemens's work and thought. One is supposed to sense in the cachet of "Mark," perhaps, Clemens's superhumanism and grand old humor. But a great humorist, per se, has done nothing to deserve such treatment. Clemens has a right to his dignity just as any other great writer has. One can just as tastefully refer to Joyce as Jim or to Tolstoy as Lev Nikolayevich.

As for the public reception of the book called by DeVoto *Letters from the Earth,* far from being found unacceptable to the community at large, as Clara Clemens had feared, it was excerpted by *Life,* it received many favorable reviews and it soon became a best seller. The book was published at a time when the question of whether God is dead was already being discussed publicly and when increasing numbers of believers felt that God had deserted man or that it was no longer possible to have a personal, direct experience of God or a proof of his existence. A year later, when the chapters on religion appeared, the United Press International released a long story about them, which was featured by newspapers throughout the country. The story included comments by church leaders. The churchmen deplored Mark Twain's views and called him bitter and confused. One churchman pitied him. But there was nothing like the explosion which Clemens was sure would occur "this side of 2006." His reading was encyclopedic in certain areas but not intense and not, in the last sense, sophisticated, as may be seen in the fact that he regarded religion as something sacrosanct and criticism of it as not fit for public discussion. He was his own voluntary censor in the cold war which he thought he was conducting with the religious thought of his time. He was conservative in matters of religion and sex and had an outmoded understanding about the shockability of the American public, traits or attitudes which he seemed able to inject successfully into Paine and Clara Clemens.

In May 1958, under contract to Harpers to gather, arrange and edit *The Autobiography of Mark Twain,* I went to Berkeley to work in the Mark Twain papers in the library of the University of California. While there I studied the five chapters on religion in the autobiographical typescript and encountered the notation that they had been omitted from *Mark Twain in Eruption* at the request of Clara Clemens. Neither Harpers nor the Mark Twain Estate had placed any restrictions on my use of materials for my edition, nor had they or Mrs. Clara Clemens Samossoud indicated to me that certain portions of the autobiographical typescript had been suppressed. I believed that technically the restrictions placed on Bernard DeVoto by Mrs. Samossoud did not apply to me, but morally, because of what I had learned from the pencilled notations, I felt obliged to remind her that she had denied to DeVoto the right to publish the chapters almost twenty years ago. At the same time I asked her for permission to include them in my edition of the autobiography. Mrs. Samossoud, who was eighty-four, replied June 6.

"I presume you refer to that portion of the M.S. which was called 'Letters from the Earth.' My purpose in refusing its publication was prompted solely by my desire to protect my father's wishes as far as I was able to estimate them. When he wished to publish any of his writings there was nothing in the way of his doing so. Certainly his withholding anything from the public eye was not his fear of 'shocking people.' If anyone can be shocked into a state of truth or wisdom, let him be thoroughly shocked. It would take a long letter to describe my father's ready condemnation of his own extravagant expressions of convictions which through their imbalance could give false impressions. In my small book about my experience with Christian Science, written two years ago, I made a point of quoting Father's approving remarks about Mrs. Eddy and her great work for mankind's comfort; remarks that flatly contradicted his diatribes previously launched against Mrs. Eddy in his book on Ch. Science.

"I know that Father agreed with the attitude that the size of an individual's genius and intellect was only important in a large way as it affected mankind for *good* or *evil*. Why otherwise did he spend so much effort on studying the wrongs of accepted conventions or the sins inflicted on the people of conquered countries? The most steadfast occupation of his thoughts displayed the urge to help victims of injustice and misfortune.

"That I personally *agree* with his attacks on most of the Bible and the humanized concept of God has no bearing on this situation which must be divested of all personal considerations. I am very sorry that I cannot write what you would wish me to, but my feelings towards my father have not weakened since 1940."

In a postscript Mrs. Samossoud wrote, "Of course Father *was* innately *religious*."

I replied that the manuscript to which I had referred was not "Letters from the Earth" but part of the autobiographical dictations and soon thereafter sent her four of the five chapters on religion: the dictations of June 19, June 20, June 23 and June 25, 1906. The fifth chapter, dictated June 22, 1906, by some error had not been sent to me by the library of the University of California in Berkeley and I promised Mrs. Samossoud that I would send it along as soon as I received it. Her reply was dated July 6, 1958.

"I find the first selection (God of the Testaments) utterly delightful and completely true for anyone who thinks at all. Though powerful in expression this chapter includes such charm-

ing humour. The second section also is fascinating and the portion about the immaculate conception is profoundly convincing,
in case the reader needs convincing along that line. I heartily
agree with everything 'Mark' says about the Christianity of the
Bible and find nothing harmful in that kind of fact-revealing.
The thing I have always wondered about is mankind's acceptance of Biblical assertions, as though voiced by *God Himself*,
and therefore undeniably true. This weakness I don't remember
Father's calling attention to. But my memory may be inexact(?).

"In Christian Science so much stress is laid on the *statement*
that God made the world and called it 'good,' thus precluding the
possibility of evil anywhere. Now my letter is growing too long.

"The parting of your and my ways comes partially when Mark
offers his feeling about the 'real God' derived from a broader personal attitude and then switches sharply into tirades against the
very man-made God that Biblical 'cusses' have shaped Him into.
Of course there is so much wonderful writing and truth in these
pages following, that I wish they might be used somewhere else—
not just where Mark has started to let some cheer into the depressing darkness. How I wish you and I could talk! I feel
incapable of setting on paper the things I feel about the heavy
weight of tragedy in these many pages with *no relief*. And my
thoughts are too many to go into a letter. At the same time I
believe Father is in sympathy with them! At present the two
last sections shrink the portrait of Mark Twain both as artist and
man. He would not choose to deluge thousands, maybe millions
of souls, in massive sadness when they are struggling away from
the agonies of human finitude into a wider, *enlightening* realm
of charm created by the God-comforting gift of Imagination
and extensive Intuition. Quite falsely Mark appears as an almost
malignant searcher for evil instead of for good. In these chapters
he does not present any balance between the perfection of
Beauty in God's creative genius and the evidence of ugliness—
which latter may be the invention of Beelzebub completely unrelated to the wonders of *spiritual* power.

"In the last sections there is too much great writing to admit of
cancellation, but I do think Father would himself transfer or

scatter it into other portions. Father actually relished *joy* as a sublime treasure definitely incompatible with evil in any form. He said: 'Don't part with your illusions. When they are gone you may still exist but you have ceased to live.' And these very illusions may eventually be revealed as a higher *Reality*.

"Father enlarges on the 'punishments' inflicted on man without knowing whether they *are* punishments. What goes on in the invisible source of existence is an *unyielding Mystery*. In 'The Mysterious Stranger' and other of his writings, Mark has gone so explicitly into the superiority of the beast over man that I doubt whether the public needs any more of that viewpoint, which was never anything but a *mood* easily proved by his outpouring of admiration for man's phenomenal intellect at other times.

"I am going to ask the Citadel Press to send you my 'Awake to a Perfect Day.' It is not long, besides you need only read the parts referring to Mark's *genuine* religious nature. I don't want Father to ever appear as a dark Angel. But danger lies where condemnation is feverish without the accompaniment of constructive ideas.

"I am keeping the M.S. a day longer so that my husband can read it.

"With many friendly wishes,

"Cordially yours
"Clara C. Samossoud

"*Later*

"My husband is even stronger than I in his feeling *against* publication of those two sections! Among many other things he points out that the communists would make *generous* use of such a weapon as Mark Twain's attack on God. They would advertise it all over the world. Jacques also emphasizes the fact that this land is definitely *religious;* that the signs of it are so universal that tremendous resentment of Father's sacrilege would sweep through all circles—political, religious, and social. A lamentable attack on Father would ensue. My husband also wisely remarks that this material was not to be used until Father, through death, was 'safe from public opinion.' But Mark Twain has *not* died.

His words and thoughts live as a potent influence. Therefore those sections must be deleted much as I hate to disappoint you."

Before I could reply to this letter I received another one, dated July 8.

"Dear, oh dear! What confusion and confounding disorder! I sent you the M.S. today with a letter that is completely *bla*. In driving towards the effort to *save* parts of the M.S. I lost the main point of it all! The 'later' portion of my letter applies to every line of the material you sent me. *None* of it can see the printing press; we certainly are not going to place my blessed father and superior character on the side of the *all-good-destroying Communists*. What a kind of Hades that would be—Mark Twain an *upholder* of the Soviet Regime. My dear husband alone has protected the American nation from that revolutionizing disaster. What a narrow escape! No, dear Mr. Neider, in these disorderly times none of my dear Father's assaults on the Citadel of Spirit (however faultily presented to mankind) can be published.

"If the remaining selection from Berkeley is in the same vein don't trouble to send it."

I wrote: "Naturally, from my point of view it is regrettable that such fine and important writing by your father must remain unknown except to scholars. Intellectually it seems to me a pity that the community at large is not permitted to judge how deleterious the chapters are by being exposed to them. . . . The other day, by a coincidence, I found samples of the chapters printed in Paine's biography (Vol. III, pages 1354–57). I had not noticed them previously."

On July 24 Mrs. Samossoud wrote:

"Doubtless you felt that I adopted an almost Mark Twainious extreme of expression in prophesying what the communists would stage in the way of triumphant shows if they actually got my father on their bandwagon, yet certain it is that they would make drastic use of such an advantage; and I would be bombarded with questions and demands for explanations from countless newspapers, magazines, not to mention a deluge of letters. The passages you refer to in Paine's biography were written at a vastly different period of mankind's history. The horrors today of Russian communism are a hideous threat to man's higher progress along spiritual lines. Is any other viewpoint valid?"

When I met her in San Diego March 28, 1959 I was impressed by Mrs. Samossoud's physical and mental vigor. She was bent with age and had pathetically thin small hands but her dark eyes were lively, although she was in pain from an old neuritis, which caused her to press a hand against the left side of her breastbone occasionally. During our hour of conversation (Mr. Samossoud was also present) I expressed as diplomatically as I could the hope that she and her husband would not consider the matter of the religious chapters closed just because the *Autobiography* had recently been published but would reconsider the advantages of allowing them to be published, perhaps in a second edition of the *Autobiography*. When the Russians later in the year unexpectedly gave my edition considerable publicity by attacking it in their chief literary journal and then by permitting me to defend myself in the same journal, I kept Mrs. Samossoud and her husband informed of these events and sent them a copy of the published exchange between me and the Russian critic, noting the fact that the suppression of the religious chapters had given the Russians propaganda ammunition against the *Autobiography*. I urged the point that publication of the chapters would be the best refutation of the Russian claim that America was censoring and suppressing Mark Twain. But as far as I could judge, the Samossouds were politely adamant in the matter.

Meanwhile I was involved in matters relating to the so-called Mark Twain literary trademark. Mark Twain himself had made a claim for a trademark in his pseudonym, for example on the copyright page of *Life on the Mississippi,* published in 1883. Clemens, who had been legally victimized by publishing pirates in Canada and in England, was more aware than most American authors of the inequities and inconsistencies in various copyright laws and was prolific and vociferous on the subject of legal mistreatment of writers, pointing out, for example, how differently real property was regarded and treated as against copyrighted property, and urging longer copyright protection in literary

works, especially in the United States. But whether he actually
believed he could successfully circumvent the copyright statutes
of his own country by means of a claimed trademark is a moot
point. Possibly using his approach as a precedent, Harper &
Brothers and the Mark Twain Estate requested the payment of
fees for the right to reprint works by Mark Twain already in the
public domain, reasoning that although it was permissible to reprint such works without a fee if the name Samuel L. Clemens
was used as the author, it was not permissible to use the protected
name of Mark Twain without payment of a fee. I myself had had
occasion to pay such a fee and it seemed that I would have to do
so again before long but on a larger scale. I asked the Patent
Office just what kind of a literary trademark resided in the name
Mark Twain and learned that there were twelve Mark Twain
trademarks, for such goods as citrus fruits, work shirts, cigars,
coal, gin, boots and watches, but that there was no registration
for literary properties. The information from the director of the
Trademark Examining Operation was unequivocal: "We have
rechecked our records from 1881 to date and fail to find any
record of a registration for the mark 'Mark Twain' for books
etc."

I had been considering writing an article about Mark Twain
and copyright and had inquired about the literary trademark
partly in connection with the article. My correspondence with
the Patent Office seemed to indicate that the subject was more
complicated than I had imagined. I wrote to the chairman of the
board of Harpers and outlined what I had discovered, asking for
enlightenment. The chairman replied that Harpers was informed
by the lawyer for the Mark Twain Estate that the name Mark
Twain was trademarked and suggested that I address any inquir-
ies directly to the lawyer, which I did. The day after I sent my
letter to the lawyer the latter telephoned me to say that the Estate had registered the Mark Twain trademark in all the states
but that the Estate had not yet been able to register it with Washington because the Federal Government had a rule that a name
must be in business use for a number of years before it was eligi-
ble for registration. The cogency of this seemed to escape me,

for the name Mark Twain had been in "business use" for at least
three-quarters of a century. I suspected that the Federal Government felt that one ought not to have his cake and eat it too in
such a matter: that one ought not to enjoy the time-limited copyright protection of a Congressional statute while at the same time
enjoying trademark registration protection for what might turn
out to be, in legal terms, perpetuity. The lawyer said that all this
was "hush-hush" and that I was like one of the family. He said
that the money obtained from Mark Twain's work was "Clara's"
sole support and that she needed money. I thought I recalled reading in the *New York Times* that her income the previous year
from her father's works and properties was around $57,000 and
that the principle amounted to about half a million but being uncertain of these figures I did not mention them. The lawyer said
that the Estate could probably tie up anybody with lawsuits on the
basis of state registration.

That same day I inquired of the Department of State of the
State of New York if the name Mark Twain was a registered
trademark for books and other literary materials in New York
State and was informed by the department of Miscellaneous Records that the name Mark Twain had been registered on August
2, 1946 by the Estate of Samuel L. Clemens, deceased, and that the
registration had expired on August 2, 1956. The mark was not
presently of active trademark record. I notified both the lawyer
for the Estate and the chairman of the board of Harpers of that
fact but did not receive a reply to my communication. Three
weeks later I wrote to the chairman again, pointing out that I
was planning to edit for Doubleday *The Complete Humorous
Sketches and Tales of Mark Twain* and enclosing a list of the
titles I would use. I said that the material without exception was
in the public domain and that therefore there was no problem of
permissions but that perhaps there was a problem regarding the
use of the name Mark Twain. I added, however, that inasmuch
as it was clear to me that the name Mark Twain was not a registered trademark and never had been as far as the Federal Government was concerned, if I was to pay for the use of the name what

actually would I be paying for? I did not hear from the chairman, therefore I wrote to him again five weeks after my last letter. He explained that he had not written because he had hoped to speak with me some time on my return to New York, that he had been thinking a good deal about the Mark Twain situation, that he was having a further investigation made and that he would be glad to talk with me about the matter at any time. I saw him in his office September 21. He said that the matter disturbed him and that it had begun to disturb him before my involvement in it, that till now he had accepted the reasoning of the Estate in the matter but that he could no longer go on doing so, that he was obtaining legal advice from another source and that he did not know what the answer was at this time. When I referred to two current paperback editions of *Huckleberry Finn,* one acknowledging the trademark, the other not, he said that one company had paid, the other hadn't. He assured me that there would be no fee in connection with my edition of Clemens's sketches. On December 13, 1960 he informed me by phone that he had told the lawyer for the Estate that Harpers would no longer collect fees for the use of the name Mark Twain and that the lawyer had said it was going to "ruin Clara." I said I doubted very much that it would ruin her.

On October 28, 1960 I raised the subject of the chapters on religion once more with Mrs. Samossoud. I asked if she and Mr. Samossoud would consider publishing the rejected chapters in an appendix of a contemplated second edition of the *Autobiography.* Her reply startled me.

"My husband's objection to publishing Father's unsympathetic attacks on God, was that if I were still living, I would have to face the many types of resentment hurled at me by those who disagree with these splenetic outbursts of Father's. My objection was merely that I think the word of a famous man should be to *uphold* rather than destroy the vision of something so spiritual and needed as God.

"I should hurry up and die and thus the coast would be entirely clear. I personally advise their (his writings on this subject) appearance in print, simply because I don't wish to be an intruder in this matter and because if Father were living he probably would say 'go ahead.'

"This is a non-committal letter, dear Mr. Neider, which you and Harpers better interpret as you think wisest."

Despite Mrs. Samossoud's characterization of her letter as "non-committal" it seemed clear to me that she had finally opened the door to the publication of the long-suppressed chapters. 1960 was a year of many Mark Twain celebrations, for it was the 125th anniversary of his birth and the 50th anniversary of his death. I suspected that its spirit had influenced Mrs. Samossoud's thinking on the question of further suppression. I phoned my editor at Harpers and gave her the news. Mrs. Samossoud wrote to me again November 21. "Jacques or I will write Harpers and give them the permission they want. Possibly we have already written them. I am a bit vague. Someone wrote me the other day that I was regretfully preventing the publication of Father's most important opinions, which I had forgotten all about. Then Jacques explained that he had objected to their publishing a controversial subject from which the painful results would naturally come to my door. It's already in the past now so we can act oblivious to the whole incident."

On December 2 I received a phone call from one of the editors of *Look,* who said that the magazine was interested in the possibility of publishing the chapters on religion and therefore wanted to see them. I relayed this information by telephone to Harpers and to the lawyer of the Estate. The latter said that to publish the chapters was to give aid and comfort to the "Commies," as he put it. He said he was a religious man and didn't like to see religion trampled. I replied that in my view Mark Twain was a profoundly religious man and that only such a man would get so worked up about details of religious theory and practice. I outlined the chapters (the lawyer had not read them) and said that the Russians knew their contents fairly well from Paine and that to continue suppressing the chapters was only to help Russian propaganda against us. The lawyer inquired several times if there was any money to be made out of the affair "for Clara's sake." I said I did not know. He said that after all, *Look* appeared to be interested in the chapters. I replied that I could not gauge the extent of *Look's* interest, nor did I know anything about their rates.

On December 7 I was informed by my editor at Harpers that Harpers had received formal permission from Mrs. Samossoud to publish the chapters on religion. Next day I learned that Mrs. Samossoud's letter of permission was a sweeping release for all the suppressed Mark Twain manuscripts, not only for the chapters on religion. On December 13 I again spoke by phone with the Estate lawyer. He asked how much money was involved in magazine publication of the chapters. (*Harper's Magazine* was also interested in the chapters.) I said that undoubtedly *Look*, if they took the chapters, would pay a good deal more than *Harper's* was prepared to pay. He asked, "Can we trust *Look* not to swipe the stuff if we send it to them?" I said that the chapters, being still unpublished, were protected by common-law rights and that anyhow it was impossible for me to conceive of *Look's* "swiping" anything. Two days later I had another conversation with him, in which he said that John Fischer, editor of *Harper's Magazine*, had called him and had spoken about the prestige of publishing the chapters in the magazine. The lawyer told me that he didn't "give a hoot" about the prestige, that his job was "to make money for Clara" and that he wanted to get as much for the chapters as he could. He said he thought he might ask $10,000 for them from *Look*. I said that struck me as an impossibly high figure. He asked if *Letters from the Earth*, the suppressed manuscript edited by Bernard DeVoto many years ago, might make money. I said it might if it were issued as a trade book but that it wouldn't if it were issued in a scholarly edition by a university press.

On January 3, 1961 I had a phone conversation with my editor at Harpers. She said that she had read the religious chapters and was worried about them. She said she didn't like them, they were so different in tone from the rest of my edition of the autobiography, which was a "family book." She said the chapters on religion were lacking in Clemens's usual sense of humor. She said it really was too bad about the timing: the chapters would have shocked people if they had been published when Clemens wrote them, but now they were not shocking, yet they would offend just as many people. She said that maybe it would be best if all the suppressed materials appeared in one book. She said she just didn't know. On the 27th I wrote her the following letter:

"I have read the religious chapters once again and have thought about them for a few days. It's my opinion that they belong in the *Autobiography* and not in another volume, and I hope that you and Harpers will decide to include them in a second edition.

"The fact that they are humorless and severe does not make them untypical. Mark Twain had two sides—the jolly, funny one, and the serious one which was often colored by his gift of invective. My edition of the autobiography amply exemplifies the second side—in the attacks on Bret Harte, on Webster, on Mrs. Aldrich, and in the several biting comments on man.

"It is easy to see my edition as a 'family book' but that is after the fact, for if I had been allowed to include the religious chapters originally I would certainly have done so, and the book would then have acquired a tone different from the one it has now. The important thing is that Mark Twain is a giant of American letters, and all effort ought to be made to publish everything he wrote, regardless of how we may feel about a particular piece. I think it would be a mistake to make an exception of these chapters by publishing them in a volume other than the one for which they were intended.

"Obviously the chapters are going to offend people, but that is what Mark Twain intended them to do. He wanted to shake up people's thinking in an area where he thought they desperately needed it. We have waited so long to bring these chapters to the public. Now that Clara Samossoud has finally consented to their release it would be a shame to stand in the way of their proper presentation. To publish them elsewhere than in the *Autobiography* would be to invite speculation and comment on why we side-stepped doing what is clear and forthright and expected of us. In an age in which Bertrand Russell is a best seller these chapters may find fewer people who are shocked than some of us may think."

To which my editor at Harpers replied that she wouldn't resist inclusion of the chapters in the *Autobiography* but that she wished a bit wistfully that the subject hadn't come up. On March 14 she wrote that she was still sitting on the chapters and still hoping that a graceful way out of the dilemma would present itself. Near the end of November I asked her what had become of the chapters and if Harpers had plans for their publication. She replied that there were no plans but that Harpers would publish *Letters from the Earth*, which in her opinion said everything that was said in the religious chapters but with artistry and humor, an opinion with which I disagreed.

On August 24, 1962 the *New York Times* printed a story about the forthcoming publication of *Letters from the Earth* detailing how Mrs. Samossoud had come to agree to its publication and mentioning the fact that I planned to publish the chapters on religion in a magazine and that two magazines had already declined the chapters as being "too inflammatory." The editor of *The Hudson Review* read the story while vacationing in Maine, phoned me and asked to see the chapters in order to consider them for publication. In September I wrote to my editor that I still believed that the chapters belonged in *The Autobiography of Mark Twain* but that it seemed to me the least we could do, if Harpers did not wish to issue a revised edition of the *Autobiography*, was to publish the chapters in pamphlet form. I said the chapters would pain some people but that it wasn't our task to create an image of Mark Twain, but only to report him accurately. To which she replied that she was resistant to the chapters, whose tone was "so ugly." She said, however, that she would review the matter with as open a mind as she could muster. On September 24 I informed her that *The Hudson Review* had purchased the chapters and would publish them in October 1963 in accordance with the desire of Harpers to have a full year elapse between the publication of *Letters from the Earth* and the magazine appearance of the chapters. I told her that I did not think that the tone of the chapters was ugly.

My editor reread the chapters and early in October reported that the opinions in the chapters didn't seem now as "gratuitously offensive" as they had on first reading. I told her that I was more than ever impressed by the chapters' cogency, courage, noble utterance and by their anthropological view of religion and man. Late in October she suggested that they be published in a centenary edition of Mark Twain's works, which would be brought out over the next dozen years or so. She thought this was "the perfect solution" to book publication, a scholarly presentation in the original context. I replied that it seemed to me the issue was clear: it was because the chapters had been suppressed for so long, and their suppression and the lifting of the ban made widely public, that it was a matter of some urgency that they be published. To leave their publication up to "the next dozen years or so" was hardly suitable, in my opinion. In her next letter, dated November 6, she informed me that there was no assurance that the chapters would be included in the centenary edition. Mrs. Samossoud died November 20, 1962, and I suspected, ironically, that I had lost an important ally in my efforts to find a permanent printed place for the chapters.

In March 1963 I wrote to the lawyer for the Estate, saying that I had tried in vain to persuade Harpers to publish the chapters either in a new edition of the *Autobiography* or in a separate brochure, and I asked him how he felt about my finding another publisher for the chapters. I did not receive a reply. In October I wrote to him again, saying that Harpers had once more declined to publish them, and informing him that a New York publisher had expressed interest in publishing them as a pamphlet. The lawyer replied that he would discuss the matter with Harpers. I wrote to him October 30.

"Just to confirm your telephone call to me of about 6 P.M. yesterday, in which you stated that you had talked with Evan Thomas of Harpers and that the feeling at Harpers is that the publication of the chapters on religion as a pamphlet or brochure would hurt the sales of *Letters from the Earth*, and that consequently Harpers does not wish the chapters published in such form, either by themselves or by anybody else.

"I wish to state for the record, as I did yesterday on the phone, that I can't understand how the sale of a tiny pamphlet could

hurt the sale of a large book, and one which has been a best seller for a year or more.

"Perhaps at some future date Harpers will no longer entertain
this belief and perhaps at such a time they or some other publisher
will publish the chapters with your consent."

That is where the matter stands at this writing, to the best of
my knowledge.

Princeton
June 1966

POSTSCRIPT, JULY 16, 1966

Since writing this essay I have learned of the existence of an
important law case with a direct bearing on the so-called Mark
Twain trademark question: Clemens v. Belford, Clark & Co.,
known as "the Mark Twain case." In it Clemens sued the defendants for publishing *Sketches by Mark Twain* in 1880 without his
permission. He did not claim infringement of copyright, for apparently the sketches were in the public domain, but argued
instead that he had the exclusive right to the use of the nom de
plume or trademark of Mark Twain and that the defendants
could be enjoined from using this name without his consent.
Clemens lost the case. The opinion of the court, rendered January 3, 1883, was that an author does not have and cannot acquire
a better or higher right in an assumed name than he has in his
Christian or baptismal name and that he has no exclusive property in his published work except when he has secured and protected it by compliance with the copyright laws.

THE NOTEBOOKS

IN THE SUMMER of 1964, when I returned to Berkeley to work in the Mark Twain Papers, which include Clemens's notebooks, I carried with me a false notion of the contents of the books, a notion probably shared by most if not all students of Clemens's works who had not studied the originals. The notion was that the notebooks did not reflect certain important aspects of Clemens's life and career as accurately and as bluntly as one might expect. I was puzzled by the discrepancy, for it seemed that the notebooks, being more private even than letters, and spanning Clemens's entire professional career, should reveal without question those business crises which were well known from his letters and biography, crises which finally marred his domestic life and which were, in a sense, disguises for more profound spiritual crises: failing literary powers, a failing artistic conscience (which had not been strong to begin with), and an increasing acceptance of and indulgence in the dubious gifts of the gilded age. My false notion was due to Albert Bigelow Paine's *Mark Twain's Notebook*. That was the title, instead of *Mark Twain's Notebooks*, which Paine gave the volume for some reason best known to himself. Published in 1935 on the occasion of the 100th anniversary of Clemens's birth, the volume is still, more than three decades later, the sole edition of the notebooks.

It is a puzzling one. There seems to be a profound disagreement between Paine's comments in the text and his comments in the foreword. In the text there are clear indications that the edition is in many respects an anthology (for example, Paine sometimes summarizes entries), a fact which contradicts some of the remarks in the foreword. Paine disarms the reader by assuring him in the foreword that he has reproduced the originals faithfully. He states, "A good while ago I wrote a biography of Mark Twain. In that book I drew briefly here and there upon the set of journals, diaries, or commonplace books which through a period of nearly fifty years [Clemens] had kept and, what is still more remarkable, preserved. These little books are now offered in full." And again, "The entries, whatever their interest, or lack of it—are as he left them." And in an afterword he says, "And so the record closes. It is Mark Twain—at his best and at his worst. I cannot discover anything more to add, and I am not prompted to take anything away. Those who have wanted Mark Twain as he was—to himself, and to those nearest him—have him now—in his daughter's memories, *My Father, Mark Twain,* and in these desultory memoranda, the fitful record of fifty years."

Unfortunately these statements are not true. Paine omitted much from the originals, both matter that probably interested him, such as the sarcastic remarks on genius in the notebook of December 1866—January 1867, and matter that probably bored him, such as the lists of chores and the lists of names and addresses in the later notebooks. A comparison of the originals with Paine's edition shows that Paine abridged sections which he included, and often edited sentences and punctuation, sometimes with only the vaguest of hints to the reader of what he had done but often with no hints at all. He rarely referred to the notebooks specifically. He lumped them together to create the sense of a narrative, intervening with comments whenever he pleased, making many or few selections as his purpose or his intuition dictated, and often giving only a general idea of the dates of entries. His book was divided into chapters with chapter titles. An example of his unacknowledged editing can be seen by referring to the notebook of April–August 1885. He quotes an entry on wit and humor. This is how he presents it: "Wit and Humor—if any difference it is in duration—lightning and electric light. Same material, apparently; but one is vivid, brief, and can do damage— the other fools along and enjoys elaboration." The original is subtly different: "duration" is underlined and "the other" is "tother." The original entry continues. Clemens discusses his belief that there is no humor in *The Pickwick Papers* except for the kind a clown makes in a circus. He also discusses the difference between English and American humor, saying that English humor is conscious, American humor ostensibly unconscious. But Paine gives no indication that the entry has been abbreviated and that he has omitted significant material.

Another example may be found in the notebook of October 1890—June 1891, which contains a note for a continuation of the Tom-Huck saga. It appears in Paine's volume in the following form: "Huck comes back sixty years old, from nobody knows where—and crazy. Thinks he is a boy again and scans always every face for Tom, Becky, etc. Tom comes at last from sixty years' wandering in the world, and attends Huck and together they talk of old times; both are desolate, life has been a failure, all that was lovable, all that was beautiful is under the mold. They die together." The note in the original is quite different: the punctuation is different, "attends" is "tends," "talk of old times" is "talk the old times," and Tom like Huck returns at sixty rather than after sixty years of wandering in the world. These two examples are far from being isolated ones. Paine had an itchy finger when it came to editing Clemens. He even took liberties with Clemens's novels, as I have noted elsewhere. His version of the notes taken on the famous around-the-world trip makes it seem as though Clemens was interested almost exclusively in making literary observations, whereas in fact the originals have a considerable freight of non-literary material. Sometimes Paine omits almost an entire notebook, as in the case of the notebook of May 1886—May 1887. The latter, full of feverish business notes, is admittedly depressing but it is necessary for a full portrait of Clemens.

Paine's volume offers only vague suggestions of the fact that during and after Clemens's best creative years Clemens was seriously at odds with himself, quick-money fevers and a public personality having a considerable and increasingly deleterious effect on his literary work. The money fevers so distracted him from literary concerns that the latter probably often lost their stature and flavor in his imagination, and the enjoyment of being celebrated and lionized ate away at his time, encouraged his love of theatrics (which affected his literary work), and encouraged

the further expansion of a public personality antithetical to the
needs of a private, creative one. From Paine's edition one re-
ceives the impression of a writer whose notebooks from beginning to end are of one tone and piece—the tone of vigorous and
vivid notes, which one might expect from a great writer—but
this is because Paine edited the notebooks to create such an impression, not only by selecting what he considered to be and
what sometimes was the cream, but also by suppressing parts
which could hardly be called literary or "life" notes. Wherever
Clemens's notes degenerated into appointment notes, notes about
contracts, stocks and bonds, about lectures and lecture ideas;
wherever they were names and addresses, lists of chores, travel
schedules, fragments of business letters; wherever they were the
fever of a publishing business rising with the publication of
Grant's memoirs and failing with the publication of Sherman's,
and the mania of a get-rich-quick typesetter scheme, Paine either
quietly omitted them or greatly subordinated them. But wherever they reinforced the image of Clemens as a devoted laborer
in the literary vineyard, Paine included and sometimes emphas-
ized them.

A cavalier editor with a proprietary attitude regarding
Clemens, Paine also stated in the foreword something of wider
concern than the notebooks themselves. "A superstition, nursed
and nourished by a number of persons—most of them too young
to have known Mark Twain, too perverse to accept the simple
and the obvious, is that because of restrictions laid upon him by
his wife, by W. D. Howells, and later by those to whose care he
trusted his manuscripts, he has not been permitted to have his
say. Now this is a good way from the truth. Mark Twain had
his say; as much as any author could have it, thirty, forty, fifty
years ago. When restricted at all it was chiefly through his own
expressed wish to observe the conventions and convictions of
that more orthodox, more timid and delicate (possibly more immaculate) day." This was begging the question, which was not
whether Clemens had his say during his lifetime but whether he
had it afterwards, while in the hands of Paine and of Clara
Clemens. It was also a piece of effrontery in view of the fact

that Paine knew better than anyone else that Clemens's writings
on religion, among other things, had been and were still being
suppressed.

It would be a formidable task, far exceeding the limits and purpose of this essay, to catalogue Paine's omissions and changes.
However, in order to correct the impression left by Paine's edition, it may at least be worth while to describe the contents of
the originals briefly, with probably (but not intentionally) an
emphasis on the kind of materials that Paine omitted.

Clemens's notebooks were not literary, bookish.[His mind, eye
and ear were alert to people, to the vernacular, the sounds of
things, delighting in anecdotes, dialect, tales, yarns, and of course
humor. These traits and predilections can be seen in his early
"professional" notebooks—the Sandwich Islands books of 1866,
the book of December 1866—January 1867 concerning a voyage
from San Francisco to New York via the Isthmus, and the Holy
Land Excursion notebooks of 1867. The books are extremely
vivid. I call them "professional" because Clemens clearly kept
them for professional use—in newspaper correspondence, in
lectures, and in writing sketches, stories, essays and books. The
two notebooks of his piloting years are, by contrast, strictly business books, detailing, for his own use only, the business of piloting on the Mississippi. A typical entry from them reads: "Hove
lead at head of 55—no bottom—ran no channel in it. 8 ft. bank
on pt. opp. Densford's—or rather up shore at head of timber."

Occasionally Clemens's notebooks illuminated him. In the
notebook of the spring and summer of 1877 he describes how he
left New York by ship at 3:30 of a May afternoon (he was on
his way to Bermuda for what he claimed was his first actual
pleasure trip) and how blazing it was in the harbor and how,
beyond the harbor, cold rain fell. He put on his sealskin coat and
tied the collar with a silk handkerchief. This was the dandified
theatrical side of him, which he had enough money now to indulge. Generally his notebooks are not introspective or interior,
they do not often talk about himself, they usually deal with aspects of the outer world which interested him and with which

he seemed to have peculiarly intimate relations. He liked to note
the slang names of things, bits of dialogue, quick descriptions,
whatever would help him to remember and whatever strongly
impressed him. His descriptive talent grasped Bermuda readily
as he noted the white roads, the white chimneys like sugar, the
white cakelike houses looking seamless and jointless as they
gleamed in the dull green vegetation. The 1877 trip became the
basis of "Some Rambling Notes of an Idle Excursion" but the
notebook for the trip contains no sign of the crazy dialogue
which begins that effective sketch. The missing dialogue seems
like a symbol of something missing in the notebooks. There are
glimpses of Clemens but the essential, revealed Clemens is not
present. The Clemens mystery persists wherever one tracks the
man down, probably for the reason that there was no mystery in
any fabricated sense, the ambiguity, the incommensurability, being as actual, although not as evident, to its possessor as to its
pursuers. One wonders if Clemens revealed himself anywhere in
his surviving papers, if he revealed the extent of his premarital
sex life, for example, or the extent to which he was on stage in his
most private moments, the extent to which he was Clemens the
performer on the one hand and Clemens the private practitioner
of his craft on the other, a writer unlike those others who are
not split by the possession of a pseudonym and a public personality.

In his best notebooks he is alert to all kinds of professional
possibilities: journalism, literature, language, his past experiences
(he often draws on his reservoir of experience in the notebooks).
He will jot down a note for a telephone farce (later expanded and
published), or for *The Prince and the Pauper,* or for a biography of Whitelaw Reid (with whom he was feuding and whom
he meant to assassinate in print, an intention which he was ex-
ceptionally qualified to give substance to, what with his gift of
invective; but he ran out of steam on the project), or for his
autobiography, or he will put down comments on towns,
people, customs, or sarcastic reflections on old, great paintings.
He will set down thoughts, reflections, ideas for stories; in the
same notebook he will jot down names and addresses, notes on

moving around Germany, appointment notes. He will urge himself to give American drygoods clerks *"rats"* and to quote some
of their insolence to ladies, whom he is always ready to tilt a
lance for, provided they are not French; he is a persistent moralist operating on a rather Victorian spectrum of ideas. He will
make a note on a blue jay yarn (the yarn will become *the* blue
jay yarn in *A Tramp Abroad*), on the German language, and
will even, despite his claimed tolerance, set down an occasional
slur against Jews. Later he will note compliments about Jews but
fall into the old prejudice that Jews never work with their
hands. His notebooks are markedly proper. They rarely contain
off-color matter. It is as if he expects his mother or his wife or
his daughters or the good queen herself to peek into them. This
is one of the ways in which he seems to betray his bohemian
years in the West, and the tradition of irregularity exemplified
by other writers of his time, such as Bret Harte. In the notebook
of October 1878—January 1879, in which he is gathering materials for *A Tramp Abroad*, many notes are written in the tone of
the projected travel book, and the "I" is usually disappointing,
it is usually the "I" of the book. In the next notebook he mentions
calling on Turgeniev in Paris in May 1879 and having a cup of
tea out of Turgeniev's samovar, and Turgeniev's calling on him
and giving him one of his books (unnamed by Clemens) and of
his giving Turgeniev *Tom Sawyer*, but what he thought of
Turgeniev and of Turgeniev's book (if he read it) he does not
say. One suspects that they were not in the arena of his interests,
that they were too literary, too self-conscious (he was impatient
with self-consciousness) for his tastes.

He is sarcastic about *Tom Jones*, which he calls disgusting and
which he accuses of a poverty of invention. He calls communism
idiocy because in his opinion property would never stay divided
equally, it would require redivision every three years. He says "it
takes a heap of sense to write good nonsense." By 1880 and 1881
he seems, judging by the notebooks, rather badly disorganized,
bric-a-brac threatening to engulf his creative hours, yet we
know that these were still very creative years, therefore we
must use the notebooks cautiously as a guide to his literary

powers. There are notes on things to be done, addresses of people, business notes, names of people and places. The notebook for 1882, which records the excursion he made on the Mississippi in preparation for completing *Life on the Mississippi*, is a relatively good one, although he is still jotting down chore notes, or cracks against the French, or against Reid. He tries on titles for size (Abroad on the Great River, Abroad on the Father of Waters, Abroad on the Mississippi) and notes that literary people are "low" and that human nature can best be studied in villages, where people wear fewer disguises than in cities. The most obvious instance of the notebooks containing "objectionable" matter occurs in a dictated (and therefore perhaps somehow protected?) notebook, dictated to his secretary Roswell Phelps on the Mississippi trip. This notebook is in general freer than most and contains "God damn," "bitch," "whore," "son of a bitch," and "piss." It is rich in other respects also, containing anecdotes, much about pilots, details of Bixby's experiences as a war pilot (Horace Bixby, who taught Clemens the river), details of family feuds, etcetera. Much of it was used in *Life on the Mississippi*.

By 1883 and 1884 Clemens's money mania appears to be in full swing. He wants to invent something that will make a quick million, or write a play that will be an instant success. He considers writing a play based on "The £1,000,000 Bank-Note" and another about America in 1985, when the Pope was the temporal as well as the spiritual despot of the United States, when the United States was dominated by an aristocracy and primogeniture, and when Europe was republican. There is much about games in the notebook, including notes for a game to study history by. And there are notes on Paige of the ill-fated typesetter machine. The notebook of October 1884—April 1885 contains entries about General Grant and the latter's memoirs (which Clemens is planning to publish) and about a reading tour that Clemens makes with George Washington Cable. It contains lists of stocks and dividends, lists of people's names, ideas for lectures, lists of things to be done by Clemens and of things for others to do. He is apparently determined to continue the saga of Tom and Huck: he considers having Huck ship on a Mississippi river boat as a cabin boy so he, Clemens, can memorialize the great river in story form; he considers having Tom, Huck and Jim experience his (Clemens's) Missouri campaign in the Civil War. In the notebook for April–August 1885 he is still concerned with the Grant memoirs. And he wants to get Redpath, his lecture agent, to shorthand his (Clemens's) autobiography, and he means to see if there is a patent for indenting a waffle form in asphalt pavement. He writes "Son of a ----!" and "H-l" in the privacy of his notebook. The next book, August 1885—January 1886, has much about the Paige machine, about patents, patent laws, contracts, ideas for exploiting this or that. The notes begin to seem frantic. Always they list things to be done. And there are fragments of letters which Clemens means to write. The notebook for May 1886—May 1887 is again full of business, business, in the midst of which he notes cryptically, "Bring down Tolstoi," leaving the reader to wonder if he means to attack Tolstoy or to bring down a volume by the great writer.

So it goes: irritations about money matters, querulousness with Charley (Webster), notes on sales of books, and many questions to be asked of various correspondents. Occasionally there are literary notes: bits of dialogue, a phrase or two to suggest an anecdote, brief phrases to note a yarn or an idea. In 1888 he makes notes for *A Connecticut Yankee* but they are interrupted by feverish notes on the Paige machine. Eureka! he cries. For on Saturday, January 5, 1889, at 12:20 P.M., he sees a line of movable type composed by the Paige machine and almost goes into ecstasies over what he takes to be an historic event, forgetting that his excitement is generated more by his hope of making millions with the invention of a compositor than by his hope of making history with it. He lists the people present at the awesome event. Two days later he notes, in almost tremulous tones, that the first proper name set by the machine was William Shakespeare. Great writer and great humanitarian, Clemens is also a vulgarian, a seeker of rococo opulence, a chaser of the fast buck, a native son of his age. The Paige machine was destined to bleed him almost dry. No wonder he said he hated the past because it was so humiliating. In the following notebook there is again a general confusion of things: sentences in German, lists of songs, a poem, and endless Paige matters. His relations with Paige and with the latter's machine punctuate the notebooks for a number of years. The machine breaks down; a substantial sum of money (it is always substantial) is needed for parts and repairs, which Clemens supplies; Paige tinkers; and Clemens learns to despair of ever gaining profit or wisdom from the experience.

A note on Tom and Huck in a notebook of 1890 and 1891 seems to reflect his increasing gloom, whose cause is not limited to any particular troubles or combination of troubles of his mature years but which rather seems to have been present, in a muted degree, in his Hannibal years. This is the note referred to earlier, in which Huck returns to the village at the age of sixty (Clemens is fifty-five). The same notebook contains notes on a reading given at Bryn Mawr and notes on publishing distractions and difficulties. When Clemens goes to sea his notes perk up temporarily. The sea has a salutary effect on him, if for no other reason than that he is removed from the scenes of his money fever. He comments on the ship, the ocean, his quarters, and records bits of heard dialogue. In Europe there are literary and travel notes, but not for long. Soon there are chores, chores. The book for March 1893—July 1894 has an extended memorandum on his dealings with Paige, banking notes, an observant note on the cackling of a hen, bare travel notes, German phrases and sentences, ideas for new editions (to raise money), and more business, more names, addresses, notes on stocks.

The next five books, of March 1895—July 1896, are from his round-the-world trip and overlap chronologically. He gathers materials for the travel book he plans to write, which will become the mediocre (for him) *Following the Equator*. There are notes on train travel across the U. S., ideas for stories, notes on readings, a draft of a letter to Kipling, remarks on sunsets, comments on Australian towns, remarks on the French, New Zealand notes. The notes are increasingly preoccupied with the effluvia of life. Occasionally one encounters a brighter moment, as when Clemens hopes for a heavy storm because of "a menagerie of mannerless children" on board when he sails from Wellington, or as when he writes that he read *The Vicar of Wakefield* and some of Jane Austin (sic) during the past year and found them "thoroughly artificial." The book for January–April 1896 is more leisurely than the recent ones and contains notes on the ship's captain, on a juggler, on ants and religion, on missionary work, on tailors being idiots, on the Indian Ocean. But one still increasingly senses that his notes are no longer vital. Too much time has been and still is being and will be consumed in moving about, in lectures, in being celebrated, until at last Clemens seems incapable of making any but superficial notes and, perhaps but not probably, any but superficial observations. When he reaches London and begins writing *Following the Equator* his notes (of September 1896—January 1897) improve considerably. He is interested in diseases of man, in maxims, in man's failure to reason, in dream humor, and as usual in continuing the Tom-Huck saga. There is a note on the bus-horses of London, on sheep-runs, sharking, London villages, English speech, and on matters relating to his physical comfort, such as a temporary insufficiency of blankets. There are many notes on Susy, his favorite child, who had died recently and suddenly of spinal meningitis.

The succeeding notebook contains remarks on conscience, the duality of character, Vienna, a visit to a Countess Bardi (evidencing his headiness, almost his fawning, when it came to family titles, despite his sarcasm about them in some of his writings), ideas for stories and lectures, and notes on the "real" God and on nature. There is an incident which typifies Clemens's speculation madness. He gets terrifically excited over the Szczepanik designing-machine for carpets and immediately takes options on it, convinced that this time he'll make his elusive millions. The matter fades and isn't mentioned in the later notebooks. There is a note for what will become his fragment "The Great Dark," a list of Americans (many of whom are very wealthy), there are chores, ideas for articles and stories (he's taking stock, trying to raise money) and an extensive note for a "new Huck Finn," with the kind of Tom Sawyer shenanigans which so delight Clemens. The book of June 1897—August 1899 records his life in Vienna, the cost of servants and meals, and includes notes on the Austrian parliament, on radicals and conservatives, and many maxims and aphorisms. From 1900 on, the notebooks are even less literary than recently. They contain social and business appointments, notes on stocks, bonds and contracts, and various chores. There are names and addresses galore, lists of sums earned, and publishing matters. The notebook of 1904 contains a pathetic note on the death of his wife, written June 5th, immediately after the event. The last extant notebook, of 1905–1908, is mostly blank. It records some names, some ideas for what were probably meant to be speeches, and a few literary notes.

Princeton, New Jersey
July 1966

THE SKETCHES

I AM WRITING this introduction* in October of 1960, five or six weeks prior to the 125th anniversary of Mark Twain's birth. (He was born in Florida, Missouri on November 30, 1835. He died April 21, 1910, just a little more than half a century ago.) This has been an unusual Mark Twain year, with many celebrations of his life and work on both the popular and the esoteric fronts. There have been television shows, spreads of text and photographs in national magazines, and the issuance of various books and articles.

Mark Twain's popularity has not always been as intense in his own country as it has been the past couple of years, and particularly during the present one. As recently as four years ago, when writing the introduction to his *Complete Short Stories*, I had occasion to complain, "Here is a man, a very great man, a national monument, you might say, who has been dead these forty-odd years without having had his stories collected, when lesser men, just recently dead, or still living, have had that mark of honor offered them by the publishing world and the public."

It was not merely that an edition of his collected stories had been overlooked, which was the case. It was also that certain editors in high places believed his vogue had waned to the extent that such an edition would amount to an expensive hobby. The success of the collected stories has made it possible to issue this volume of sketches as a companion volume.

A friend of mine, a novelist who was born and raised in Missouri and who has long been a student of Mark Twain, recently wrote me that he had been reading some current deep analyses of Mark Twain's works. As a result of his reading, which left him alternately astonished and numbed, he decided, "I have pretty

* To *The Complete Humorous Sketches and Tales of Mark Twain*, Doubleday, 1961.

well given up writing any book about Mr. Clemens. I am
a charter member of the Mark Twain and No Hogwash Society
[he used a more pithy and less polite term], and the perfessers
have sifted the old man's ashes back and forth until there's nothing left but some sour-smelling talc. All the time the perfessers
are trying to figure out what Mark Twain meant by this or that.
Hell, he wrote about as clearly as anyone could write and I see
no reason to doubt that he meant what he said. There's a perfesser wrote a book in which Huck's trip on the raft symbolized
Sam's journey west in the stage coach, and the purpose of the
journey was search for a father. Keee-rist! Another perfesser
wrote a book for which he did an astonishing amount of research. Of course a lot of the research adds up to nothing important but, being a scholar, he had to put it all in."

Some of the deep analyses are removed from the reality by a
distance of not less than several light-years. Mark Twain was not
that remote from reality, nor did he have all those anemic
theories flowing in his veins. He knew the reality as well as any
writing man of his time and better than most. His works, when
observed without coyness and without a succession of mirrors,
show it.

Mark Twain's sketches never won for themselves the illustrious reputation won by his other kinds of writing, but no one
interested in American humor can long remain indifferent
to them. They comprised a substantial share of his literary apprenticeship and developed so thoroughly into a flair of genius
that they made their way into his important books long after he
had decided he had broken their spell. As with the short story he
was long on hodgepodge in form and short on French neatness.
It is often not easy to say which is a story and which a sketch,
and sometimes it is not possible. In the long run it makes little
difference, for fortunately his minor works carry the impress of
his literary features so strongly that they possess an intrinsic
value quite apart from any which they might have gathered to
themselves by being more akin to the usual genres.

Some of Clemens's well-wishers were embarrassed by his
sketches and were ready to consign them to oblivion. Paine,

for example, in discussing a collection of items entitled *Sketches New and Old*, published in 1875, said, "Many of them are amusing, some of them delightful, but most of them seem ephemeral. If we except 'The Jumping Frog,' and possibly 'A True Story' (and the latter was altogether out of place in the collection), there is no reason to suppose that any of its contents will escape oblivion." Its contents included such tales as "My Watch," "Political Economy," and "The Experience of the McWilliamses with Membranous Croup," all published in the volume of collected stories. The remainder are included in the present volume. So much for Paine's clouded crystal ball. Howells praised the book in the *Atlantic* on its publication, however. The sketches are a minor side of Mark Twain, but it ought to be noted that they are a particularly brilliant and representative side.

He began writing them at an early age, before he left Hannibal, and the newspapers of the day made their publication possible. The blights of bigness and sameness had not yet come to the papers. There were no press associations and no syndicates. Each paper had an intimate, personal, local tone rare today and reflected the personality of its editor, also of the town or area in which it was read. Today a reader's only, slim hope of a hearing is in the Letters to the Editor section of the editorial pages. In those earlier times the papers welcomed contributions from its readers, particularly pithy paragraphs from clever men. If you were clever enough you could work your way up to whole sketches. The reward was a haven from anonymity.

It was not only a question of appearing in your local paper. Because papers did not jealously guard their copyright status, if you were good other papers would pick up your items and reprint them along with your name, and your fame might spread over a whole region, as it did in the case of Mark Twain. Those paragraphs of comment, news, observation, hoax, skit, and sketch were Clemens's apprenticeship on the American literary scene, although it is doubtful that he ever regarded them in so portentous a manner. He used what was available to him in outlet and in matter, and the result is that his beginnings and his career were so different from those of the masters of the

predominant New England school and from those of the emerging Henry James. If anyone strayed into literature (the phrase is
Thomas Mann's as applied to himself) it was Mark Twain.

But anonymity was only the first part of the reward. Later
there was payment in greenbacks and in gold. Thus did Clemens
write sketches for the Hannibal *Journal*, the New Orleans *True
Delta*, the *Territorial Enterprise* of Virginia City, Nevada,
the San Francisco *Morning Call* and *Alta California*, for the
Californian and the *Golden Era* and the Buffalo *Express* and
the *Galaxy*. Beginning in the fifties, he continued writing these
sketches into the seventies. He traveled a familiar road to fame,
the road of Artemus Ward, Josh Billings, and Petroleum Vesuvius Nasby, all humorists, all commentators—and all lecturers
and showmen. For once one's fame was established in the para-
graphic way the lecture circuit beckoned with its gold as it
competed with other forms of entertainment—with the minstrel
show, the music hall, the variety show, the circus.

The humorous lecturer in those days was invariably a show-
man and invariably "quaint" in matter and style. He availed
himself of the appurtenances of showmanship: pseudonyms,
advance agents, puff advertisements, colored lithographs, and
quaint posters. The poster announcing Mark Twain's first lecture, held in San Francisco in 1866, contained the following
information:

Maguire's Academy of Music/Pine Street, near Mont-
gomery/The Sandwich Islands/Mark Twain/(Honolulu
Correspondent of the Sacramento Union)/Will Deliver A/
Lecture on the Sandwich Islands/at the Academy of Music/
On Tuesday Evening, Oct. 2d/(1866)/In which passing mention will be made of Harris, Bishop/Staley, the American missionaries, etc., and the absurd/customs and characteristics
of the natives duly discussed/and described. The great volcano
of Kilauea will also/receive proper attention./A Splendid
Orchestra/is in town, but *has not* been engaged/Also/a Den
of Ferocious Wild Beasts/will be on exhibition in the next
block/Magnificent Fireworks/were in contemplation for
this occa-/sion, but the idea has been abandoned/A Grand

Torchlight Procession/may be expected; in fact, the public are/privileged to expect whatever they please./Dress Circle, $1.00 Family Circle, 50¢./Doors open at 7 o'clock. The Trouble to begin at 8 o'clock.

Lectures had a wide audience, for they were written up in the newspapers and often quoted at length. Just as Mark Twain the lecturer was aggrandized by Mark Twain the writer of sketches, so the writer of sketches benefited from the lecturer, by the creation of a greater market for his wares. And just as the lectures were influenced by the competing forms of entertainment, so they in turn influenced them. The sketches in particular established Mark Twain's fame as "the wild humorist of the Pacific slope" and "the moralist of the Main." In the sketches we find more than mere echoes of the variety shows he no doubt enjoyed during his years of piloting on the great river (he did not pilot showboats, but they flourished on the river in his time) and of the Negro minstrel shows he so loved. The "nigger show," as it was known, with its formalized dialogue between the middleman (who was the straight man) and the end men Tambo (for tambourine) (also Banjo for banjo) and Bones (for castanets) made itself felt in Clemens's early writings, and even in his later ones. "When the Buffalo Climbed a Tree" from *Roughing It* is an example of what I have in mind.

Long after the minstrel show gave way in popularity to the variety show, Clemens, an old man, wrote nostalgically: "Where now is Billy Rice? He was a joy to me and so were the other stars of the nigger show—Billy Birch, David Wambold, Backus and a delightful dozen of their brethren who made life a pleasure to me forty years ago and later. Birch, Wambold and Backus are gone years ago; and with them departed to return no more forever, I suppose, the real nigger show—the genuine nigger show, the extravagant nigger show—the show which to me had no peer and whose peer has not yet arrived, in my experience. We have the grand opera; and I have witnessed and greatly enjoyed the first act of everything which Wagner created, but the effect on me has always been so powerful that one act was quite sufficient; whenever I have witnessed two acts I have gone away physically exhausted; and whenever I have ventured an entire opera the result has been the next thing to suicide. But if I could have the nigger show back again in its pristine purity and perfection I should have but little further use for opera. It seems to me that to the elevated mind and the sensitive spirit the hand organ and the nigger show are a standard and a summit to whose rarefied altitude the other forms of musical art may not hope to reach." And he continued in the same vein, recalling the color and the technique of the minstrel show.

It is all right to scout around for devious influences on Mark Twain's work, but it is downright foolish to neglect obvious native sources of his humor.

Mark Twain's first book was *The Celebrated Jumping Frog*, a collection of sketches. He referred to the title story as a sketch in a letter to Bret Harte written in May 1867, the month of publication of the book. "The book is out, and is handsome. It is full of damnable errors of grammar and deadly inconsistencies of spelling in the Frog sketch because I was away and did not read the proofs; but be a friend and say nothing about these things. When my hurry is over, I will send you an autograph copy to pisen the children with." He mentioned the book in a letter to his mother: "As for the Frog book, I don't believe that will ever pay anything worth a cent. I published it simply to advertise myself—not with the hope of making anything out of it." The book contained twenty-six sketches in addition to the title story.

His next book was *The Innocents Abroad*, published in 1869, which included four sketches. "Mark Twain's Burlesque Autobiography and First Romance" appeared in 1871, a pamphlet-sized little book. *Roughing It*, in 1872, included nine sketches. In 1874 a thin volume of sketches appeared under the title *Number One*. It was presumably the first in a series but the other numbers failed to materialize. *Sketches New and Old* was published in July of the following year. (The title was *Sketches Old and New* on the cover and *Sketches New and Old* on the title page.) A few of the pieces were new, but most were reprinted from the magazines and newspapers for which Clemens had been writing the past several years. "Answers from Correspondents" was in part from the *Californian*, "To Raise Poultry" was from the Buffalo *Express*, "My First Literary Venture" was from the *Galaxy*, "Information Wanted" was from the *New York Tribune*, "The Siamese Twins" was from *Packard's Monthly*, "Concerning Chambermaids" was from the New York *Weekly Review*, "Honored as a Curiosity" was from the Sacramento *Union*, "Curing a Cold" was from the *Golden Era*, and so on.

According to Paine, Clemens gave up the writing of sketches in 1871, when he relinquished his humor column in the monthly *Galaxy*. Around this time he also sold his one-third interest in the Buffalo *Express*. He was pressed for time now and wanted to devote himself more thoroughly to the writing of books. His old sketches kept appearing in his books, however—in *Punch, Brothers, Punch!* (1878), *The Stolen White Elephant* (1882), *The £1,000,000 Bank-Note* (1893), and several others. At the same time new sketches were written for the travel books— thirteen for *A Tramp Abroad* (1880), two for *Life on the Mississippi* (1883) (but one of these was lifted from a novel in progress), and two for *Following the Equator* (1897).

Mark Twain's sketches contain his brand of humor in what is perhaps its purest form. Here more than elsewhere he indulged in fun for its own sake. It is true that in his *Autobiography* he denied that he had ever been a humorist of the "mere" sort, but his practice belied him. In a discussion of a pirated edition of *Mark Twain's Library of Humor*, he said, "This book is a very interesting curiosity, in one way. It reveals the surprising fact that within the compass of these forty years wherein I have been playing professional humorist before the public, I have had for company seventy-eight other American humorists. Each and every one of the seventy-eight rose in my time, became conspicuous and popular, and by and by vanished. A number of these names were as familiar in their day as are the names of George Ade and Dooley today—yet they have all so completely passed from sight now that there is probably not a youth of fifteen years of age in the country whose eye would light with recognition at the mention of any one of the seventy-eight names. . . . In this mortuary volume I find Nasby, Artemus Ward, Yawcob Strauss, Derby, Burdette, Eli Perkins, the 'Danbury News Man,' Orpheus C. Kerr, Smith O'Brien, Josh Billings and a score of others, maybe two score, whose writings and sayings were once in everybody's mouth but are now heard of no more and are no longer mentioned. . . . Why have they perished? Because they were merely humorists. Humorists of the 'mere' sort cannot survive. Humor is only a fragrance, a decoration. Often it is merely an odd trick of speech and of spelling, as in the case of Ward and Billings and Nasby and the 'Disbanded Volunteer,' and presently the fashion passes and the fame along with it. There are those who say a novel should be a work of art solely and you must not preach in it, you must not teach in it. That may be true as regards novels but it is not true as regards humor. Humor must not professedly teach and it must not professedly preach, but it must do both if it would live forever. By forever, I mean thirty years. . . . I have always preached. That is the reason that I have lasted thirty years. If the humor came of its own accord and uninvited I have allowed it a place in my sermon but I was not writing the sermon for the sake of the humor. I should have written the sermon just the same, whether any humor applied for admission or not."

The reader need only read the present sketches to see that Mark Twain, fortunately, did not always consider it necessary to "preach." Nor did he always consider humor only a fragrance. Is laughter indeed only a fragrance, and is frowning the substance of life? Some of Mark Twain's "merely" humorous things *have* survived "forever"—because of their play of fancy, their wit, their fresh and always idiomatic prose. The vogue of coy illiteracy practiced by Ward and Billings was bound to die, if only because it represented not a way of seeing life but a way of exploiting tricks of style and manner. Clemens saw life as a strange and comic affair, and that is why his humor needs no surface help. Also, his statement notwithstanding, he was graced by the power to enjoy the comic aspect of things for its own sake, and to enjoy laughter as few have enjoyed it, with invective when he was aroused, but for the most part with a kindliness which makes the use of his great gift seem little short of epic.

New York
October 1960

THE STORIES

Nᴏᴛ ʟᴏɴɢ ᴀɢᴏ I happened to be reading Mark Twain's *Roughing It*, when I was piqued by his habit of inserting yarns of pure fiction in a non-fictional work, yarns tossed in just because they were good ones which he had in his head at the time. I counted five yarns or stories in *Roughing It* and wondered if there were others in some of his other non-fictional books. Sure enough, there were: two in *A Tramp Abroad*, three in *Life on the Mississippi*, and three in *Following the Equator*. "What a curious habit!" I thought. But Mark Twain is full of curious habits, both personal and literary, and you either love him or you don't, regardless. It is just his unconventionality, as a literary figure as well as a man, which makes him so appealing to those who like him.

"Strictly speaking, however, these yarns don't belong in the books which house them," I thought. "They belong with his other tales, the stories which are plainly recognized as such. They ought to be included in his collected stories. Let's see if they are." And so I went across the street to the Columbia University library, where I discovered, to my surprise, that his stories had never been put together apart from essays, anecdotes and the like.

Here is a man, a very great man, a national monument, you might say, who has been dead these forty-odd years without having had his stories collected, when lesser men, just recently dead, or still living, have had that mark of honor offered them by the publishing world and the public. Why? Is it because he is not a good writer of stories? But he is acknowledged to have written some great stories and I believe it is generally conceded that as a story writer he is among our best. Is it because his output was so large, varied and popular that his stories have been overshadowed—by the novels and travel books? Or is it because he is not a formalist and did not himself publish his short stories purely as such?

During his lifetime his stories appeared in volumes which I can only call hodgepodge, containing as they did anecdotes, jokes, letters, essays—all sorts of serious and humorous non-fiction along with the fiction. Mark Twain was a man who was very easygoing about border lines. Some of his short pieces fluctuate between fiction and fact. And he was a fellow who had very definite notions about the appeal of the grab bag. When he was a publisher himself he got Howells to edit a collection of accounts of true adventure. Howells put the pieces together according to a scheme, but after Clemens had looked at it he gently advised Howells to mix the things up, give them variety, so that the reader might be surprised. A formal scheme was about as appealing to him as a tight collar. This differed con-siderably from the French notions popular at the time and popular today. Perhaps it is his unconventionality, his insistence on formlessness, which has left his stories in the lurch.

Mark Twain was not unconscious of this formlessness. Whether he was rationalizing some literary defect or not when he was defending it, I do not know. I know he had a philosophy about it. Six years before his death, when he was dictating frag-ments of his autobiography, he felt impelled to explain the prac-tice of dictation. His explanation illuminates his general writing beliefs. I have quoted the following passage in the essay on the autobiography. With the reader's indulgence I should like to quote it again, but in a less abbreviated form.

"Within the last eight or ten years I have made several attempts to do the autobiography in one way or another with a pen, but the result was not satisfactory; it was too literary. With the pen in one's hand, narrative is a difficult art; narrative should flow as flows the brook down through the hills and the leafy wood-lands, its course changed by every bowlder it comes across and by every grass-clad gravelly spur that projects into its path; its surface broken, but its course not stayed by rocks and gravel on the bottom in the shoal places; a brook that never goes straight for a minute, but goes, and goes briskly, sometimes ungrammatically, and sometimes fetching a horseshoe three-quarters of a mile around, and at the end of the circuit flowing within a yard of the path it traversed an hour before; but always going, and always following at least one law, always loyal to that law, the law of narrative, which has no law. Nothing to do but make the trip; the how of it is not important, so that the trip is made.

"With a pen in the hand the narrative stream is a canal; it moves slowly, smoothly, decorously, sleepily, it has no blemish except that it is all blemish. It is too literary, too prim, too nice; the gait and style and movement are not suited to narrative. That canal stream is always reflecting; it is its nature, it can't help it. Its slick shiny surface is interested in everything it passes along the banks—cows, foliage, flowers, everything. And so it wastes a lot of time in reflections."

In almost any other writer's work it is easy to say, "This is a short story, whereas that is not." Take the cases of Joyce, Mann, James, Hemingway, Kafka, Lawrence. There is no hesitation about it: a short story belongs to a particular genre and has a relation to the whole of fictional writing in the same way that a water color has to the whole of painting, or a song to the whole of composition. Even in Chekhov it is easy to say what is a short story and what is not. I say "even" because his stories are so gentle in their shading, so clearly lacking in formalism (although not in form), that he of all the writers mentioned might cause some trouble in this respect. But in Mark Twain's case it is quite another matter. I have the sense that Clemens wrote primarily to satisfy an audience rather than the requirements of a genre. Whatever came to mind that aided his cause was grist for his mill. This is why we find sketches in which it is not possible to distinguish between fiction and fact.

He rarely bothered about the niceties of fiction. Fiction has a tone all its own, which the literary artist reveres. For him it is in a special sense greater than reality; it shapes reality, controls it. It is inconceivable to think of a James or a Flaubert inserting raw material, untransmuted, unmodulated, into his fictions. For Mark Twain such problems were beside the point. He simply disregarded them, although he was quite aware of them, a great deal more aware than he was accustomed to admit. Clemens had enough of the frontier spirit to dislike "form." Form was likely to be something eastern; or if not eastern then something worse: European. Henry James went to Europe to seek form, to saturate himself in it, the form of old societies, old art, old manners and buildings. Clemens went to Europe to poke fun at it and to make us laugh. The product of the frontier thought he could see where form was growing hollow and becoming a fraud.

Whatever a short story may be—and this is not the place to attempt to say exactly what it is or should be—we can say with some assurance what it is not. It is not a fragment of autobiography or biography; it is not a report, unalloyed, of a historical event; it is not a joke or a hoax pure and simple; it is not a moral sermon, whether taken down from the pulpit or not; it is not, in short, any of the small bits of writing which used to be produced in the old West for newspaper and magazine fillers and of which Mark Twain turned out a healthy share. A short story is something which, through the long process of evolution, has come to exist in and for itself. It has laws of its own, it is sovereign in its field. And it was already sovereign when Mark Twain began to write.

Clemens had the artistic temperament without too much of the artistic conscience. His genius was essentially Western, its strength the land, the people, their language and their humor. What he lacked was a studied Eastern conscience to refine the great ore he mined. Perhaps such a conscience would have inhibited and eventually ruined him. Probably he knew best what was necessary for him. What he had, he had in great measure: the naked power of the man with the gift of gab. He knew what a yarn was, and what it was for, and what to do with it. He did not think that a good yarn needs prettifying, and he told it straight, without trimmings. His high jinks are remarkable— his love of mugging, of monologue, dialect, caricature. He is a great proponent of the tall story, piling details on until the story comes crashing down. At his best he is uproarious, and he is often at his best in his stories.

It has been said that his stories are an important part of our literary heritage. It would be difficult, if not impossible, to dispute this statement successfully, presuming one cared to try. They are also part of our folklore. Mark Twain is our writer closest to folklore, our teller of fairy tales. The Jumping Frog story is a living American fairy tale, acted out annually in Calaveras County. "The Man That Corrupted Hadleyburg" is part of our moral heritage. These tales, together with several others, among them "The $30,000 Bequest" and "The £1,000,000 Bank-Note," have been anthologized many times. Others—tales of moral indignation such as "A Horse's Tale," and tales meant to shock, for example, "Captain Stormfield's Visit to Heaven," are no less powerful and important for being less popular. Who are our short-story writers? Irving, Hawthorne, Poe, James, Melville, O. Henry, Bret Harte, Hemingway, Faulkner, Porter—these are names which come to my mind without reflection, although my taste does not run to O. Henry and Harte, and finds much to quarrel with in Faulkner. Mark Twain's ranks high among them.

Clemens is a dangerous man to write about. Unless you approach him with a sense of humor you are lost. You cannot dissect a humorist upon a table. Your first stroke will kill him and make him a tragedian. You must come to Clemens with a smile. That is his prerogative: that he can make you do so or fail. A great American critic wrote a study of Mark Twain which was brilliant. The only trouble with it was he thought he was describing Mark Twain, when all along he was describing somebody else—himself, probably. The critic did not have a sense of humor, and his error was comparable to that of the tone-deaf critic who wrote on Beethoven. In Mark Twain it is not the line-by-line detail which is great, nor the day-by-day life—it is the mass, the contour, and the fragrance of a personality.

He poured his writing out in a stream, showering upon it all his gifts. Sometimes it carried everything before it but at others it failed naively. He was not the sort of versatile writer who is equally good at everything he puts his hand to. It is difficult to believe that he could have written fastidious travel essays like Hawthorne's or the delicate, subtle criticism of James; yet at times he appeared to be attempting both. He carried a broadsword which he sometimes tried to use on butterflies. He wrote very rapidly and was as proud as a boy of his daily output. He did not strive for the polished effect—or, rather, he strived for it too seldom. When his mood changed he stopped writing and put a manuscript away, sometimes for years. He was not a good judge of his work. Being essentially a man of humor, he was rarely humorless regarding himself in relation to his work. He was unlike Flaubert and Proust and James in this respect. To be humorless regarding oneself—or at least regarding one's work —can sometimes be a great advantage. To be well balanced does not guarantee better-grade work.

There is, in a good deal of his writing—in the Hadleyburg story, for example—a kind of naiveté which one feels is literary, a sort of refusal to infuse prose with the sophistication of the mature man. This no doubt reflects in some measure an attitude he had to the act of writing and to the nature of his audience. Writing was not the whole man. It may have even been at times the lesser man; and the audience, one seems to perceive, like his family, was largely composed of women: naive women, sheltered from the realities of a man's world. The moral pressure in Mark Twain's work is generally considerable; but the purely literary, the aesthetic, pressure is occasionally so low as to form only a trickle. This aesthetic pressure, impossible to define, is what is necessary to the creation of a work of art. In some cases it stems from moments of transcendent well-being, in others from the depths of frustration or despair; but whatever the causes, the pressure must be there, inside one, for the effect to be made. Too great a pressure may be as devastating to a work as too little, although writers like Mark Twain are more likely to suffer from too little.

In Clemens's case there is often something pleasant in even the lesser pages, precisely because of the low pressure: he is relaxed and his mood is infectious. He rarely tries to overreach himself, to strain after an effect of greatness. This lesson of being relaxed while writing, although a dangerous one for young writers, is an invaluable one for the mature ones. The right balance of pressure when one is about to sit down to work—one's health, one's relation to the material, one's linguistic resilience at the moment, the play of one's mind—is really what is called inspiration: the balance is everything: the container, which is one's own complex state, must exactly suit the thing contained, which is the raw material about to be transfigured into art. It is a pity that Mark Twain did not often take the pains to find the just balance for himself. But if he did not, he at least substituted another virtue. He says somewhere, wryly, that he had the habit of doing and of reflecting afterward. One contrasts this habit with an opposite one, the habit of reflecting to the point of disease, often found in the later works of Melville and James, as well as in portions of the works of Thomas Mann and Marcel Proust.

Mark Twain does not strive to be an artist—*artiste*, he probably would have called it with a grin. He would have felt more comfortable wearing the term journalist. He grew up a journalist, like Dickens, and was one of those hearty nineteenth-century scribblers who strayed into literature almost without realizing it. He had the journalist's instinct, in the way Defoe had, and in the way Hawthorne and James did not. This is not necessarily a handicap in the creation of literature. In so far as it stimulates a sense of audience, a sense of common scene, and the use of native speech and lore—in so far, that is, that it inspires one to attempt a colloquy in common terms but with uncommon genius, it is a definite and rare gift. Its limitations are likely to be great also, the limitations of the known, and especially what is known to the particular group. Mark Twain's writing was almost always a means to an end. He had few impersonal objectives in mind in the way of form, experiment, texture, design. He had the common touch and knew it was a blessing. He was enriched by it and made world-famous.

He possessed in a limited degree the craft discipline of the writer who *sees* his prose, who carefully examines it, watching for design and effect, while at the same time listening to its music. Flaubert and Joyce were writers who intensely saw, and it is by no accident that we find in their work a brilliance of visual images. The visual intelligence can act as a tight check on the aural one; the latter may run wild, like a weed, until one is writing sound for its own sake. James in his later phase dictated much of his fiction, and as a result his work of that period is marked by prolixity, dilution, and sometimes a vagueness of meaning. Of course, it can be argued that he adopted dictation to satisfy the requirements of a genius which was declining. The trouble here is that it would be a difficult task to chart and to prove the actual falling off of his genius apart from the mannerisms which had begun to afflict it. One wonders if the visual sense in literature, especially in terms of formal design, has not overreached itself in our century with the production of works like Joyce's *Ulysses*, Mann's *Joseph and his Brethren*, and parts of the great Proust novel, and if the impetus to their excesses was not at least partly the excesses of the aural sense, as witnessed in a writer like Dickens.

It is a large part of Mark Twain's greatness that he heard so well. His dialogue is extraordinary. One sometimes wonders if he had a phonographic memory. His ability to imitate styles of speech, with a vast array of accurate detail, is truly remarkable. Paine has written: "At dinner, too, it was his habit, between the courses, to rise from the table and walk up and down the room, waving his napkin and talking—talking in a strain and with a charm that he could never quite equal with his pen. It is the opinion of most people who knew Mark Twain personally that his impromptu utterances, delivered with that ineffable quality of speech, manifested the culmination of his genius." Mark Twain and the oral tradition: both are related to the frontier. Yet some of his chief faults stem directly from this side of his genius—an occasional looseness of texture, a kind of stage or vaudeville timing for effect, an overindulgence in burlesque, a sense as if he were lecturing from a platform. Early in his public career he achieved success as a lecturer and as a maker of speeches, and no doubt this success, this practice, this buttressed confidence in a talent he long must have known he possessed, had a crucial influence upon his work.

There is a certain transparency in Clemens's work, like that to be found in fairy tales. One senses the machinery behind the silken screen. But in this very transparency there is a kind of potency also found in the fairy tales, a foreknowledge of events, a delight in repetition, in the spelling out of the known, a sort of tribal incantation. There is also something abstract in certain of his fictions, some sort of geometric approach to the art of narrative which, to the modern reader, is not quite satisfying. I refer to pieces like *The American Claimant* and *The Tragedy of Pudd'nhead Wilson*. The latter is a very imperfect work whose imperfections are traceable to its conception, or rather misconception, a fact which Mark Twain himself has revealed at some length. But when he speaks out of his own mouth, with the drawl and idiom and dialect, as he does in so many of his stories, he is unique, inspired, zany, wonderful.

This man loved a gimmick the way the frontier loved a practical joke. He claimed to be the first private user of the telephone; the first author to use a typewriter; the first author to dictate into a phonograph recording machine. He fooled around with inventions with the passion of an inveterate gambler, and lost his shirt. A literary gimmick sometimes caused him to lose his literary shirt. His favorite of his own books was his *Joan of Arc*, which purports to be the recollections of a friend of Joan's. It is sentimental and dull, as it was likely to be, not being done in Mark Twain's own voice and style.

It is a fact that Clemens, like many other nineteenth-century novelists, is sometimes guilty of padding. This is often due to the economics of book production of his day. The two-volume work, often sold by subscription, often serialized, was as much the thing in those days as it is not now. If a man had only a book and a half in him, that was too bad; he had to get up the half somehow or throw in the towel. The effect of this can be seen all the way from Dickens to James. Forgetting this, we are likely to recall the size of nineteenth-century novels and think, "There were giants in those days." There *were* giants, but the fact remains that many of the novels of the previous century can stand pruning, from our point of view.

There is a new kind of padding which has come to flower in our own century, a kind not due to economics of book production, a kind which almost deliberately flies in the face of economics—the padding of Joyce, Proust, Mann, Faulkner. I suspect this sort has as its motive a gentle and harmless variety of megalomania, the desire to fill up culs-de-sac in such a way that no one can add a pound to them. It is time that the novel of elegant proportions returned to fashion and worth—the novel which by its intensity, elasticity, form and overtones achieves what the older ones have achieved through bulk. A whale is not by definition superior to a shark.

It is almost needless to add that in the story the impulse or the need to pad was at a minimum, and that consequently there is more economy of effect in Mark Twain's stories than in most of his book-size works. One might even say that he felt most at home in the story, that it was the form most congenial to him, lover as he was of the yarn. It was the form which most effectively brought out his particular "voice." Some of his full-size books are more like a series of yarns strung together than works with an indigenous structure.

Despite his great successes he remained an unfulfilled, unintegrated writer of uncertain taste. In *A Tramp Abroad*, for example, his desire was often for serious description of scene, influenced by the beauty of the landscape and the fact he had kept accurate notes. This conflicted with a desire to be funny, or a nervousness because he feared his reader's attention was flagging. He broke up his descriptions with unfunny insertions of outlandish foreign words and phrases, creating a hodgepodge that was in poor taste, dull, and an affront to his considerable descriptive talents. His autobiography is a good example, although a late one, of his uncertain taste. He did not—he could not—write it in sequence, but drifted here and there, wherever idle memory (not always dependable) and a wandering stream of associations led him, at times lingering over minor events and hurrying past important ones. It is an important and neglected American document, justly neglected inasmuch as it is almost unreadable in its present form, the sequence of events garbled, and bits of daily journalism thrown in from the period in which he was composing it. And yet at its best it is remarkable and needs only a skilled hand to put it together properly. It is ready to emerge as a classic of its kind, although at present it is in the stage of being raw material. Twain did not always recognize the difference between raw material and the polished product, just as Henry James, inversely, sometimes mistook the polish of his prose for the material of life itself.

Mark Twain at his most balanced is likely to be found in his letters, where he could be himself, without having to please what he believed to be his audience and to satisfy his audience's demand (whether real or imaginary) for more of the Twain brand of humor. He was in a sense the slave of his audience; or, more justly, the slave of what he conceived to be his duty toward his audience. When Clemens is truly himself he is magnificent. How beautifully, how truly, how movingly he can write in the midst of deep emotion, as when he set down his thoughts immediately after the death of his daughter Jean. There is no false tone, no striving in his prose then. You sense he is a *man*, unique and great, honest, noble, in some ways sublime.

His best books, with the exception of his travel books, are those with a Western scene; and his travel books largely owe their humor, their geniality and their wisdom to his Western orientation. The sentimentality of the frontier, which ranged all the way from an exaggerated regard for females to the most deadly sort of sadism; the lack of form in social behavior, together with certain codes of behavior which smack of juvenile delinquents; the relative contempt for the written as against the spoken word; the racy language; the attitudes toward dudes and the East, the two being almost synonymous; the impatience with the ways and principles of law—all these characteristics of the American frontier are to be found in Mark Twain's best work. They are also to be found, in somewhat more disguised form, in the work of his star descendant, Ernest Hemingway.

A man from Missouri, Clemens said "Show me" skeptically to Europe and the world. This was a novel concept to the East, where reverence for Europe among literary men was in vogue, as it is today. Paris, Rome, London are still considered the seats of literary learning; or if not learning, of literary practice; or if not practice, of literary conscience. Clemens knew better. To the Westerner Europe seems remote, and its concerns—its stale concerns—seem almost perversely imagined, or at any rate like a long-forgotten but still-remembered dream, a bitterness on the tongue, a haunting disquiet in some dim corner of the mind. The climate and the great spaces speak eloquently of today and to-morrow. Europe, like the East, is a pallid yesterday.

Clemens could be sardonic in turning the tables and exposing a bluff. It had been fashionable, up to his time, for Europeans, some of them prominent literary figures like Dickens, to write sarcastic reports on the "raw" United States. Clemens, a self-appointed ambassador, returned the compliment with interest, offering a tongue-in-cheek view of the American as progressive, the European as a piece of baroque humanity. The salt in the wound was that there was much truth in this view, as Hawthorne had already hinted in his *English Note-books*. Mark Twain never struck upon a happier symbol than the German language, which he satirized so penetratingly and with such wit that even many Germans laughed and appreciated the truth of what he implied. Clemens has a wonderful wisdom. He is so essentially sane that it is exhilarating to be in his company. By his way of life he seemed to say, "I am of the tribe of writers but I am saner than they. I know how to savor life." You expect a man like that to live a long life. He did, like Tolstoy, and like Tolstoy he managed very often to write without contrived effects.

It has happened in other countries that what was once looked upon condescendingly as being unworthy of art became, almost overnight, the body and soul of the highest art. It happened in Germany and in Russia early in the last century. I believe it will happen in our own country when Western legends and myths, Western folklore, become the basis of a sophisticated art. There is no lack of snobbism among Eastern intellectuals toward Western materials. Some academic writers and critics, who enjoy Western films, deride the notion that in the more serious realm of the novel the same materials can be used to good and true effect. The frontier may be closed, finished; no doubt it is—the geographical one. But there are other frontiers—the frontier of a cultural *tone*, for example. These are important also. They contain elements which the geographical frontier created or inspired. The frontier has gone underground, and if this is a calamity to the adventurer it is not necessarily so to the artist, in particular the writer. There is a free-swinging sense of things in the West which has long been missing in the East. The ghost of Europe hovers over the East.

It seems to me that the West will produce a great and fertile literature and that this literature, although it will be free in tone and speech in a way the New England literature could not be, will nevertheless be sophisticated, will know what it is about, will understand the meaning of heritage and tradition as well as of rebellion, and of its place in the great stream of literature and the arts. That it has not come into its own during the last half-century need not be held against it. Its practitioners are unfortunately parochial, and either unnecessarily resentful of the East or afraid of it. Perhaps the greatest and most successful users of Western materials will not be Westerners at all. They need not be. They may very well be Easterners.

Clemens's personal influence during his lifetime was great. His literary influence has also been considerable, not only among humorists but also among American novelists. Hemingway's prose of action and his language of speech owe much to Mark Twain's work. Hemingway himself has said that American literature begins with one book, *Huckleberry Finn*—an obvious exaggeration in his fashion, but indicative of his regard for Mark Twain. Clemens is a muscular writer, he is par excellence the writer who calls a spade a spade, the writer who is intent on making an accurate correspondence between reality as he has experienced it and reality as it emerges in his books. This too is what Hemingway is after. It is Hemingway's passion. What makes him great is that he has had the vision to sense where in this complex world he can come to grips with what, for him, is a real experience; the courage to seek these places out and, in James's term, saturate himself in them; and the passion to find the words—the fresh words, in his own style—to fit his experience. Like Mark Twain, Hemingway gives the impression of being only incidentally a great writer. The writing follows upon his life. This is far from the example of James and Flaubert, who seemed to live only for their work and whose passion, morality, intelligence and religion were dissolved and sacrificed in their work.

Twain's fashion has dimmed in the last forty years. He is seen to belong to another era, the era of chromos and linsey-woolsey, of an extraordinary optimism, of a degree of national self-criticism rarely now enjoyed. Despite his frontier manliness he is too frilly, too juvenile, too surrounded by females to entirely please the national taste. But he is a solid monument in American letters and an invaluable lesson for our young novelists. That lesson is: do not neglect your native sources; remember that yesterday's journalism may become tomorrow's literature; steep yourself in the living speech; and do not forget that the life of humor is long and that the Muse does not insist you wear a frown when you work.

Pacific Palisades, California
July 1956

LIFE AS I FIND IT

W ITH ONE EXCEPTION, none of the items in this book,* although many are of considerable importance, was included in the august and expensive version of Mark Twain's collected works subtitled the "Definitive Edition" and issued more than a decade after his death. Whether they were included in any of the earlier and less comprehensive editions I have not troubled myself to discover, but I have seen enough of those editions to doubt it. The exception was "The Indignity Put Upon the Remains . . . ," which Paine rescued from the files of *The Galaxy* magazine and which he reprinted as one of the many appendixes of his biography of Clemens, issued almost half a century ago and later included in the Definitive Edition.

The Definitive Edition is eccentric in a few other respects. Volume XIX contains "Speech on the Babies" (pp. 397–401) and "Speech on the Weather" (pp. 402–6). Volume XXVIII contains the same speeches but with abbreviated titles: "The Weather" (pp. 53–57) and "The Babies" (pp. 58–62). These are only examples, not the complete record.

It is a curious fact of Mark Twain scholarship and publishing that fifty years after his death it is possible to put together a volume such as the present one, in which a large majority of the items make their first appearance in book form.

A glance at my sources will show the reader that I have revived many of the items which Mark Twain wrote for *The Galaxy*. *The Galaxy* was a literary monthly which flourished from 1866 to 1878 and which ended its career by merging with —or rather, being absorbed by—the *Atlantic Monthly*. The being absorbed by the *Atlantic* was not without its irony, inasmuch as the original intention of the founders of *The Galaxy* was to

Mark Twain: Life As I Find It, Doubleday, 1961.

establish a New York rival to the prestigious Boston *Atlantic*. Boston in those days was dominant in the field of American letters and published the leading quarterly, the *North American Review*, as well as the leading monthly, the *Atlantic*. The *Atlantic* habitually devoted a large part of its space to New England writers and matters and was regarded in certain quarters as having an exclusive attitude toward New York.

In its time *The Galaxy* published many of the interesting writers of the day, including Henry James, Walt Whitman, Trollope, Turgeniev and Bret Harte. Despite its several attempts it failed to persuade James Russell Lowell, that *Atlantic* lion, to contribute. The magazine was founded and edited by two New York brothers. It first appeared in 1866, and by the spring of 1870 was able to boast of having Mark Twain as a monthly contributor. Clemens conducted a humorous department which he called "Memoranda." It is worth noting that his department appeared near the end of each issue and was in double columns per page, whereas most of each issue was in single columns. It was not a good billing for one who was already enormously popular as a result of the publication of *The Innocents Abroad*. Mark Twain's first contribution appeared in May 1870 and his final one in April 1871. In the latter he wrote in explanation: "For the last eight months, with hardly an interval, I have had for my fellows and comrades, night and day, doctors and watchers of the sick! During these eight months death has taken two members of my home circle and malignantly threatened two others. All this I have experienced, yet all the time been under contract to furnish 'humorous' matter once a month for this magazine. . . ." It was only part of the story. He was being pressed for time, he wanted to devote himself to writing the more profitable books, and he was hoping to leave journalism as a regular occupation.

The Galaxy's editors continued the humorous department under the name of "Galaxy Club-Room." It became a miscellany of material supplied by several writers. In 1873 the magazine abandoned its attempt at a special department of humor.

A number of the pieces in the present volume appeared in a

book of limited circulation issued in 1919, whose title was *The Curious Republic of Gondour and Other Whimsical Sketches.* I have reprinted them because in some instances the text of this book is at variance with that of the original published text, and because the pieces deserve to be better known.

"Open Letter to Commodore Vanderbilt" is a brilliant example of Mark Twain's early social criticism and personal invective. It appeared in *Packard's Monthly* in 1869 and has been reprinted only once, I believe, as a pamphlet of very limited circulation. Its facts may at times be vulnerable—as a reader wrote to *Packard's* in defense of the Commodore—but this probably did not disturb Clemens and need not bother us much now. I am happy to be able to print the piece in book form for the first time—in the English language. I must add "in the English language" because it is possible that it is already in volume form in the Soviet Union. When I spoke last November with a Professor Mendelson of Moscow, a Russian scholar interested in Mark Twain, he informed me that "Open Letter to Commodore Vanderbilt" would be included in the new Soviet twelve-volume edition of Mark Twain's works. One could see that the Russians had been busy looking up the uncollected pieces with the desire to add to the canon of Mark Twain's criticism of America.

I was informed that the Soviet edition would include "quite a few works" that have not appeared in American editions, among them "The Curious Republic of Gondour" and "King Leopold's Soliloquy." Professor Mendelson was in a position to give me accurate information, for he was a member of the editorial board in charge of publishing the twelve-volume edition, for which there are 300,000 subscribers. Eight volumes have already been published, he said. About one third of the final volume will be devoted to the autobiography and will include chapters from my edition. Although my edition was blasted in Moscow, with the charge that the hitherto unpublished chapters which it contained were of "poor quality," these same chapters were judged fit to print in the collected works, after having been published in *Crocodile*, a Russian magazine of large circulation, and in *Hammer and Sickle*, an Estonian magazine—without a kopeck of royalty either to me or to the Mark Twain Estate. The Russians refuse to sign a copyright treaty with us. I wonder if the twelve-volume edition will contain any of the fiery articles on copyright which Clemens got off in his lifetime.

"Goldsmith's Friend Abroad Again" is a story which deserves to be much better known. "The Noble Red Man" is a peppery bit of satire which has never been reprinted and which is easily as good as many of the essays or articles in the collected works. "The Coming Man" is—— But let the reader judge for himself whether these stories, sketches and articles are worth preserving.

"King Leopold's Soliloquy" was written as a savage protest against the excesses of King Leopold II's rule in the Congo territory. It appeared (1905) at a time when much of the Western world had already been aroused to the consequences of Leopold's personal rule in the Congo, but Clemens's voice had a stature that sharply focused general attention on the evident injustices. The pamphlet elicited countercharges from Brussels that it contained inaccuracies, which was no doubt true, but truer was the long and unexampled exploitation of a primitive people for the enrichment of a modern sovereign who claimed to be a devoted Christian. Eventually Belgium took over the administration of the Congo and instituted various reforms. The current confusion, violence and hatred of whites in the Congo has a background of Belgian colonization and rule, abetted by the great powers (including the United States), which it is not pleasant to contemplate.

The illustrated pamphlet sold for 25¢. It had a gray cover containing a motif of a crucifix and a butcher's knife crossed, with the motto, "By this sign we prosper." The proceeds of the sale of the pamphlet were donated by Clemens to the Congo Reform Association. An Englishman connected with the association, E. D. Morel, had, in 1904, brought to Clemens's attention the deteriorating situation in the Congo. Morel wrote a few years later: "I can see him now, pacing up and down his bedroom in uncontrollable indignation, breaking out ever and again with his favourite exclamation, 'By George!'; or with some rapid, searching question."

I have included a sampling of newspaper interviews, with the full knowledge that Mark Twain was on the whole distrustful of interviews. They are obviously not to be regarded in the same light as his signed work. Nevertheless, many of them sound authentic, some were dictated or signed, and a number contain valuable information. All of them amuse, and they bring back those days in which Mark Twain played a conspicuous part. I believe this is the first collection of interviews to be published. I have not attempted to be inclusive or to go far afield. I have merely tried to show something of what the old files contain.

New York
March 1961

APPENDIX

THE BEARS

BY DAVID CROCKETT

"The Bears" is composed of four separate hunting tales which are to be found in the anonymous Sketches and Eccentricities of Col. David Crockett of West Tennessee, *a volume entered for copyright in the name of J. & J. Harper in the Clerk's Office of the Southern District of New York November 14, 1833. A variant edition,* The Life and Adventures of Colonel David Crockett, of West Tennessee, *was entered for copyright in the same year by J. S. French, the presumed author of the book, in the Clerk's Office of the District Court of the district of Ohio. I have made one narrative of the four tales and have edited them.—C. N.*

WELL AS I told you it's been a custom with me ever since I moved to this country to spend a part of every winter in bear hunting unless I was engaged in public life. I generally take a tent, pack horses and a friend 'long with me and go down to the Shakes, where I camp out and hunt till I git tired or till I git as much meat as I want. I do this because there's a great deal of game there; besides, I never see anybody but the friend I carry. I like to hunt in a wilderness, where nobody can disturb me.

Sometime in the winter of '24 or '25 a friend called to see me to take a bear hunt. I was in the humor, so we got our pack horses, fixed up our tent and provisions and set out for the Shakes. We arrived there safe, raised our tent, stored away our provisions and commenced hunting. For several days we were quite successful. We brought our game to the tent, salted it and packed it away. We had several hunts and nothing occurred worth telling save that we killed our game.

But one evening as we were coming along, our pack horses loaded with bear meat and our dogs trotting after us, old Whirlwind held up his head and looked about, then rubbed his nose

agin a bush and opened. I knew from the way he sung out 'twas
an old he bear. The balance of the dogs buckled in and off they
went right up a hollow. I give up the horses to my friend to
carry 'em to the tent, which was now about half a mile distant,
and set out after the dogs.

The hollow up which the bear had gone made a bend and I
knew he would follow it, so I run across to head him. The sun
was down now. 'Twas growing dark mighty fast and 'twas cold,
so I buttoned my jacket close round me and run on. I hadn't gone
fur before I heard the dogs tack and they come a tearing right
down the hollow. Presently I heard the old bear rattling through
the cane and the dogs coming on like lightning after him. I run
on. I felt like I had wings, my dogs made such a roaring cry.
They rushed by me and as they did I harked 'em on. They all
broke out and the woods echoed back, and back. It seemed to
me they flew, for 'twasn't long before they overhauled him and
I could hear 'em fighting not fur before me. I run on but just
before I got there the old bear made a break and got loose. But
the dogs kept close up and every once in a while they stopped
him and had a fight. I tried for my life to git up but just before
I'd git there he'd break loose. I followed him this way for two
or three mile, through briars, cane and such stuff, and he
devilled me.

Once I thought I had him. I got up to about fifteen or twenty
feet of him. 'Twas so dark I couldn't tell the bear from a dog
and I started to go to him but found there was a crick between
us. How deep it was I didn't know but it was dark and cold and
too late to turn back, so I held my rifle up and walked in. Before
I got across, the old bear got loose and shot for it, right through
the cane. I was mighty tired but I scrambled out and followed
on. I knew I was obliged to keep in hearing of my dogs or git
lost.

Well, I kept on, and once in a while I could hear 'em fighting
and baying just before me. Then I'd run up but before I'd git
there the old bear would git loose. I sometimes thought 'bout
giving up and going back but while I'd be thinking they'd begin
to fight agin and I'd run on. I followed him this way 'bout, as

near as I could guess, from four to five mile, when the old bear couldn't stand it any longer and took to a tree, and I tell you I was mighty glad of it. I went up but at first it was so dark I could see nothing. However, after looking about and gitting the tree between me and a star I could see a very dark looking place and I raised up old Betsy and she lightened. Down come the old bear. But he wasn't much hurt, for of all the fights you ever did see, that beat all. I had six dogs and for nearly an hour they kept rolling and tumbling right at my feet. I couldn't see anything but one old white dog I had. But every now and then the bear made 'em sing out right under me. I had my knife drawn, to stick him whenever he should seize me. But after a while bear, dogs and all rolled down a precipice just before me and I could hear 'em fighting like they were in a hole. I loaded Betsy, laid down and felt about in the hole with her till I got her agin the bear, and I fired. But I didn't kill him, for out of the hole he bounced and he and the dogs fought harder than ever. I laid old Betsy down and drew my knife but the bear and dogs just formed a lump, rolling about, and presently down they all went agin into the hole.

My dogs now begun to sing out mighty often. They were gitting tired, for it had been the hardest fight I ever see. I found out how the bear was laying and I looked for old Betsy to shoot him again but I had laid her down somewhere and couldn't find her. I got hold of a stick and begun to punch him. He didn't seem to mind it much, so I thought I would git down into the crack and kill him with my knife. I considered some time 'bout this. It was ten or eleven o'clock and a cold winter night. I was something like thirty mile from any settlement. There was no living soul near me except my friend, who was in the tent, and I didn't know where that was. I knew my bear was in a crack made by the Shakes but how deep it was and whether I could git out if I got in were things I couldn't tell. I was setting down right over the bear thinking, and every once in a while some of my dogs would sing out as if they wanted help. So I got up and let myself down in the crack behind the bear.

Where I landed was about as deep as I am high. I felt mighty

ticklish and wished I was out. I couldn't see a thing in the world
but I determined to go through with it. I drew my knife and kept
feeling about with my hands and feet till I touched the bear. This
I did very gently, then I got pretty fur up. I stuck it into him. He
sunk down and for a moment there was a great struggle. But by
the time I scrambled out everything was gitting quiet and my
dogs, one at a time, come out after me and laid down at my feet.
I knew everything was safe.

It begun now to cloud up. 'Twas mighty dark and as I didn't
know the direction of my tent I determined to stay all night. I
took out my flint and steel and raised a little fire. But the wood
was so cold and wet it wouldn't burn much. I had sweated so
much after the bear that I begun to git very thirsty and felt like
I would die if I didn't git some water. So, taking a light along, I
went to look for the crick I had waded. As good luck would have
it I found the crick and got back to my bear. But from having
been in a sweat all night I was now very chilly. It was the middle of winter and the ground was hard frozen for several inches
but this I had not noticed before. I agin set to work to build me
a fire but all I could do wouldn't make it burn. The excitement
under which I had been laboring had all died away and I was so
cold I felt very much like dying. But a notion struck me to git my
bear up out of the crack, so down into it I went, and worked until
I got into a sweat agin. And just as I would git him so high that if I
could turn him over once more he'd be out, he'd roll back. I kept
working, and resting, and while I was at it it begun to hail
mighty fine. But I kept on, and in about three hours I got
him out.

I then come up almost exhausted. My fire had gone out and I
laid down and soon fell asleep. But 'twasn't long before I waked
almost frozen. The wind sounded mighty cold as it passed along
and I called my dogs and made 'em lie upon me to keep me warm.
But it wouldn't do. I thought I ought to make some exertion to
save my life and I got up, but I don't know why or wherefore,
and begun to grope about in the dark. The first thing I hit agin
was a tree. It felt mighty slick and icy as I hugged it, and a notion
struck me to climb it. So up I started, and I climbed that tree for

thirty feet before I come to any limb, and then slipped down. It was warm work. How often I climbed it I never knew but I was going up and slipping down for three or four hours, and when day first begun to break I was going up that tree. As soon as it was light I saw before me a slim sweetgum, so slick it looked like every varmint in the woods had been sliding down it for a month.

I started off and found my tent, where sat my companion, who had given me up for lost. I had been distant about five miles. After resting I brought my friend to see the bear. I had run more perils than those described. I had been all night on the brink of a chasm, where a slip of a few feet would have brought about instant death. It almost made my head giddy to look at the dangers I had escaped. My friend swore he would not have gone in the crack that night with a wounded bear for everyone in the woods. We had as much meat as we could carry, so we loaded our horses and set out for home.

I was setting by a good fire in my little cabin on a cool November evening—roasting potatoes, I believe, and playing with my children—when somebody halloed at the fence. I went out and there were three strangers, who said they come to take an elk hunt. I was glad to see 'em, invited 'em in, and after supper we cleaned our guns. I took down old Betsy, rubbed her up, greased her and laid her away to rest. She is a mighty rough old piece but I love her, for she and I have seen hard times. She mighty seldom tells me a lie. If I hold her right she always sends the ball where I tell her. After we were all fixed I told 'em hunting stories till bed time.

Next morning was clear and cold, and by times I sounded my horn and my dogs come howling 'bout me, ready for a chase. Old Rattler was a little lame. A bear bit him in the shoulder. But Soundwell, Tiger and the rest of 'em were all mighty anxious. We got a bite and saddled our horses. I went by to git a neighbor to drive for us and off we started for the Harricane. My dogs looked mighty wolfish. They kept jumping on one another and growling. I knew they were rum mad for a fight, for they hadn't had one in two or three days. We were in fine spirits and going 'long through very open woods when one of the strangers said, "I'd give my horse now to see a bear." Said I, "Well, give me your horse," and pointed to an old bear about three or four hundred yards ahead of us, feeding on acorns. I had been looking at him for some time but he was so fur off I wasn't certain what it was.

However, I hardly spoke before we all strained off, and the woods echoed as we harked the dogs on. The old bear didn't want to run. He never broke till we got most upon him. But then he buckled for it, I tell ye. When they overhauled him he just rared up on his hind legs and boxed the dogs 'bout at a mighty rate. He hugged old Tiger and another till he dropped 'em nearly lifeless but the others worried him and after a while they all come to and they give him trouble. They are mighty apt, I tell ye, to give a bear trouble before they leave him. 'Twas a mighty pretty fight. 'Twould have done anyone's soul good to see it, just to see how they all rolled about. It was as much as I could do to keep the strangers from shooting him. But I wouldn't let 'em, for fear they would kill some of my dogs. After we got tired seeing 'em fight I went in among 'em and the first time they got him down I socked my knife into him. We then hung him up and went on to take our elk hunt. You never seed fellows so delighted as them strangers was. Blow me if they didn't cut more capers, jumping about, than the old bear. 'Twas a mighty pretty fight but I b'lieve I seed more fun looking at them than at the bear.

By the time we got to the Harricane we were all rested and ripe for a drive. My dogs were in a better humor, for the fight had just taken off the wiry edge. So I placed the strangers at the stands through which I thought the elk would pass, sent the driver way up ahead, and I went down below. Everything was quiet. I leaned old Betsy 'gin a tree and laid down. I s'pose I had been lying there nearly an hour when I heard old Tiger open. He opened once or twice and old Rattler give a long howl. The balance joined in and I knew the elk were up. I jumped up and grabbed my rifle. I could hear nothing but one continued roar of all my dogs, coming right towards me. Though I was an old hunter the music made my hair stand on end. Soon after they first started I heard one gun go off, and my dogs stopped, but not long, for they took a little tack towards where I placed the strangers. One of them fired and they dashed back and circled round way to my left. I run down 'bout a quarter of a mile and I heard my dogs make a bend like they was coming to me. While I was listening I heard the bushes breaking still lower down and started to run there.

As I was going 'long I seed two elk break out of the Harricane 'bout one hundred and thirty or forty yards below me. There was an old buck and a doe. I stopped, waited till they got into a clean place, and as the old fellow made a leap I raised old Bet, pulled trigger and she spoke out. The smoke blinded me so I couldn't see what I did. But as it cleared away I caught a glimpse of only one of 'em going through the bushes, so I thought I had the other. I went up and there lay the old buck a kicking. I cut his throat and by that time the Tiger and two of my dogs come up. I thought it strange that all my dogs wasn't there and I begun to think they had killed another. After the dogs had bit him and found out he was dead old Tiger begun to growl and curled himself up between his legs. Everything had to stand off then, for he wouldn't let the devil himself touch him.

I started off to look for the strangers. My two dogs followed me. After gitting away a piece I looked back and once in a while I could see old Tiger git up and shake the elk to see if he was really dead and then curl up between his legs agin. I found the strangers round a doe elk the driver had killed. One of 'em said he was sure he had killed one lower down. I asked him if it had horns. He said he didn't see any. I put the dogs on where he said he had shot and they didn't go fur before they come to a halt. I went up and there lay a fine buck elk. Though his horns were four or five feet long the fellow who shot him was so scared that he never seed 'em. We had three elk and a bear. So we managed to git it home, then butchered our game, talked over our hunt and had a glorious frolic.

One day I was out hunting with a friend and I was going 'long down to a little Harricane 'bout three mile from our tent, where I knew there must be a plenty of bear. 'Twas mighty cold and my dogs were in fine order and very busy hunting, when I seed where a piece of bark had been scratched off a tree. I said to my companion, "There's a bear in the holler of this tree." I examined the sign and knew I was right. I called my dogs but to git at him was the thing. The tree was so large 'twould take all day to cut it down and there was no chance to climb it. But upon looking about I found that there was a tree near the one the bear was in, and if I could make it fall agin it I could then climb up and git him out. I fell to work and cut the tree down but, as the devil would have it, it lodged before it got there. So that scheme was knocked in the head.

I then told my companion to cut away upon the big tree and I would go off some distance to see if I couldn't see him. He fell to work and he hadn't been at it long before I seed the old bear poke his head out. But I couldn't shoot him, for if I did I would hit him in the head and he would fall backwards. So I had to wait for him to come out. I didn't say anything but it wasn't a minute before he run out on a limb and jumped down.

I run as hard as I could but before I got there he and the dogs were hard at it. I didn't see much of the fight before they all rolled down a steep hill and the bear got loose and broke right in the direction of the Harricane. He was a mighty large one and I was 'fraid my dogs would lose him, 'twas such a thick place. I started after him and told my friend to come on. Well, of all the thick places that ever you *did* see, that bear carried me through some of the thickest. The dogs would sometimes bring him to bay and I would try for my life to git up to 'em but when I would git there he would git loose. He devilled me mightily, I tell ye. I reckon I went a mile after that bear upon my hands and knees, just creeping through briars, and if I hadn't had dear-leather clothes on they would have torn me in pieces.

I got wet and was mighty tired stooping so much. Sometimes I went through places so thick I don't see how anything could git through; and I don't b'lieve I could if I hadn't heard the dogs fighting just before me. Sometimes I would look back and I couldn't see how I got along. But once I got in a clear place. My dogs, tired of fighting, had brought the bear agin to bay and I had my head up, looking out to git a shoot, when the first thing I know I was up to my breast in a sink hole of water. I was so infernal mad I had a notion not to git out. But I begun to think it wouldn't spite anybody, so I scrambled out. My powder was all wet except the load in my gun and I didn't know what to do. I had been sweating all morning and I was tired but I harked my dogs on and once more I heard 'em fighting. I run on and while I was going 'long I heard something jump in the water. When I got there I seed the bear going up the other bank of the Obion River. I hadn't time to shoot him before he was out of sight. He looked mighty tired. When I come to look at my dogs I could hardly help from crying. Old Tiger and Brutus was setting on the edge of the water, whining because they couldn't git over. I had a mighty good dog named Carlow. He was standing in the water ready to swim. I observed as the water passed by him it was right red. He was badly cut. When I come to notice my other dogs they were all right bloody and it made me so mad that I harked 'em on and determined to kill the bear.

I hardly spoke to 'em before there was a general plunge, and each of my dogs just formed a streak going straight across. I watched 'em till they got out on the bank, when they all shook themselves. Old Carlow opened and off they all went. I set down on an old log. The water was right red where my dogs jumped in and I loved 'em so much it made me mighty sorry. When I come to think how willingly they all jumped in when I told 'em, though they were badly cut and tired to death, I thought I ought to go and help 'em.

It was now about twelve o'clock. My dogs had been running ever since sunrise and we had all passed through a Harricane, which of itself was a day's work. I could hear nothing of my companion. I whooped but there was no answer. I concluded he had been unable to follow me and had gone back to the tent. I looked up and down the river to see if there was a chance to cross it but there was none. No canoe was within miles of me. While I was thinking of all these things my dogs were trailing. But all at once I heard 'em fighting. I jumped up—I hardly knew what to do—when a notion struck me to roll in the log I had been setting on and cross over on that. 'Twas a part of an old tree, twelve or fifteen feet long, lying on a slant. I got an old limb, straddled the log with my feet in the water, and pushed off. 'Twas mighty ticklish work. I had to lay the limb across, like a balance pole, to keep me from turning over, and then paddle with the hand that wasn't holding the rifle. The log didn't float good and the water come up over my thighs. After a while I got over safe, fastened my old log to go back upon, and as I went up the bank I heard my dogs tree. I run to 'em as fast as I could and sure enough I seed the old bear up in a crotch. My dogs was all lying down under him and I don't know which was the most tired, they or the bear.

I knew I had him, so I just set down and rested a little. And then, to keep my dogs quiet, I got up and old Betsy thundered at him. I shot him right through the heart and he fell without a struggle. I run up and stuck my knife into him several times up to the hilt, just because he devilled me so much. But I had hardly pulled it out before I was sorry, for he had fought all day like a man and would have got clear but for me.

I noticed when the other dogs jumped on him to bite him old Carlow didn't git up. I went to him and seed a right smart puddle of blood under him. He was cut into the hollow and I seed he was dying—nothing could save him. While I was feeling about him he licked my hand. My eyes filled with tears. I turned my head away, and to ease his suffering plunged my knife through his heart. He yelled out his death note and the other dogs tried to jump him. Such is the nature of a dog. This is all I hate in bear hunting. I didn't git over the death of my dog in some time. I have a right to love him to this day, for no man ever had a better friend.

After resting awhile I fell to work and butchered my bear. I think he was the largest I ever seed. Then what to do I didn't know. I was about, as near as I could tell, four mile from the tent and there was a river between us. To leave my bear I couldn't do after working so hard. But how to git him across was the question. Finally I determined to carry him over on the same log

I crossed on. I cut him up, threw away some of him, and brought at four turns as much as I could tote and put it on the bank. The river was about three hundred yards from where I killed the bear and 'twas hard work to git him there, I tell ye. After I got it there I put a piece on my log, straddled it and brought it over, then went back and kept doing this way till I brought it all over. But 'twas a hell of a frolic and I paid mighty dear for my meat. I packed it away in the crotch of a tree to keep anything from troubling it and started for my tent. The sun was most down and though it was a cold winter day and I had been wet all the time I wasn't cold much. I think that was the hardest day's work I ever had and why some of my frolics haven't killed me I don't know.

I got to my tent an hour or two in the night, where I found my companion with a good fire. He seemed mighty glad to see me, for he didn't like staying there by himself. I told him what sort of a day I had had of it and he could hardly b'lieve me, so I told him I would take him next morning and show him. I then dried myself, got warm and went to sleep. Next morning we got our pack horses and went after my bear. 'Twas all safe and we brought it to our tent and salted it away. My dogs was so much worsted by the fight and I was so sore from it that we concluded not to hunt any more that day. My powder was all spoiled. My friend hadn't much. So next morning instead of going hunting we bundled up all our things and set out for home.

'Twas more than a day's journey, so the first night we camped about ten mile from my house. Having no powder at home, I told my friend if he would stay in the tent till I come back I would go over the river to a little store about twenty mile off for a keg of powder which the merchant had promised to git for me. He agreed to do it and the next morning I left my dogs with him and went down to the river, where I knew there was a crossing place. I got down pretty early and the log I expected to cross on was almost under water and the river still a rising. But I thought as I was so fur on my way I would go over. The log didn't reach all the way across, but where it stopped a small tree grew up and leaned over the bank, so that when I quit the log I had been walk-

ing on I had to climb the little tree to git to the bank. I fastened
my rifle to my back, climbed up and got over safe. I noticed all
these things because I knew I'd have to wade when I come back.

Well, off I went to the store. I got there just about sundown
and met with a right jolly set. So instead of going back I stayed
there and frolicked with them and made shooting matches for
two or three days. I then got my powder and one morning before
day started off for my tent. The weather had turned much colder
while I had been absent and a smart snow had fallen, which made
it mighty bad walking. I got to the river about two hours by sun
and as I expected the river had risen and my log was covered.
The water had risen considerably but I didn't know how much.
I knew it wouldn't do to stay there, for I should freeze. There
was no log to float across on and my only chance was to git back
as I got over. I slung my keg of powder to my back and climbed
down the little tree till I got to my log. This I found by feeling,
and the water was about three feet over it. I kept feeling 'long
and got over safe. 'Twas a mighty trying time, for right under
the log was twenty feet deep and if I had made one false step
'twould have been all over with Davy Crockett.

I had left old Betsy on the other side so I had to go back for her
and pursue the same plan to git over. I got ready to start agin in
about an hour and then I had to go through a wide swamp to
strike the path leading to my tent. The water, from the rise in the
river, was all over the swamp and I had to wade all the time. And
what made it worse, there was ice all over, which wasn't strong
enough to bear my weight but made it mighty hard to git along.
Just as I had started off I saw where something had broke the ice
and a notion struck me 'twas a bear and I determined to follow it.
I kept on about a mile, most of my time knee-deep in water, when
I struck the highland and found I was right in the path to my
tent. What I thought was a bear was some friends who had been
down to the river to look for me. I took their tracks and about
dark I got to my tent. 'Twas full of people and they were mighty
glad to see me. I had stayed away so long that my friends thought
some accident had happened to me and had gone to my house to
git help to look for me. They told me that my family was in a

great disturbance, believing I had been drowned. So to quiet 'em we all bundled up and went to my house that night.

Well I had been at home some time. The weather was so cold I didn't care much 'bout hunting. And Rees and a friend of his come over to my house one evening and asked me if I didn't want to go down to the Shakes and take a bear hunt. I told 'em I didn't care much about it but if they wanted to go I'd go with 'em. So next morning we fixed up, got our pack horses and off we started for the Shakes. We pitched our tent right on the bank of one of those lakes made by the Shakes and commenced hunting. We were tolerably successful. There was nothing strange about any of our hunts, only bear hunting is always the hardest work a man can be at. We killed our game and salted it away as usual and on the third day 'twas so cold and there was so much snow on the ground that we all come to our tent earlier than usual.

We made us a good fire and were lying 'round it when Mr. Mars, who had been to Mill's Point, rode up. He got down and told us that he was obliged to be at the land office very early next morning and if we would set him across the lake there 'twould save him the trouble of riding 'round it, which was about twenty mile out of his way. There was an old flat lying on shore but we all told him we couldn't, 'twas too cold and we were tired. But he kept begging us, saying he was obliged to be there. And after a while he pulled out a bottle of whiskey and passed it 'round. We soon emptied it and it made me feel in a heap better humor. So when Mars fell to persuading us agin I said I'd set him across if one of the others would help me. Rees said he would and Mars being in a great hurry we went down to the lake, and gitting his horse in we pushed off.

'Twas a mighty rough establishment, oars and all. The oars were covered with ice and the old flat had a good deal of snow in it and she leaked mighty bad. But I thought she would carry us over, so after we had started off, Mars said if we carried him straight across he would have to swim a slue and there was so much mushy ice in it he didn't believe he could git his horse across. But if we would land him up the lake he could get on safe.

To go straight across was about a mile but to go where Mars wanted us was about three. However, we were all in a right good humor and the sun was rather better than two hours high, so we agreed to land him where he wished.

We pulled away and just as we got 'bout the middle of the lake his horse made some motion in the boat and set her to leaking worse than before. I told Mars she'd sink if he didn't bail her, so he took his hat and went to work. We pulled as hard as we could and Mars worked mighty hard but the water run in as fast as he could git it out. By and by, though, we got to the bank and just as Mars went to lead his horse out the whole bottom went down. It had only been pinned on and the weight of the horse broke it loose. Rees and I was a little wet and when we got upon the bank we didn't know what to do. Mars looked half-frozen with his wet hat and his horse was shivering. He had to ride about fifteen mile or a little upwards before he could git to a house. And we were there without a horse, separated by a lake from our tent, and had nothing to strike fire. Mars said he could do nothing for us, for he was all but froze and must go on, as he had a long way to ride and 'twas getting late. I told him 'twasn't worthwhile for him to stay and off he started. We looked at him till he got out of sight and we didn't know what to do.

Well, there was Rees and I shivering and we must either git back to our tent or freeze to death. I recollected there was a canoe right opposite to where we begun from but 'twas two mile to that place and then to git to it we would have to cross the very slue which Mars had been afraid of swimming. This was the only chance. I told Rees 'twasn't worthwhile to consider—that there was no two ways about it, we must do it or die. So off we started. When we got to the slue 'twas as Mars said, covered with mushy ice and about thirty or forty yards across. We were mighty cold and it made the chills run over me to look at it. I called to Rees and told him as he was tallest he must go first. He didn't speak but waded right in. He seemed to think 'twas death anyhow and was resigned to his fate. I watched him as he went along. It kept gitting deeper and deeper till for nearly twenty yards he walked along with nothing out but his head. After he got out I started in and for nearly twenty yards I had to tiptoe and throw my head back and the ice just come along to my ears. 'Twas this soft ice made of snow. I didn't speak. We were too near dead to joke each other.

We went down to the lake and there we found the canoe. 'Twas nearly full of snow and water and I set to work to clean her out. When I thought 'twould answer I called to Rees to come on. He didn't answer me and I went to him and shook him but he was fast asleep. I endeavored to rouse him up but I couldn't make him understand anything so I dragged him 'long and laid him in the canoe. I then straddled one end, put my legs as deep as I could in the water to keep 'em from freezing, and paddled over.

Our friend we had left at the tent had a fine fire. I could see it some time before I got ashore and it looked mighty good. He had been preparing for us, as he knew we would be very cold when we got back. I hailed him as I run the canoe ashore, to come take out Rees, for, says I, I b'lieve he's dead. I got up and thought I would jump out and started to do so but come very near breaking my neck, for I couldn't step more'n 'bout six inches. I got out. I couldn't do any good by staying there and I left my friend pulling poor Rees out and started for the fire. I soon got to walking right good and felt the fire before I got to it. But I was hardly at it before I begun to burn all over. I kept turning round but my pains only grew worse. I was suffering torments and I quit the fire.

I turned towards the canoe. Our companion had poor Rees in his arms, his feet dragging the snow, coming towards the fire. I didn't say anything to him, for I didn't know what to say. But while I was looking on I recollected that there was a mighty big spring not fur off and a notion struck me to go and git into it. The sun was just down and the sky looked red and cold as I started off for the spring. When I got there I put my legs in and it felt so warm that I sat right flat down in it and I bent down so as to leave nothing out but my mouth and the upper part of my head. You don't know how good I did feel. I wasn't cold anywhere but my head. I sometimes think now of that frolic and I b'lieve the happiest time I ever spent was while

I was in that spring. I felt like I was coming to. 'Twas so warm and everything around me looked so cold. How long I remained there I don't know but I think an hour or two. 'Twas quite dark when I got out.

I went to my tent and there I saw poor Rees wrapped up in some blankets and laid before the fire, his friend watching over him. He was dull and stupid and had not spoken. The fire had no other effect on me than to make me feel comfortable. I took off my clothes, got dry, went to sleep and never had any trouble. But all our attention couldn't get poor Rees entirely well. We stayed with him two or three days and then carried him home. But he never walked afterwards. That frolic sickened me with hunting for one while.